FLY *to* LET

CADOGANguides

Contents

Author's acknowledgements

Given the wide geographical area that this book covers, it necessarily draws widely not just on my own research, but also on copious published material from a variety of different sources, including banks and other financial institutions, real estate industry organisations, reference books and even estate agents! Several people have also provided invaluable assistance by sharing with me their particular expertise on certain countries: Claire Brown (of Claire Brown Realty) helped on Thailand, Bali and the Far East; Tom Pattinson on China; Tom Walker on Morocco; Justin Sparks on the Czech Republic; Imre Karacs on Hungary; and Graham Platts on France. My wife, Roberta, shared with me her knowledge of her native Italy and also provided some useful more general comments on the manuscript. So, too, did Elisabetta, Alexander and Matthew.

This project would never have got off the ground if it had not been for Carey Scott, former editor of the 'Home' section of the *Sunday Times*, who championed the fly-to-let columns out of which this book has grown. Thanks also to John Witherow, Richard Caseby and Sean Ryan for allowing me time away from my day job to write this book.

Despite my best efforts, some errors will inevitably have crept into the text. I, of course, take full responsibility for them.

About the author

Peter Conradi is one of Britain's leading writers on foreign property. He writes the 'Fly to Let' column in *The Sunday Times* and edits a weblog on overseas property on the Times Online website. He is also the newspaper's property editor and is a former foreign correspondent, based in a number of different countries. Although he now lives in London, he still travels widely to research foreign property markets. He is married with three children.

Cadogan Guides
2nd Floor
233 High Holborn
London WC1V 7DN
info@cadoganguides.co.uk
www.cadoganguides.com

The Globe Pequot Press
246 Goose Lane, PO Box 480, Guilford,
Connecticut 06437–0480

Cover photographs: *front* © StockShot/Alamy,
Nicholas Stubbs/Alamy, Barry Mason/Alamy,
MedioImages/Getty; *back* © Misha Gordon/Alamy
Cover design: Sarah Rianhard-Gardner
Editor: Linda McQueen
Proofreader: Mary Sheridan
Indexing: Isobel McLean

Produced by **Navigator Guides**
www.navigatorguides.com

Printed in Great Britain by Biddles Ltd
A catalogue record for this book is available from
the British Library
ISBN 10: 1-86011-343-5
ISBN 13: 978-1-86011-343-7

The author and publishers have made every effort to ensure the accuracy of the information in this book at the time of going to press. However, they cannot accept any responsibility for any loss, injury or inconvenience resulting from the use of information contained in this guide.

Please help us to keep this guide up to date. We have done our best to ensure that the information in it is correct at the time of going to press. But places are constantly changing, and rules and regulations fluctuate. We would be delighted to receive any comments concerning existing entries or omissions. Authors of the best letters will receive a copy of the Cadogan Guide of their choice.

Introduction: Getting Started

By the standards of any impulse buy I have ever made, it was certainly the biggest – and perhaps even the most reckless. Within 12 hours of setting foot for the first time in Bratislava, the picturesque capital of little-known Slovakia, I had made an offer to buy a flat. We are not talking about peanuts, either. I was committing myself to invest just over £100,000. In return, I would become the proud owner of a large two-bedroom apartment with wooden floors and high ceilings in a wonderful period building just opposite the British embassy in the smartest part of town.

A bargain? No, in all truth, I probably paid slightly over the odds. But let's talk again in five years. You probably haven't noticed, but Slovakia is actually one of Europe's most dynamic and fastest-growing economies, and property prices, it seems, can only go up. In the meantime, after a few licks of paint and a new kitchen, the flat has been let to a diplomat who pays enough rent each month to cover the 90 per cent mortgage that a Slovakian bank was surprisingly willing to grant me after one brief meeting and the provision of a minimal amount of paperwork.

My behaviour may be rash – but I am far from alone. Britons, of course, have been buying property abroad for decades, a vestige, so my Italian wife tells me, of that old empire spirit: even if we do not colonise foreign countries any more, we can at least buy small chunks of them. Traditionally, though, Britons have looked to sunny places like the south of France, Tuscany or the Spanish *costas* in search of a holiday home or a place for early retirement.

I, by contrast, have no intention of living in Bratislava, or even spending anything longer than the occasional long weekend there. It may be a pleasant enough little place on the banks of the Danube with its own 15th-century castle, a fine historic centre and some stylish bars and cafés. But the motivation behind my purchase is purely commercial. And I am far from alone.

A decade or so after rising property prices and a greater availability of mortgages created the buy-to-let market in the UK, increasing numbers of Britons (and Irish) are trying the same thing abroad. Drawing on their experience at home, they are jumping on planes to places they had previously never heard of in search of the kinds of rental income and capital growth that are distant memories in Britain.

Such is the buzz that I used my own experience as the starting point for a column in the *Sunday Times* looking at the phenomenon, which we, snappily enough, have dubbed 'Fly to Let'. After Bratislava, I have since travelled to Tallinn, Warsaw, Brussels, Berlin, Venice, the Bulgarian coast and even Dubai to see what Britons are buying and why. And I feel as if I have only just scratched the surface. In fact, there's so much to say about the subject that I've decided to put it into the book you now have in front of you.

Questions, Questions

So where to start? As a budding fly-to-let investor you must first ask yourself a few basic questions about your investment aims and what you can afford. Your answers will determine not just where you put your money but also the kind of property that you buy.

The former Communist countries of central and eastern Europe, such as Poland, the Czech Republic – and, of course, Slovakia – are attractive for those hoping for a reasonably fast return on their money. Anyone buying in Warsaw, Prague or Bratislava in the last few years will have achieved rental returns of 7–10 per cent – more than enough to cover borrowing costs – and enjoyed annual double- digit rises in the value of their property. Although yields have fallen back in most places during the last year or so, the overall trend in prices is still upward, albeit at a more modest pace.

These markets are maturing, however, and, although still good value, they may not satisfy those out to make a quick buck. Such investors might look instead at buying an 'off-plan' – that is, not yet completed – flat in Bulgaria, perhaps, or else in Dubai, where the market was so hot in 2004 and 2005 that apartments in some of the most sought-after developments were changing hands three or four times even before they were finished. This meant handsome profits for those with the nerve to get in early. There has been similar frenzied buying in parts of America, too. The best in all three places may already be over. As I discuss in the chapters on Bulgaria and Dubai, there are concerns in both places of possible over-supply as the huge numbers of buildings commissioned in the last couple of years or so come on stream. In America, meanwhile, rising interest rates mean the great property boom in Florida and other parts of the country might be entering its final phase.

If all this seems too much like a pyramid scheme, there is money to be made closer to home. In France, a system called leaseback takes away much of the risk by allowing you to buy a property and then immediately lease it back to the developer. The annual returns are respectable rather than spectacular, but your flat or house will almost certainly be worth substantially more when the scheme matures than it is now, and there are significant tax breaks. There are also hopes of good capital gains: the French property market has been one of the strongest in western Europe in recent years and looks likely to continue its upward path. Alternatively, if you really want to go against the herd, why not buy in Germany, where, almost alone in Europe, prices have been stagnating or even dropping? Bizarrely, some districts of Berlin, the capital of the richest country in Europe, are now cheaper than the equivalent parts of Prague or Riga. If, as many experts suspect, the German market has finally bottomed out, buying now could be a shrewd investment – although you might have to wait 10 years or so to see real results.

So where will it all end? Certainly, nowhere these days is too far or exotic for the intrepid British or Irish property investor. What about Shanghai, where the Communist government has been presiding over property speculation with a distinctly capitalist flavour? Or maybe Bangalore, India's technology hub, or the northeastern coast of Brazil? I haven't heard anyone seriously offering Baghdad yet, but I bet that five (or should that be 10?) years from now, some enterprising agent will be marketing prime property in the centre of the Iraqi capital on the premise that the only way for prices is up. Getting adequate insurance may be tricky, though.

As for me, I'm sticking with my pad in Bratislava for the moment. But whenever I pitch up in a new city I can feel myself calculating rental yields and instinctively reaching for my cheque book. There's something to be said for impulse buys.

How to Use this Book

This book is split into two sections: in the first I discuss various theoretical aspects of property investment, and in the second I look at some of the more interesting parts of the world in which to put your money. It has not been possible to include every country in the world. Thus you will not find a chapter on Japan, Norway or sub-Saharan Africa. Nor have I written about the former Soviet Union. In the case of some countries, this is because it is neither easy nor attractive for foreigners to invest in property there; with others it is just too difficult to obtain reliable information about their real estate markets.

Even for those countries that are covered, limitations of space mean the information included for each is strictly tied to the needs of the property investor. Although I have included a few basic figures on population size, GDP and the like, you won't find detailed descriptions of the climate (except where it is relevant as far as the letting market is concerned), the quality of medical care or the price of a pint of beer. If you want to find out about these things, then any guide book will tell you. Indeed, if you like the sound of a particular country, then the next stage would be to seek out a more specific guide to buying property in that country – of which Cadogan and other publishers produce several. Bear in mind, though, that a lot of the information you find there will date quickly. This is especially true in the so-called emerging markets of central and eastern Europe or the Middle East: mortgage products not yet developed at the time of writing might have become available in the meantime and interest rates may have fallen. Property prices, meanwhile, will almost certainly have gone up.

The Internet, too, can be an enormously useful source of information. In a first, this book has its own website, **www.flytoletguide.com**, which is developing into a leading portal for foreign property investment. The website's contents will complement and update some of the information in this book. It will also contain other exclusive material and useful links.

There is plenty of other information out there as well. Go to Google, or any other search engine, and type in the city or country in which you are interested, together with the words 'property' or 'real estate', and you will quickly come across a wealth of material, much of it in English. (Some entries will show up with 'property', others only with 'real estate'.) The sites that come up first will probably be for estate agents. These will not only contain property listings; many will also give information about your target market. (Don't forget to take some of the more bullish market predictions with a pinch of salt, though – after all, these people are trying to sell you something!) Keep searching and you should also find research reports on the property market, either by banks or other international organisations. Although often dry in tone, they will tend to be more objective and provide useful historical perspective.

Another good source is the property sections of the national newspapers. Best of the bunch, of course, is the Home section of the *Sunday Times* – and my own monthly 'Fly to Let' column. You can also read my foreign property weblog on Times Online (**www.property.timesonline.co.uk**). Other sources include *The Times*'s 'Bricks and Mortar' supplement on Fridays and the supplements in the *Independent* (Wednesdays), the *Daily Telegraph* (Saturdays) and the *Sunday Telegraph*. For a more international perspective, try the *Wall Street Journal Europe* on Friday and the *Financial Times* on Saturday.

None of this, of course, should be a substitute for your own research. Before buying anything anywhere, I would suggest at the very minimum visiting the country(!). Be wary, too, of agents' promises about how easy it will be to let your property and how much you are likely to receive in rent. (I speak from bitter experience here: I ended up letting my Bratislava flat at only just over half the monthly rent that the agent who sold it to me assured me I could easily achieve.) One tactic might be to approach another agency, posing as a tenant: if they already have large numbers of vacant properties on their books similar to the one that you are planning to buy, alarm bells should start to ring. Proper legal advice is also even more of a must when buying in an unfamiliar place than it is at home.

Agents Offering Property in Various Countries

See the chapters on individual countries in Part Two for more agents.

- **Assetz, t** (0161) 456 4000, **www.assetz.co.uk**. Off-plan property for sale in France, Spain, Cyprus, Bulgaria and Germany.
- **Classic International, t** (01697) 741671, **www.classicinternational.co.uk**. Off-plan and 'second-hand' property for sale in a variety of locations including Spain, Italy, Cyprus, Florida and the Caribbean.

- **Letterstone, www.letterstone.com, t** (020) 7384 7488. London-based company offering off-plan property in Central and Eastern Europe.
- **Prime Location, www.primelocation.com/foreign-property.** Site with properties for sale and rent across the world from a number of different agents.
- **Property Frontiers, www.propertyfrontiers.com, t** (01865) 202700. Properties for sale in various locations including Shanghai, Bulgaria, Dubai, Barbados and Brazil.
- **Savills, www.savills.com, t** (020) 7499 8644 (London office). Leading property consultant and real estate agent, offering property across the world.
- **Someplace Else, www.someplaceelse.co.uk, t** (020) 7731 2200. Off-plan properties for sale in a number of places including Brazil, Latvia, Montenegro and Belize.

A Disclaimer

I have endeavoured to ensure that all the information contained in this guide is accurate at the time of printing. Some markets are moving especially fast, though, and prices, interest rates and other figures may have changed by the time you read this. So, too, may laws and other regulations governing property ownership. In any case, before taking any investment decision, you should seek professional advice.

In other words, while happy to take credit for any good deals secured and money made as a result of reading this book, neither I nor Cadogan Guides will be in any way responsible for any losses, financial or other, or hardships suffered if things go wrong!

Good luck, and happy hunting!

Part One: Why Fly to Let?

Location, Location, Location

02

If you have got this far, you are probably not still flicking through this book in the shop, but have bought it and are serious about buying an investment property abroad. Before you go any further – and certainly well before reaching for your cheque book – you should be clear about your objectives and act accordingly. However cheap the property and small the amount of money you put in up front, this is still a major financial commitment – in the case of most people, the second biggest commitment they make after buying their own home. For that reason, it is not something to enter into lightly or without doing some homework first.

The reason most people are getting into fly-to-let is to make money. Some have done well from the housing boom in Britain (or Ireland) and want to replicate their experience abroad. Others have missed out at home and see the booming foreign markets as a chance of making up lost ground. But what kind of money are you trying to make? Are you looking primarily for something that will generate income – as an alternative to a deposit account in a bank? Or maybe you are not so bothered about income but are more interested in capital gains. And what kind of gain: a quick, speculative one, or are you looking at 10 years or more? You may perhaps see your investment as an alternative pension. There are other questions, too, like how much risk you are prepared to run and, perhaps more importantly, how much effort you are ready to put in. The answers to these questions will inform both the location and type of property you buy.

Location and Market Trends

So how do you choose? Some people may have already decided on a particular country or area because they have links with it or perhaps intend to live there in the future. It is an attractive idea: buy a house in France or Spain, let it for 20 years while the tenants pay off the mortgage, and eventually retire there. If you are one of those buyers, then you probably know already where you want to buy and might be tempted to skip the rest of the chapter. That could be a mistake. However much you may be wedded to a country or a region, you will regret your decision if it is a bad place to invest. Indeed, if the place you plan to live in has sluggish or falling property prices, you may be better renting there and investing your money in a place elsewhere with more dynamic prices. It might be a little bit more complicated, but it could ultimately be a lot more profitable.

With international property, just as with domestic property, location really matters. In fact, it is even more important, because once you start to compare different countries rather than different parts of Britain you have to bring in factors like exchange rate movements, different interest rates, varying economic performances and so on. Make a bad choice of city or, worse, country, and, however perfect your property, you will have made a bad investment. The converse is also true. This table shows how average property prices differed dramatically between 1997 and 2005 in a selection of countries.

Movement in Property Prices 1997–2005

Hong Kong	−44%
Japan	−28%
Germany	0%
UK	155%
Spain	171%
Ireland	196%
South Africa	263%

Put another way, imagine you had bought an average property in one of those countries for £100,000 in 1997 and sold it in 2005. This is how much you would have received for it (excluding taxes and any other such costs):

Price on Selling Property in 2005 after Buying in 1997 for £100,000

Hong Kong	£56,000
Japan	£72,000
Germany	£100,000
UK	£255,000
Spain	£271,000
Ireland	£296,000
South Africa	£363,000

Given these huge variations, it pays to choose your country carefully. This is not simply taking the best-performing country and assuming it will continue doing equally well. As the small print says, past performance is not always a guide to what will happen in the future. One way of using the past, though, is to study the factors that influenced previous rises in a place and see the extent to which they are present in a particular location today. Although only an imperfect predictor of future performance, it will at least lead you to ask the right questions before you buy.

If we are looking at emerging – rather than mature – markets, which are where most people agree the real money is made, then we find that they tend to follow a similar trend. As the rough graph below shows, prices are relatively stable at first and then start to pick up at an accelerating rate. They continue

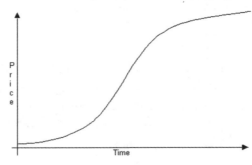

rising, but the rate of climb gradually lessens, until eventually they are going up at a moderate rate, perhaps in line with the overall growth of the economy. No single market will perform in precisely the same way and prices will oscillate around the line, often quite dramatically. But the message is clear: as a buyer keen to maximise capital gains, the time to be in the market is when the curve is beginning to become steeper.

Alise Crossick, who with her husband, Jonty, has been a highly successful investor first in the British buy-to-let market and subsequently abroad, uses the analogy of a party. No one wants to be the first one to arrive because there will be no one much else to talk to, but get there too late and you could be left with the washing up. The ideal time to be at the party is in the middle when it is in full swing. The only problem is timing your arrival correctly. And so it is with the property market.

All this theory is fine, but before actually deciding what to buy, you must make an important decision: are you intending to buy a property in a town or city that is suitable for continuous all-year-round use or instead looking for something by the sea, in the countryside or in the mountains that is intended as a holiday let? The distinction is not a black-and-white one, especially given the growing popularity of cities as destinations for long weekends. A small flat in the middle of Prague, for example, might offer good returns if let all year round to a young Czech couple. The same property could also be let by the week or even by the night to British or American tourists. The same is true in a number of other places. For simplicity, though, let us initially consider the two categories of property and the factors that influence them separately.

Properties for Long-term Lets

In a market-based economy, the price of everything – property included – is influenced by supply and demand. If the demand grows for a particular kind of property, then its price will go up, while if the supply of that kind of property increases then, provided demand remains the same, its price will go down. In reality, matters are much more complicated than that. In most cases, too, we are talking about increasing and decreasing *rates* of price growth rather than absolute rises and falls. It nevertheless provides a simple framework that might help you opt for one place over another.

Factors that Influence Demand for Property

So what kind of factors influence demand for property? The following points do not constitute an exhaustive list, but rather a selection of the most important. Their relative importance will vary according to time and place.

Income and Unemployment

This could be the most important one of all. The reason why house prices are higher in Britain than in Bangladesh is largely because the average Briton earns much more than the average resident of Bangladesh and is able – and obliged – to pay more for somewhere to live. It is as simple as that. It will also account for differences over time: the faster a country's economy grows, the faster incomes and house prices will go up, too. For this reason, a country like Latvia, whose economy has been growing at a blistering 7–8 per cent a year, is an especially attractive proposition. Closely linked with this is the level of unemployment: any rise in the jobless figures will push down incomes, and this, in turn, will have a depressive effect on house prices. Both income and employment levels can vary widely within a country, though. Typically, those living in the capital will be the most affluent and property prices will be the highest. (Exceptions to this are countries like Germany and Italy, where the respective capitals of Berlin and Rome are not their commercial or financial capitals.) Britain has been a good example: the boom in London's economy pushed up prices there in the mid to late 1990s, widening the differential with less economically active parts of the north of the country. As the British example shows, though, a ripple effect out from the capital meant other areas subsequently played catch-up. Such a phenomenon is also to be expected in the emerging markets of central and eastern Europe, which are still clearing up the problems left behind by more than 40 years of Communism. While much of the action still appears to be in the capital cities, where the money and jobs are concentrated, property prices in secondary cities could begin to grow faster as they develop, too.

Population Changes

Property is not just a financial asset, it is also somewhere to live. If the population of a country is growing, then this will push up the demand for housing, and so prices, and vice versa. The effect can be quite localised: while the total number of people may be stable, there can still be considerable movement into some areas, cities or districts. London, again, is a good example (even if the inward movement of young people in search of well-paid jobs in recent years has been offset, to some extent, by the departure of older people with families). Equally important are changes in the structure of society: much of the rise in demand for property in developed countries results from the gradual disappearance of the traditional extended family of grandparents, parents and children living under one roof. Young people these days strike out at an earlier age to live on their own; the divorce rate has risen and there are more and more elderly people living alone. This increases the overall need for housing, but tilts the demand away from large family homes towards smaller units. As the number of elderly people rises, so too will the demand for bunga-lows, ground-floor flats and buildings with lifts.

Interest Rates

Given the price of housing, most people in countries with developed banking systems do not buy for cash, but spread out the cost over 15, 20 or more years with a mortgage. For this reason, any small changes in interest rates is important – not just in affecting monthly mortgage repayments, but also in determining property prices. A cut in interest rates will push up prices (by making debt more affordable) while a rise will have a depressive effect. It will also affect the relative attractiveness of buying and letting: if it costs less to borrow, many people previously happy to rent will buy instead.

One of the clearest examples of the effect of falling interest rates has been in the southern European countries that joined the euro in 1999. Italy and Spain traditionally had relatively high inflation and interest rates, but had to cut both in the run-up to the launch of the single currency. It is no coincidence that prices in both countries have been booming since the late 1990s, but have been stagnant in Germany, which already had low interest rates. Price rises in the new EU members of central and eastern Europe have also been driven by the fall in the cost of borrowing there which, until recently, was in double digits. In Britain, by contrast, the rises in interest rates that occurred from 2003 to 2005 helped slow the market. Prices in Britain, in fact, are especially sensitive to rate changes, not only because so many of us are mortgaged up to the ears – but also because mortgages traditionally have a variable rate. The effect is not so immediate in countries such as the United States or much of western Europe, where fixed rate loans are more common.

The Availability of Mortgages

In Britain, we take it for granted these days that almost anyone can take out a mortgage: 90–100 per cent loans means you don't have to spend years saving for a deposit, while self-certification means you may not even need a regular job. The amount of money you can borrow relative to income has grown substantially, while specific buy-to-let mortgages allow you to buy second, third or even fourth properties. A generation ago all of this would have seemed very exotic indeed, and there are few countries that have gone as far as Britain. Most, however, are moving in this direction: according to the report *The View from the Rooftops: Prospects for Europe's Mortgage Markets* in September 2005, by Citigroup Equity Research Europe, Europe's mortgage market almost tripled from €1.5 trillion in 1990 to €4.4 trillion in 2004, with the figure likely to rise to €6 trillion by 2009. Substantial differences remain, even between developed countries: while mortgage debt is around 76 per cent of GDP in Britain, the figure drops to 53 per cent in Germany, 27 per cent in France and just 15 per cent in Italy, where traditional attitudes to debt still prevail. In many central and eastern European countries, where mortgages are a relatively recent phenomenon, it can be as little as 5 per cent. Although it could be years before mortgage debt in these countries reaches western European levels, the growing availability of home loans will encourage people to buy, pushing up prices.

Indeed, the rise in the market in the Baltic states of Estonia, Latvia and Lithuania is due not only to strong economic growth but also to the mortgage boom. An investor who gets into a market before loans are widely available or when the process is only just beginning will therefore be in line for handsome gains (even though investors will have to raise their own finance elsewhere). The flipside is that this will eat away at the long-term rental market and push down yields; why would an Estonian family, for example, want to rent a family house in Tallinn from a foreign investor when they could buy one with a cheap mortgage – and benefit from any capital gains? The rental market will not disappear completely, though: in Britain, for example, although there is not much long-term letting (apart from that of homes owned by councils or housing associations) there are always people who want to rent, perhaps because they are only staying in an area for a short time or have had a change in domestic circumstances like a divorce.

Government

The actions of governments can do a lot to affect the demand for housing. The most basic way is the extent to which they create a stable, peaceful environment with respect for the rule of law. If a country appears on the brink of a Communist revolution, or if property there can be confiscated by the whim of a state official, then foreign investors will be wary of putting in their money – or demand a hefty risk premium before doing so. One useful indicator of whether a country is really politically stable – or just gives the impression of being so – is the number of times and how smoothly power has been transferred from government to opposition in recent years. The more often this has happened, the better.

The former Soviet bloc countries are a good example of this: investing in Poland or Hungary just after the fall of the Berlin Wall seemed perilous to many people. Now that they and their neighbouring countries are fully fledged members of the EU, it does not seem much riskier than putting money in France or Spain. Part of the massive rise in property prices that has occurred in these countries since the 1990s can be attributed to these changed political circumstances. For the same reason, many will still be wary today of investing in countries deeper in the former Soviet bloc such as Moldova or Georgia, or in the Middle East or Latin America. EU membership itself is vitally important. While Brussels may be viewed with scepticism by many in Britain, for those on the outside, membership looks like a ticket to the promised land. Large amounts of

EU and private investment money flow into a candidate country in the run-up to membership, followed by even more during the years after it has joined. Merely preparing for membership can force countries to make beneficial changes to their economic and legal systems; the setting of a membership date can also have a strong psychological effect. Property prices surged in all 10 countries that joined the EU in 2004, while the prospect of membership is underpinning strong rises in Bulgaria and Romania, which are due to join in 2007, and in Croatia, which will follow shortly afterwards.

The actions of government will have an effect on property prices on a day-to-day level, too. The most direct way is through the tax system. This can have an indirect impact on property prices through changes in income tax or value added tax (VAT), which, in turn, will influence economic growth. Governments can also change the way property is taxed or alter rules governing the tax treatment of mortgage interest. In Britain, for example, it was widely assumed that the government's apparent intention to allow people to buy residential property with their self-invested personal pensions (SIPPs) from April 2006 would have given a boost to the market, until Gordon Brown, the chancellor of the exchequer, unexpectedly ruled it out in December 2005.

Other kinds of government policies can also have an effect. A decision to push the development of a particular region – or particular city – can boost demand for property there, by encouraging business and workers to move in. This is especially the case if it is accompanied by an investment of public money, which in turn brings improvements in infrastructure. In Europe, this means not only watching national government policy, but also European Union policy. A decision by Brussels to grant an area so-called Objective One Status will typically be followed by large injections of public money. At a more local level, the building of a university will boost demand for property for students.

The Olympic Effect and Other Special Events

The residents of London's East End are already salivating at the effect that the 2012 Olympics will have on property prices, not just because of the Games themselves, but also because of the investment in transport and other infrastructure in the run-up to the competition. The Bulgarian ski resort of Bansko is hoping for the same effect if it succeeds in its bid to host the 2014 Winter Olympics. Indeed, with the possible exception of Athens, which comprehensively mismanaged the 2004 Olympics, property prices have increased in most cities that have hosted recent Olympics. Valencia in southern Spain has already benefited from the decision to stage the America's Cup there. Other major sporting events such as the World Cup can also have an effect – which could bode well for Germany, which is hosting the competition in 2006. As shown by the experience of Liverpool, so, too, can a decision to designate a place as a European City of Culture.

Local Factors

You may start your property search by looking at countries, but do not forget that, ultimately, you are buying an individual flat or house in a specific place. This means looking not just at broad issues like government economic policy or interest rates, but also at things specific to the region, city or even district in which you are buying. The opening of a new underground station near your apartment block will boost demand; a new motorway or high-speed railway line will open up an inaccessible part of a country and turn a sleepy village into a booming commuter town. Conversely, plans for a nuclear power station in the neighbourhood may put off buyers. Sometimes these will already be factored into the price by the time you come to buy, but you should still do as much research as possible.

Tastes, Fashions and Expectations, or the 'X Factor'

Any economic theory based on treating humans as entirely rational beings is bound to have some serious shortcomings; this is especially the case with property. Demand in a certain area rises sometimes simply because that area has become fashionable, often for reasons that are not entirely clear or logical. Look at Notting Hill in west London, which in the course of a couple of decades or so has gone from being a virtual no-go area to one of the most exclusive parts of the capital, at least partly because of the film set there. The same is true for districts of Paris, New York or any other major city. Once an area has become fashionable in this way, it can quickly take off and other people move in for the simple reason that they are convinced prices must go up. Trying to make sense of the swings of the British housing market would sometimes require the skills of a psychologist rather than an economist. Indeed, with time, the mere expectation of rising prices can create demand of its own. The boom on the Bulgarian Black Sea coast is an example of this. Many of the Britons eagerly snapping up flats in Sunny Beach and the other resorts are doing so not because they are especially keen on Bulgaria or want to spend their holidays there, but because they have seen how prices have already risen and expect them to continue to do so. There is always the danger that investors will put their money into what is little more than a pyramid scheme. There is sense in moving with the herd – or at least being aware of what the herd is up to – but warning bells should start to sound if you are too close to the back. If they suddenly change course, it may be too late before you realise what has happened.

Factors that Influence the Supply of Property

As any economist will tell you, demand is only one half of the equation. You must also look at the supply of property as well. In any market-based economy, developers will respond to increases in demand – and consequently in price – by trying to build more properties. The more they are able to build, the less prices will tend to rise in response to any given increase in demand. So which factors influence supply?

Availability of Land

As the old maxim puts it, buy land – they're not making it any more. That being said, there are important differences between areas. Compare Texas and Manhattan. If demand for property rises sharply in Texas, there is little to stop builders from building more houses, thereby dampening price increases. Space in Manhattan, however, is finite, meaning those who want to buy there will have little alternative but to outbid rival purchasers, driving up prices. The same is true of the beautiful historic centres of many continental European cities, such as Venice or Prague, and of front-line seaside property. Once the seafront is completely built up, you cannot build more houses there – except in Dubai, where they got round the problem by constructing giant man-made islands.

Government Policy and Planning Law

Government policy will affect the supply of property as well as the demand for it. One of the main ways is via planning laws: soaring real estate prices in the London area have been due in part to successive governments' maintenance of the green belt around the city. Relaxing the rules would lead to more building. The same effect is at work in resort areas. In Bulgaria, for example, local authorities have introduced restrictions on building too close to the seashore in a belated attempt to prevent a repetition of some of the worst excesses of the Spanish *costas*. There have been similar moves in Croatia. The more effectively this is policed, the more of a premium it will put on the price of property already been built in these restricted areas.

Besides changes in planning laws, there are a number of other ways that authorities can influence the actions of builders, principally through the tax system and provision of subsidies. By manipulating VAT, for example, they can also change the relative attractiveness of building new homes from scratch or renovating existing ones.

Properties for Holiday Lets

Holiday properties will be influenced by many of the above factors, although their relative importance will differ.

Factors that Influence Demand for Property

The Economy

A booming economy in the destination country will drive up the cost of flats and houses along with the general price level. As the locals become more affluent, they, too, might start buying or renting second homes in holiday destinations. Indeed, this should be the profound hope of British investors buying on the Bulgarian Black Sea coast. An emerging Bulgarian middle class might provide some – although not many – of the much-needed end users for the myriad new developments.

Important, too, is the economic situation within the country from which second-home buyers and holidaymakers come. A slowdown in the British economy, for example, can have a dampening effect on property prices in regions of Spain or France popular with British second-home buyers. It will also reduce the flow of tourists ready to rent those properties. The continuing woes of the German economy, meanwhile, appear to have had a dampening effect in some southern European markets, both by reducing the flow of potential new buyers and prompting some Germans who bought a few years ago in Croatia and Spain to sell.

Transport Links

Transport links are also of crucial importance, given that the attractiveness of a particular area as a holiday or city break destination is highly dependent on the ease and the cost of getting there. The explosion in the buying of foreign property by Britons in recent years has coincided not only with a sharp drop in the price of air travel but also with the opening up of direct routes to provincial airports in destination countries.

France provides probably the best example of this 'Ryanair effect': the decision by that airline to fly directly from Britain to little airports like Carcassonne, Pau or Rodez, which had hitherto been served only by domestic flights, has led to a mini-boom in such areas. Important, too, is the growth in flights originating not only in London but also in provincial British airports such as Liverpool or Southampton. There have been claims that the opening of such a route could add as much as 20–25 per cent to prices in an area in a year. For the same reason, the arrival of low-cost carriers in Croatia and on the Bulgarian Black Sea coast, hitherto relatively poorly served by scheduled flights, is bound to have an effect on tourist numbers and property prices.

Before investing in an area, therefore, it is worth spending a little time poring over airline schedules, almost all of which you can find online these days. Remember, though, that a route can be axed from one day to the next – as some British second-home owners found to their cost when Ryanair took over its smaller rival, Buzz, in 2003. The disappearance of a route may be merely incon-venient for those using the property themselves; for those relying on rental income, it will be nothing short of disaster, since many potential holidaymakers will simply book somewhere more easily accessible. In the longer term, the economics of the air travel industry could also be affected by changes in oil prices or by long-mooted plans to tax aviation fuel as part of efforts to combat global warming.

Climate Change

Climate change can itself have an effect, at least in the medium to long term. Low-lying ski resorts could be especially at risk if the planet is getting warmer: average temperatures need rise only slightly to shorten the season in some resorts, reducing the potential rental income from your apartment or chalet. Extreme weather, such as the Boxing Day tsunami of 2004, earthquakes and hurricanes can also have a dramatic effect, not only in terms of immediate death and destruction, but also in influencing people's holiday decisions for years afterwards. Geopolitical shocks can have a similar impact: the 9/11 attacks on the United States in 2001 had a devastating effect on world tourism. The American-led invasion of Iraq in 2003 strongly affected the number of trips made to Turkey, Egypt and other Middle Eastern countries.

Taste and Fashion

Even more than with long-term city lets, tastes and fashions are also important. For reasons that are not always clear or easy to predict, some countries and areas suddenly become fashionable, pushing up property prices and providing a windfall gain for those who have already bought. Others drop out of favour. Changing holiday patterns can play a part in this. In general, Britons and other western Europeans spend far more time on holiday than their parents or grandparents did. Increasingly, people go on long weekend city breaks or head off on adventure holidays in addition to the traditional two weeks by the sea, affecting the pattern of demand for holiday accommodation. Demographics and, in particular, the ageing of the population can boost demand for certain kinds of holiday properties and reduce it for others.

Ease of Access and Facilities

Other more specific considerations apply when choosing between particular properties to buy as holiday lets. Ease of access is one of the most important. While you may be prepared to travel for a whole day to reach your beloved cottage, those booking it for a week may not be ready to do so (unless they are specifically looking for something remote). Proximity to an airport with regular flights is therefore all-important. Location is important in other respects, too: if you are buying a property in a seaside resort, then the nearer the beach, the better. If it is in a ski resort, then make sure you are near the lifts. A good choice of bars and restaurants within easy walking distance is also a bonus – after all, people are on holiday and are there to enjoy themselves. Supermarkets and grocery stores are important, as are other facilities, especially the all-important golf courses. These have long been a major selling feature for holiday properties in Spain and Portugal and are increasingly becoming so in the rest of the world. Indeed, the opening of a new course – or merely the prospect of one – in an area will do wonders for property prices there. If you hear that one is being planned, then buy quickly!

Swimming pools are increasingly important in seaside areas. A house or villa will be much more rentable and ultimately sellable if it has one. If it doesn't, then install one. It will probably more than pay for itself. If you are buying a flat, then make sure the complex has a pool or, better still, a fitness centre and other such facilities. Also, if possible, choose a pretty home – or at least one that photographs well. Most people will decide whether or not to rent a property on the basis of a photograph and a few brief lines of description. The more attractive it looks, the more likely they are to take it. All this will be reflected in the purchase price, but it will be reflected in the resale value, too. A well-positioned property will also be easier to let if there is a glut on the market.

As a general rule, you should try and put yourself in the position of someone who is intending to rent, and try and imagine what they would be looking for. This means ensuring that the style and size of property is appropriate to the location. If you are buying in an area popular with families, then don't buy a studio. If it is in a resort popular with young people, then a cheap one-bedroom apartment could well be ideal.

The Exit Strategy

Before making any investment, pause to consider how easy it will be to liquidate it, either because you want to realise a profit or because you need the money. This is especially important in the case of property, which, in comparison with shares, is an extremely illiquid asset. When buying a flat or house, therefore, you should look to your exit strategy. This is just as true if you are buying for short-term speculative gain as if you are making a long-term investment to boost your pension. This may not seem too much of a problem if you are buying an existing flat in an established city such as Paris, Barcelona or even Prague. It does become a factor, however, if you are buying into a rapidly expanding tourist area. However superficially attractive the deal on the new-build flat you are being offered, you should still ask yourself a simple question: who will want to buy this from me when the time comes to sell? If you have any doubt, then think twice before buying yourself.

Before rushing into property, it might well be worth looking at shares, bonds or other asset classes that might give you a similar return. If it has to be property, then maybe you should also consider the growing number of financial products that allow you to benefit from increases in property prices without actually buying a house as such. And no, I don't mean timeshares, but rather various property funds and real estate investment trusts (REITs). If you choose the country and development well, then the profits can be considerable. You will also save yourself the hassle of buying, letting and managing a property at a distance. The disadvantage is that, unless you borrow against your own home, it will not normally be possible to gear up in the way that you do when you take out a mortgage to buy a house. There is also always the sneaking suspicion that a disproportionately large chunk of your profits is disappearing into the pockets of the people who run the scheme. They are nevertheless still worth checking out – even though they are beyond the scope of this book.

Another interesting and related sector in which to invest is land, especially in places such as Bulgaria's Black Sea coast or Croatia, where there is a building boom. The value of land will often rise far more quickly than the value of the apartment blocks that are built on it. The existence, in most countries, of planning regulations and different designations for land also offer the chance for owners to benefit from considerable jumps in value whenever this designation is changed. To take the example of Bulgaria, land near the sea may sell for £3–4 a square metre if it is purely agricultural, but its value could easily jump to £20 or £30 if permission is granted to change its status to residential. Multiply that by 10,000 and your initial £30,000–40,000 investment could suddenly be worth £200,000 or £300,000 – a far bigger profit than if you bought apartments.

Such gains are far from risk-free. In many less-developed countries, the rules governing the re-designation of land are often far from transparent. All too often, one field will become building land while the one next to it remains farm land as a result of a discreet bribe paid to someone in the local planning department. Also important is the proximity of water, electricity and gas. Buy a plot that is too far from the nearest village and you could face an astronomical bill for piping in the utilities.

Before allowing yourself to be sweet-talked into buying a field which is doomed to remain a field for eternity, therefore, you should seek expert advice – ideally from a disinterested local surveyor who knows the area and the country's planning laws.

The Nitty Gritty

So, you have decided you want to get into fly-to-let and, making use of some of the criteria discussed in the previous chapter, have established the country and, ideally, the city, town or region where you want to invest. The next stage is to decide what kind of property to buy. Will you go for a new build or an existing 'second-hand' house or flat? Your answer depends on how much risk you are prepared to undergo, how familiar you are with the country and how much hassle you are prepared to put up with.

New Build

A lot of fly-to-let investors gravitate towards new build. Developers in traditional markets like Spain and, increasingly, emerging ones like Bulgaria recognise the enthusiasm among British buyers for foreign property and invest heavily in promoting them. Open the Home section of *The Sunday Times* or any other property supplements and it will be full of glittering new developments. Although some will be already completed and ready to move into, others will be little more than an artist's impression – or 'off-plan', as it is known in the trade.

There are advantages to this kind of project, the greatest of which is simplicity. In most cases, you will be dealing with a British partner – or at least someone who speaks English – who will provide you with detailed information about the flat or house that you are buying, complete with floor plans. These days, most of this can be downloaded simply from the web. Property shows can also be an important source of information, even though you can find yourself under pressure to sign up for a property before you are ready; beware of sales people who tell you there is only one flat left in the block or that prices are about to go up. Developers or agents may also lay on tours to visit the property; although these can be useful, the pressure here to sign up is even greater.

If the developers are used to selling to foreigners, then they probably also have links to mortgage lenders, which should make it easier for you to raise the cash. Things should be simpler, too, when you come to let the property. A spanking new building is always attractive to potential tenants.

You are unlikely to experience the problems with legal title that bedevil some older properties, especially in Croatia and some other countries in central and eastern Europe. It is nevertheless important to employ a local lawyer, who you are sure is not linked to the project, to make sure all the paperwork is in order and necessary permissions have been obtained. An alarmingly large number of buildings in Turkey, for example, are begun without the developers having first obtained detailed planning consent. In most cases, they eventually succeed before the building is complete. If they don't, you could face serious problems, either when you go to register your purchase or later when you try to sell.

There is another, more fundamental problem, common to all new developments: you will be buying at market price. The developers will know far better than you what the properties are worth and, unless they have fallen into difficulties and are desperate to sell, you are unlikely to get a bargain. It is also important to find out how many of the other properties in the block are being bought by owner-occupiers and how many by investors. Such information should be relatively easy to obtain; some agents will even boast as part of their sales pitch how many other investors are buying, as if to convince you what a great deal it is. Such news should ring alarm bells. It is far better instead to be one of the few investors in a block otherwise filled with owner-occupiers. As those who have bought into projects in Britain specifically targeted at the buy-to-let market have found to their cost, when it comes to letting your flat, you will find yourself competing with many identical units. Short of investing heavily in extra luxurious fixtures and fittings, you may only be able to shift your property by reducing the rent – unleashing a price war that could be damaging for all.

Buying Off-plan

All the above factors – positive and negative – will be accentuated if you buy 'off-plan', which is probably the most popular way of buying new property. The precise structure will vary from development to development and country to country, but the formula is essentially the same. On the basis of detailed plans provided by the developer, you sign a contract to buy a property which will be ready at a particular point in the future and put down a deposit, typically of 10 or 15 per cent. You then pay the rest, either in a series of so-called 'stage payments' at particular times or stages in the building process, or as a single lump sum on completion. In some of the 'hotter' markets, a development will be released for sale when it is little more than a series of drawings (although hopefully one that has already received all the necessary planning permissions and been through all the other necessary regulatory hoops). When the Dubai boom was at its peak, some developments sold out completely in a few hours even though it was months before the first foundation had been laid. In other countries, developers will only start selling once they have started building – and continue to do so until they have shifted all the last units.

By buying off-plan you are effectively lending money to the developer, which, given that he will have to borrow less elsewhere, should mean you are getting your property more cheaply than if you were buying into a completed project. Where off-plans really comes into their own, though, is in a rising market, where you are effectively buying a flat tomorrow at today's price – and have only had to put down a proportion of the money up front to do so. The return on your capital invested can be spectacular. Suppose you put down a £10,000 deposit to buy a £100,000 flat due to be completed in a year's time, and assume prices are rising at a modest 10 per cent a year. If you sell your property when the block is finished at the prevailing price of £110,000, then you will have made a gross profit of £10,000 – or doubled your initial stake.

If demand is especially strong, you may not have to wait until the apartment is finished before selling it on – or 'flipping' it – to another eager buyer, providing an even quicker profit. 'Flipping' only works when developments sell out quickly and there is an expectation of rising prices; the mark-up or 'premium' that you make on your original stake will depend on how fast the market is going. In Dubai, where the practice has been prevalent, developers have tried to stamp it out – and also cash in on some of the profits – by introducing restrictions on how quickly properties can be sold on or taking a percentage of the 'premium' when they are. At the time of writing, though, it is still going strong in parts of America, where there are even websites that allow people to 'flip' online. If you think the whole process is reminiscent of a casino or pyramid scheme, you would not be entirely wrong. When the market eventually turns, latecomers will face the invidious choice of pressing ahead and buying what is now an overpriced apartment or defaulting and losing their deposit.

Regardless of whether your intention is to hold or to 'flip' your property, you should look very carefully at the way in which the stage payments are structured, since this can have a significant effect on the real cost to you during the construction period, when you are dutifully sinking your money into the project and not yet receiving any rent back in return. The later you can postpone putting in your money, the better.

In these terms, some of the best deals are in Estonia, Latvia and Lithuania, where you only have to put down 10–15 per cent on signature, with the remainder due on completion of the building, usually nine months to a year later. Terms elsewhere are rarely that good. One project in Bulgaria, for example, required a 10 per cent initial deposit, 30 per cent a month later, 45 per cent at shell stage and another 15 per cent on acquiring ownership and completing the title deeds. As an alternative, the same developer offered the option of paying 90 per cent up front and 10 per cent on completion, but with a 10 per cent discount. You would need to get your calculator out to work out which was the better deal for you. The answer will depend on whether you already had the money sitting around in a bank account earning a few per cent a year or had to raise it expensively elsewhere. Both, though, were far more attractive than a deal I saw offered on a development in Ras al-Khaimah, an up-and-coming emirate just north of Dubai. This required a 10 per cent initial payment, 15 per cent a few months afterwards, followed by steady payment of the remainder in instalments up to completion two years later. In other words, after 18 months or so you have paid over the bulk of the money but received nothing in return.

The effect of such payment structures may be mitigated, to some extent, by mortgages that kick in some time during the payment process. This is only possible in some countries, though. Since there is not yet a completed building against which to secure their loan, some banks may be unwilling to advance the money. Even if you do take a mortgage, of course, you will have to pay interest on the money even though you have no rent coming in. Another variation on the theme, popular in countries like Egypt where mortgages are neither easy nor particularly attractive, are stage payments that start during the period in which the block is being built and then continue for a year or so afterwards. Put another way: you lend the developer money while your flat is under construction but the developer effectively lends you money once it has been finished.

Before allowing yourself to be seduced by the sales patter, you should pause for a moment to think about what you are doing: you are handing over a very large sum of money – perhaps the most you have paid for anything since buying your own home – to a company with which you have never previously had any dealings, based in a country whose language and legal system are alien to you, in return for something which does not even physically exist. Scary, huh? It is only common sense to suggest that, before doing so, you should think carefully about what you are letting yourself in for – and do as much as you can to control the risks. Only a small number of developers are downright dishonest, running off with your money or selling projects for which they don't have the necessary planning permission. There have been some such cases, though, especially on the Spanish *costas*, where some British and other foreign buyers have been badly stung. Less seriously, developments may not turn out as promised, often because the finish is not up to scratch.

Despite such risks, a surprisingly large number of people will buy – or at least put down a substantial deposit – on such a property without even setting foot in the country, let alone visiting the development. It is all very well for the selling agent to assure you that the developer has a good reputation, but such reassurances do not ultimately count for that much. You probably wouldn't buy somewhere in the UK without seeing it, so why do so abroad? Most destinations, in Europe, at least, are only a few hours away by air these days. Given the amount of money you are about to put down, a long weekend there is the minimum you should invest. At the very least, it might mean you spot the dual carriageway running behind your new flat that didn't make it on to the sketches on the developer's website. Take a little more time, and you might also come across another development that you prefer or that is cheaper than yours.

Checking up on the developer could be more difficult but not impossible. One obvious way is to ask to see buildings that the company has already completed to get an idea of its work. If this is its first project, then alarm bells should start to ring. See if you can find out more about it. If it is a large, well-known company with a reputation to defend in its native country, then it will have costed the whole thing properly and will be less likely to run out of money halfway through. A small developer financing everything too tightly may run into trouble if sales do not go according to plan and, in a worst-case scenario, may go bankrupt – taking your deposit with him. Read the contract carefully, too, to check what is included. This will vary from country to country; in some places, new developments will include kitchens with or without appliances as well as bathrooms; in others, they will be little more than a shell.

Even the most rigorous checks won't protect you from someone setting out deliberately to rip you off. The notorious timeshare sharks who used to stalk the *costas* have not become extinct, despite attempts to regulate them. Some have just rebranded themselves; others are basking in the waters of the Black Sea. Don't be lulled into a false sense of security, either, by the fact that the agent you are dealing with is British or is based in Britain; he or she will often be little more than an intermediary and your contract is likely to be with a developer based in the country of purchase. Before signing anything – and particularly before handing over any money – try and establish whom you can turn to for redress if anything goes wrong. You should also get a lawyer to look through all the documentation, but not one recommended to you by the developer!

'Second-hand' Property

The more adventurous will eschew such developments for an existing building, perhaps one in need of renovation. Devotees of television property makeover shows have strong views on how they can unlock the hidden value of a property, perhaps through a little judicious knocking down of walls. The potential can be considerable, especially in the former Communist countries of central and eastern Europe. Chronic shortages of housing meant people were crammed into as small a space as possible, often with two or more families forced to share a single flat. What was a cramped and unattractive three-bedroom apartment can be transformed at a stroke into a spacious two-bedroom one, which will be far more attractive to an expat tenant or local yuppie who is not obliged to share his home with granny and two kids.

Typically, old apartment buildings in cities like Budapest or Bratislava may also have rooms opening off each other instead of from a corridor. The effect can be reminiscent of Hampton Court or Versailles. Such an arrangement may have suited Henry VIII or Louis XIV but will not go down very well with a 21st-century tenant. If you can find a way of rearranging the flat, it will become much more attractive. The kind of cutting-edge design that we have taken for granted in British cities is also slowly making progress beyond the old Iron Curtain. Although many of the locals may initially be wary, young, affluent buyers can be just as keen as their western European counterparts on living in a minimalist loft, with bare brick walls and a bed on an open-plan mezzanine platform. During a trip to Tallinn, the Estonian capital, I was greatly impressed by a former 1930s telephone exchange building, which had been converted into 14 loft-style double-height apartments, with steel doors and floor-to-ceiling windows. I was surprised to be told by the estate agent showing them to me that the man responsible was British. Julian East, whose London-based company, West One, had been in Estonia for several years, said he had bought the building from a local developer which had acquired it as a job lot with the office block next door.

The Estonians had wanted the offices but had no real idea what to do with the exchange. East, by contrast, did. Locals had been reluctant to buy off-plan, he said, but were enthusiastic once they had seen a completed show flat.

Transforming a building into six or so flats can be extremely lucrative, provided you have done your sums right. It can also be an enormous gamble and is recommended only for those with deep pockets and plenty of time and expertise. Even renovating a single flat or house is not an exercise to undertake lightly; do so abroad and it will necessarily be more complicated than at home. It is not just a question of finding a suitable builder but also, more crucially, of keeping an eye on him once he starts work. Language is an obvious barrier. One solution might be to take advantage of one of the growing band of Brits who have set up, often in the unlikeliest of places, offering to act as intermediaries. However, in my experience, those living in central and eastern Europe in particular can be a rum bunch. Usually male and middle-aged (and with a local woman several years their junior in tow), they will often promise to both provide and supervise an army of local workers to carry out your renovation work. Few are likely to have any kind of professional qualification, so take care if you are using them for anything more complicated than simple painting and decorating jobs. Otherwise, a local English-speaking architect will be a better bet. He will also be useful for helping you negotiate your way through the permissions needed, especially if you change the outside of the building.

Whoever you go with, the same basic rules of thumb apply as at home: work out in advance, down to the smallest detail, what has to be done and make sure your payments are linked to the amount of work that has actually been done rather than to time the workers have spent. Make sure, too, that at every point in the process it is you who owes the builder money rather than vice versa. There is no better motivational tool than the expectation of future payment.

In most countries, renovation costs will be far lower than in Britain. Although London seems awash with Polish plumbers and electricians, there are still plenty back home. The same is true of other such 'emerging markets'. Some of the basic materials will also be cheaper, although don't expect too much of a difference in the price of kitchen appliances. And, of course, the global law of building applies: however carefully you do your calculations, everything will also almost always cost more and take longer than it was meant to. You wouldn't expect your renovation project in London or Manchester to come in under budget, so why should it do so in Kraków or Ljubljana?

Hotel-style Developments

These are a relatively new but increasingly popular kind of development. Rather than buying a self-contained apartment, you instead purchase a hotel room. In a sense, it is somewhat akin to buying in a new build, although with the obvious difference that your 'property' is part of a hotel and run by its management. In one such recent scheme in Warsaw, investors were asked to pay £42,000 for a 20-square-metre room in a new four-star hotel under construction in the centre of the Polish capital. In return, they were promised a 12 per cent annual return over the following 10 years. The initial yield was certainly attractive, but, given the way property prices are rising in the city, it would probably look distinctly less so after five years, making a self-contained flat a much better option. You are also unlikely to be able to take out a mortgage on a hotel room in the same way as you can on a flat. There are a number of other permutations on the theme, some of them involving serviced apartments rather than hotel rooms. A more attractive one on offer in Cebu, a resort in the Philippines, did not offer any such fixed guarantee but instead pooled the money received from the rooms and, after deducting costs, shared it with the owners. Although giving less security, such a formula at least does not cap the upside potential, and would be a better bet in a rising market.

Fractional Ownership

As the name implies, this means buying a part share in a house or apartment and in return being given the right to a proportionate share in its use. In effect, it is a formalised version of the traditional practice of friends or relatives getting together and buying a property – although hopefully without the usual petty squabbles. People will buy their shares from a management company that will also typically run the building and make sure everyone behaves according to the rules. Based on fractional ownership of executive jets and yachts, the concept was pioneered in the USA in the mid-1990s and has become popular there, with developments predominantly on the coast, on golf courses and at ski resorts. Typical buyers are money-rich, time-poor professionals who are prepared to pay for luxury, but do not want the hassle and expense of maintaining a property they have time to use only for only a short proportion of the year. While some schemes are tied to a specific property, others allow people effectively to trade their weeks in one resort for time at a different location.

Although such schemes have not taken off to such an extent among Europeans, some developers in Spain have recently started to market them. Some of the Spanish schemes are much more like traditional house ownership. In one, a maximum of four owners each put up a quarter of the price of a villa and in return have 13 weeks for their own use or to let. Either a management company or the resort itself undertakes maintenance, and all owners are governed by the conditions set out in a shared ownership agreement.

Despite the clear similarities, those marketing such developments insist they have nothing in common with the much-maligned timeshares. In fractional ownership schemes, people actually own a part of the property itself and even have a title deed to prove it.

Living on Borrowed Money

04

Let us assume that you don't have a bank account awash with cash ready to be ploughed into foreign bricks and mortar. And even if you do, would you really want to buy a property outright anyway? As we will see later, from a tax point of view, if you are buying somewhere abroad that you intend to let, then, just as at home, it can be advantageous to do so with borrowed money rather than cash.

The Magic of Leverage

There is another good reason for borrowing, and that is leverage. If you are investing in a rising market, then the less of your own money and the more of the bank's that you put down, the more profit you will make. Indeed, most of the people you read about in the personal finance sections of the newspapers who have made a fortune by building up portfolios of residential property from scratch will probably have done so with borrowed money. A simple example shows what I mean.

Let us assume two people each have £100,000 and decide to buy identical flats for £100,000 each. Mr A pays all the money up front, while Ms B puts down £20,000 and borrows the remaining £80,000 at an annual 5 per cent with an interest-only mortgage. Then they both let their respective flats for a year, earning £5,000 a year in rent. At the end of a year, both decide to sell and are pleasantly surprised to see that the price of their properties has gone up to £110,000. Which of the two did better?

Mr A invested £100,000, earned £5,000 in rent during the year and then made £10,000 on the sale: in other words, his initial investment earned him £15,000 or 15 per cent. (The precise figure will be slightly different, as the £5,000 in rent would typically have been paid in the course of the year, rather than in a lump sum at the end.)

Ms B, however, put down just £20,000 of her own money. The £5,000 she received in rent was largely offset by the £4,000 she paid out in interest on the £80,000 she borrowed, but she still walked away with a very respectable £11,000 profit on her initial stake, which makes a far more impressive 55 per cent. And what about the remaining £80,000? If she had invested that in four other identical properties, they would have each earned her £11,000, too. As a result, she would have turned her initial £100,000 into £155,000, while Mr A's grew only to £115,000.

Assume, though, that both of them are so happy with the way their investments have performed that, rather than sell after the first year, they decide to hold on to their flats. Let us say that prices (and rents) go up by 10 per cent in that second year as well, while interest rates remain the same. So how will things look if they decide to sell now? Both properties will now be worth

£121,000 and each will have earned a total of £10,500 in rent (£5,000 in the first year and £5,500 during the second).

After liquidating his investment, Mr A will walk away with a total of £131,500 – a clear profit of £31,500. What about Ms B and her five properties? She, like Mr A, will have earned £31,500 on her first property, although she will have to pay two years' worth of interest at 5 per cent on the £80,000 she borrowed, taking the profit per unit down to £23,500. But she will have done the same thing with her four other identical properties as well, meaning she has earned £117,500 profit – over three and half times more than Mr A has – and turned her initial £100,000 into £217,500.

But what if Ms B had instead bought 10 flats, putting in 10 per cent of the cost of each and borrowing 90 per cent? Provided that she found someone willing to lend her all that money (and wasn't kept up all night worrying about the weight of debt), she would have done even better. If she sold at the end of the first year, then, after paying the slightly higher mortgage bill to cover the extra debt, she would have walked away with a profit of £10,500 per flat. Multiply that by 10 and she has made £105,000 profit, compared with £55,000 if she had bought 'just' five flats, and with Mr A's now not so impressive-looking £15,000. The picture over two years is even more striking: once she has made her interest payments, Ms B will be looking at a profit of £22,500 per unit or £225,000 for all 10 together, almost double the £117,500 she would have made by buying five, and more than seven times Mr A's profit.

If they decide to hold on for three years and prices continue to grow at 10 per cent a year, the difference between their respective performances will be even greater. Assuming annual price rises of 12 per cent or 15 per cent rather than 10 per cent would also considerably increase the gap between them.

The picture in real life will necessarily be more complicated: we haven't factored in stamp duty and other transaction costs and have assumed constant interest rates and steadily rising prices. There is also the question of finding a lender ready to lend you that amount of cash: although a 90 per cent loan may look reasonable compared with the income the property can generate, any bank may be a little nervous lending Ms B £900,000. Something could go badly wrong with the rental market in our hypothetical town, leaving her with voids in some of her flats and problems paying her annual £45,000 mortgage bill.

Even more importantly, we have left out the effects of tax. This can work in different ways. In most (but not all) countries, you can offset mortgage interest-rate payments against tax, which will tend to tilt the balance further in Ms B's favour, since some of the rent Mr A receives will end up in the pocket of the tax man. There is also the question of the capital gains tax which most countries will levy on the profit property owners make when they sell. Although Ms B will still be way ahead of Mr A by the time this has been paid, the amount she takes home will be substantially less, depending on the tax rate.

The overall picture is clear: in a *rising* market, the more money proportionately that you can borrow, the more profit you will make. Indeed, some people go even further than this, by remortgaging as their property rises in value. Take the example of Ms B and her 10 flats. By the end of the first year they will be worth £1.1 million in total, while her outstanding mortgages will add up to £900,000, meaning they are equivalent to 82 per cent of the value of her properties. If the bank is still happy to go up to 90 per cent loan-to-value, this could potentially allow her to borrow another £90,000, which she could use to pay for deposits on eight more flats (which have gone up to £110,000 in the meantime), further increasing her leverage and potential for profits. Indeed, Ms B could keep on doing this every year, and within a very short space of time she will have built up a very substantial property empire. This is the basis for the success of those young millionaires I was talking about at the beginning of the chapter and indeed of the various get-rich schemes sold at all those overpriced property seminars.

Before getting too carried away, though, and pondering whether to spend your retirement in Beverly Hills or Monte-Carlo, please note the emphasis that I have put on the word *rising*. Suppose property prices actually fall over time rather than rise. If each flat is worth just £90,000 at the end of the first year, then if Ms B has spread her initial investment between 10 flats, she will find that her equity has been entirely wiped out and her properties are worth precisely what she owes to the bank. (She will, of course, have made £500 a year after interest on the rent on each flat, but that is scant compensation.) If prices fall any further, then it is as if she has stepped into a time machine back to the negative equity of the early 1990s. (Mr A, who was looking a little sheepish when prices are rising, will be looking unbearably smug now, since he will have lost 'only' £10,000.)

Of course, you only make a profit or a loss on an asset when you sell it, so Ms B could simply hold on and wait for the market to recover. But add in a rise in interest rates, and a few of those rental voids, and she could run into serious financial difficulties. This would leave her with an unenviable choice between cutting her losses and selling or dipping into her savings in order to carry on – a situation in which no one wants to find themselves.

While we are on these Doomsday scenarios, there is also another potential problem for the serial remortgager when he or she comes to sell, even if prices are rising. This is because of capital gains tax. The precise rates and rules vary from country to country. But if you keep remortgaging until you have taken more out of the property than you originally paid for it, and have invested it elsewhere, then you could reach a point when you sell where you do not have enough cash to pay the tax due on your gains.

Raising the Money

So, given the clear advantage of buying on borrowed money, what is the best way of doing so? Traditionally, many people have remortgaged their home in Britain and used the equity released to buy their foreign property. Thanks to the rapid increase in prices during the mid to late 1990s, anyone who has owned a property for more than a few years is likely to have built up some equity – that is, provided they have resisted the temptation to dip into it to fund holidays or pay school fees. In many ways, this is the easiest and most hassle-free solution: all you have to do is contact your mortgage lender, and within days a cheque can be winging its way to you. In the past it has also usually been the only way to do things. British banks are understandably not prepared to lend against a property in a foreign country, while banks there have been wary of lending to non-residents.

The situation has changed in the past few years. For purchases in many (but still not all) countries, it is possible to borrow directly against your overseas property. You can do this most easily by approaching one of the many British brokers specialising in this business. They will immediately be able to tell you whether or not this is one of the countries that they cover. They will also probably charge you commission, and you may get a better deal by going directly to a bank in the country where you are buying. In more established markets, this could mean going to the local subsidiary of a British financial institution, such as Barclays or HSBC, but local operations could be just as good. Not everyone will be ready to lend to non-resident foreigners, but a surprisingly large number will be keen to have your business – even if they might not grant you such good terms as they do to residents. Typically, the maximum loan-to-value may be lower and, less commonly, the interest rate higher.

If you are buying from agents, then they might be able to recommend a bank to you, but don't automatically assume that it will be the best deal. The easiest way is to look around while you are in the country hunting for property. Most countries normally have only a few big banks, whose signs you will see around the place. (Fortunately, the word for 'bank' is very similar in many languages, which makes them easy to spot.) In most places these days, after a bit of sign language, you will be able to locate someone who speaks English. If you are trying to set up everything from a distance, then turn to the Internet. Try typing words like 'bank', 'mortgage' and the name of the country in which you want to buy into Google or another search engine, and a number of entries will come up. As a rule of thumb, those which are in English as well as the local language are more likely to be interested in lending to foreign buyers, so see if you can find a phone number and give them a call. It may be a struggle negotiating your way through the switchboard, but, in my experience, in the end you will reach someone able to help you.

Money Conversion

When you buy your property, you will probably have to convert a large amount of money from pounds into euros, dollars or another foreign currency. It may be simplest to do so through your own bank, but before doing so, check out the rates on offer elsewhere; with sums of this size, even a 1 per cent difference can save you a lot of money. Here are some companies worth checking out:

- **Crown Currency Exchange, www.crowncurrencyexchange.com, t** 0870 803 4576.
- **Currencies4less, www.currencies4less.com, t** 0871 070 5555.
- **HIFX, www.hifx.co.uk, t** (01753) 751751.
- **Money Corp, www.moneycorp.com, t** (020) 7589 3000.
- **World First, www.worldfirst.com, t** 0800 783 6022.

The advantages of borrowing directly against the foreign property itself are clear – provided, of course, that you can be confident of letting it and thus generating an income to cover your repayments. First and foremost, it will give you more leverage, which is important if you are planning to buy several properties. You may be able to finance the first investment by remortgaging your property at home, but not necessarily subsequent ones. As mentioned above, there can also be tax advantages.

Borrowing against the foreign property can be good for your peace of mind, too: if a bank in, say, Poland or Bulgaria is prepared to lend you money, then this is a sign that it has confidence in the project and in the market as a whole. If it thinks there is danger that the developer of an off-plan complex will run off before completion, then it is not going to risk their own money on it – saving yours in the process. It will also want to make sure there are no doubts about title or any other potential structural problems. Looking on the dark side, if things really do go wrong, then it is your overseas investment rather than your own home that is at risk.

In many cases, it can also be cheaper to borrow abroad than at home, especially within the eurozone, where interest rates are substantially below sterling ones. Borrow in euros to finance your house in Spain, and, at the time of writing (early 2006), you could pay as little as 3 per cent for your mortgage – substantially less than in Britain. Borrowing in France, Italy and Germany, too, can be cheap. Moving eastwards, the situation becomes slightly more complex. Although none of the 10 countries that joined the EU in 2004 has yet adopted the euro, some, such as Estonia, have already pegged their currency to it, which means that it should be possible to borrow there at eurozone rates. Others have a slightly looser link. As a result, you will typically be offered a choice of borrowing either in the local currency or else in euros.

Generally speaking, loans in the local currencies will be more expensive than in euros, although the rates for euros will themselves tend to be higher than within the eurozone countries. The more developed a country and its banking system, the lower the rates there will be. Compare, for example, the low cost of borrowing in Estonia with the 7 per cent you are likely to be charged in Bulgaria, which is not due to join the EU until 2007 at the earliest. In Croatia, where EU membership is further down the line and mortgages more difficult to obtain, it could easily be 8 per cent. In some less-developed markets, such as Turkey or some Far Eastern countries, they could be well into double figures.

To add to the choice – or confusion – you may be able, in some countries, to borrow in other currencies, too. In Poland, for example, banks are surprisingly keen to lend in Swiss francs – which seems odd, until you realise that by so doing they can offer rates below 3 per cent, which seems almost too good to be true in a country where you should easily be able to achieve yields of 6 per cent.

Before making your final choice, of course, you should bear in mind the question of currency risk. If you live and work in Britain, then by choosing to buy a property abroad at all you are automatically placing yourself at the mercy of the international currency markets. If you buy a house in the eurozone, for example, and the euro drops 10 per cent against the pound, then that will automatically translate into a loss if you sell up and change your money back into pounds sterling. For maximum peace of mind, you should make sure your income and outgoings are in the same currency. That is, if you buy an investment flat in Paris, then since your rent is likely to be paid in euros it makes sense to have your mortgage repayments in the same currency. Things necessarily become a bit more complicated if you borrow in euros against a property that you let in Bulgaria, since you will now potentially be exposed to fluctuations between the lev (the local currency) and the euro. The same will be true if you take advantage of those cheap Swiss franc loans in Poland. If the franc goes up against the euro (or the Polish zloty) then so, too, will your monthly mortgage repayments – and the total value of your debt – relative to your rental income.

If all that sounds rather complicated, the loans themselves generally aren't. The kinds of deals on offer are far more limited than in Britain, where would-be borrowers face a choice between a bewildering variety of fixed, discounted, capped and other such deals. They also tend to be of the traditional repayment type. (The British interest-only loan, with its accompanying endowment policy, has not yet made much headway across the channel.) Terms on loans can be anything from 10 up to 30 or even 40 years, depending on country. The amount you can borrow will also vary. In most places you can borrow at least 50 per cent of the value of the property and in many countries as much as 95 per cent. Other terms and conditions will also differ from country to country and bank to bank. Given the amount of money at stake, it certainly pays to do your research.

You must do some serious thinking before borrowing money, whether by taking out a mortgage against the property or remortgaging your home. Buying a £100,000 property with an 80 per cent loan might lull you into thinking that you are only risking £20,000, but that is not true: your real potential exposure is five times that. The more you borrow, the higher your repayments will be and the smaller the chance you have of covering them completely out of rental income. This is already the case for those buying today in most developed countries and is becoming increasingly the case in emerging ones as property prices rise and rents lag behind, cutting into yields. This means you will probably have to find some of the money out of your own income or savings, especially when you take voids into account. This does not mean the property is not paying its way – don't forget that with a traditional repayment mortgage part of the money you pay each month is actually reducing the value of the outstanding debt. The money must still be found, though. Think also of how you will cope if interest rates go up or the rental market collapses; do you have a sufficient financial cushion to make sure you won't be forced to sell? Before buying anything, especially on credit, make sure the numbers really stack up – and don't rely on over-optimistic forecasts from estate agents of rental yields or future capital gains.

International Mortgage Brokers

- **Blue Horizons, www.international-mortgage-network.com, t** (01733) 206628.

- **Connect Overseas, www.connectandprotect.co.uk, t** (01708) 443334.

- **Conti Financial Services, www.mortgagesoverseas.com, t** (01273) 772811.

- **Fidentia, www.fidentiagroup.com, t** 08707 496 496.

- **International Mortgage Plans, www.international-mortgage-plans.com, t** (01932) 830660.

- **Octopus, www.octopusmortgages.com, t** 0845 230 9673.

- **Propertyfinance4less, www.propertyfinance4less.com, t** (020) 7594 0555.

Letting Your Property

05

Some investors are so confident of capital gains – and also, perhaps, so averse to hassle – that they buy a property and lock it up, only to sell it when the price has risen. This may make sense in some circumstances. But not everyone can afford it and it seems a bit of a waste. If you want to do that, then fine – but make sure you are on solid ground. This, though, is the fly-to-let guide, so let's talk about the different ways of letting.

Long-term Letting

The simplest and often most profitable way of letting is long-term – to someone who will stay in your property all the year round and make it their main home. This is especially the case when you have bought in a city rather than a holiday destination. The amount of time your tenant will stay will vary from situation to situation – and can also depend on what we can call the 'renting culture'. In Britain, for example, where home ownership remains the goal of most people, renting is regarded usually as something for the young or for a relatively short period. Properties tend to be furnished rather than unfurnished. Most tenants these days are therefore on assured shorthold tenancies which run for a year but have a break clause on both sides after six months. Things can be different elsewhere. At the other extreme, in Germany, only four out of ten people own their homes and everyone else rents. Indeed, many Germans rent for their whole lives. Not surprisingly, most property is rented unfurnished and contracts usually have an unlimited duration (albeit with break clauses on both sides). Most other countries in Europe and beyond fall somewhere between the two.

First you must find a tenant. If you are buying into a large new-build complex, then the developer will probably have a letting arm or an arrangement with an organisation that can let your property for you. Indeed, before buying it is worth checking that this is the case and maybe thinking again about your purchase if the developer does not seem interested. Things could become a little more difficult if you buy a 'second-hand' property. The simplest way is to go to a letting agent, especially if the property is in a country that you don't know very well and whose language you don't speak. Good luck. Although British estate agents may rank among the least popular members of society (alongside journalists and politicians), most are fairly good at their job. You give them the keys to the flat and, provided you have not set the rent too high, then, lo and behold, some days or weeks afterwards they come up with a tenant, check his or her references and take a deposit. For this they will usually charge around 10 per cent, or more if you want them to manage it afterwards. American realtors are equally skilled. In many European countries, though, the level of professionalism can often be much lower. It is also quite common for most properties to be advertised simultaneously with a large number of different agents. In theory, this should make it easier to make tenants aware of your property. In reality, it can mean agents are dealing with far more properties than they can comfortably handle, making it difficult for them to keep track. As a result, details of your flat might be languishing, forgotten, at the bottom of a filing cabinet. Getting feedback on why your property has not yet been let may also be difficult.

Even within one city, agents will vary widely, so it pays to do your research. Take time to go to their office and see how much passing traffic they have. Look at the other properties on their books and the kinds of tenants they attract and log on to their website. Check not only how professional it is, but also whether it is in English as well as in the local language – a sign that they are targeting the expat as well as the local market. If you have bought the property from an agent and been impressed by their work, find out if they do lettings as well; if not, they may be able to recommend someone. Another good source of advice is British investors who have already bought in the same complex. Whichever agent you go for, make sure you keep badgering them – in the nicest and most charming way. The more you call and e-mail them, the more likely they are to think of your property when the next tenant comes in – if only to get you off their back.

In most places, it will be possible to take only the basic tenant-finding service. But you must also think about who is going to manage and maintain your property – which is not easy to do from afar. It is hassle enough if you have a tenant in the same city who calls late at night to complain that the washing machine has broken or that the drains are blocked. Dealing with such problems in another country at the end of a telephone is well nigh impossible. In most cases, therefore, the best solution is to have your property professionally managed, ideally by the agent who let it. It will cost you probably another 5 per cent or so of the rent, but can be well worth it for the peace of mind.

If yours is an upmarket property of interest to diplomats, approach British and other embassies directly with details, ideally accompanied by some photographs. The larger British embassies have a housing officer who helps new arrivals to find somewhere to live. So do many other countries. Even if they do not need anywhere at the precise moment you go, it is good to be on their books. With most diplomats staying in their posts for three or four years, there can be considerable turnover. Although there are exceptions, diplomats make good tenants and are unlikely to trash your property or stop paying the rent. It is also worth targeting the local offices of multinational companies. They, too, will need accommodation for expat executives, either posted for a few months or a few years. As with the diplomats, if all goes well with the let, there is a good chance your tenant will recommend the property to his or her successor.

Another way of letting your property is to advertise it in the classified section of a newspaper. If you are targeting expats, then the best bet could be the local English-language newspaper. Alternatively, just try a local newspaper, although you will have to seek advice on which is the best one to choose. If the local language is not English, then you will also need help with drafting your advertisement. Do give some thought as well to how you will cope when the calls – in Spanish, Czech or whatever the local language is – begin to come in.

The Internet is also increasingly important. Most countries these days have at least one or more property portals with listings of flats and houses for sale or to let. Find out which is the best-used one and place your advertisement there. It will be up to you to vet the potential tenants – no easy matter abroad.

Whichever method you choose, you must market your property at a realistic price. Some people start by calculating their mortgage payments, add on a percentage to cover other costs and give themselves a profit, and convince themselves that this is the going rate. This is approaching the question the wrong way round. You should do as much research as you can and price your flat and house according to what else is on the market. You may prefer to start a little higher, but if you see that you are not getting any takers, then quickly reduce your price to a more realistic level. Remember, a month's void is the equivalent of just over 8 per cent off your annual rent. If you are renting through an agent, then you should be guided by them. Some of the less scrupulous ones may try to win your business by assuring you that they will be able to get you an absurdly high rent. If, after some time, the property has still not let, then even they will probably suggest cutting the price. Such considerations are especially important in current market conditions. Despite a global real estate boom, rents have not always kept up with property prices, compressing yields. As we shall see in the second part of this book, this has particularly been the case in several central and eastern European capitals. Indeed, in some cases, rents have dropped in absolute terms because of a glut of buy-to-let properties put on the market by investors.

Once you have secured your tenant and checked their references, then you will have to draw up a contract. If you are using an agent, they will do this for you; if not, then you are on your own. Either way, you should go through the document extremely carefully. The contents will vary according to your chosen country's particular renting culture. This is especially the case for the contract's duration and the length of the notice periods. Tenants' rights will vary greatly from country to country, but you should always start by assuming that if things do go wrong you may only be able to evict them after a long legal process. If they have children they will almost certainly have more rights. It is not always possible to foresee problems, but, given how much time and money they can cost you, it is worth putting that extra bit of effort into selecting your tenants.

Short-term or Holiday Lets

Not everyone wants – or is able – to let long-term. If your property is on one of the Spanish *costas* or in the Swiss Alps, then you are more likely to let it for the season or by the week. Your return will depend on the length of the letting season which, in most cases, will be dictated by the climate. The effect on your bottom line can be dramatic. Southern Spain, Florida and Cyprus are attractive because they can be let all year round. Your weekly rates will be highest in summer, but you should be able to make money in winter from 'snowbirds' from northern Europe fleeing south to avoid the weather at home. In Dubai, Egypt or Thailand, rates will probably be at their highest during the winter months. At the other extreme is Bulgaria's Black Sea coast, which has a relatively short but intense summer season and then packs up for the winter, giving you, realistically, only three months or so in which you can let. The same is true of Croatia.

Properties in ski resorts lie somewhere in between. Normally the season begins shortly before Christmas and, depending on the height of the resort, continues until late April or May. There can be huge variations within this period, though: places with mile-long queues at the lifts at New Year or during February half-term can be eerily quiet mid-week in January. Some resorts do also target hill walkers and mountain bikers in summer; although rates will be lower, this can provide an extra boost to your income. An important advantage of putting your money into a ski property rather than into something equivalent by the sea is that you will probably be able to charge more for it per week. Bulgaria is a good example: compare the likely returns from a flat in Sunny Beach on the coast with the money generated by a flat in Bansko in the mountains. It may be because everything else to do with skiing is so expensive, but, psychologically, people seem to accept that renting an apartment on the slopes is going to cost more. Most established ski resorts are in high-cost countries like France, Switzerland and Austria, which means that, in contrast to the situation with beach holidays, you are not facing competition from cheaper destinations in emerging markets. Don't forget, though, that maintenance charges and heating bills for a property in the mountains can be higher.

Short-term letting could be an attractive option in some cities. This is not only true in out-and-out holiday destinations like Venice, but also in places such as Barcelona and Prague, which although busy working cities are popular long-weekend destinations. As a bonus, you and your friends can use the property when it is empty. Whether it is better to let long- or short-term in such a case will depend not only on the city but also on the style, size and location of a property. A smallish flat in the heart of the old town of Tallinn or Kraków could be a natural for a holiday let. Something larger, in a modern block, with a garage, 10 minutes' drive from the centre would be more suited to a long-term letter.

It can be difficult to predict in advance whether it is more lucrative to cater for holiday lets or to let long-term. A flat that would fetch £500 a month if let yearly could earn you as much as £50 a night from tourists, but how many nights a month are you going to fill it? Also don't forget to factor in the extra hassle and costs you will incur in providing what is, in effect, hotel accommodation.

If you are going down the short-term route, the simplest way is through an agent because of the work involved in managing the place. If you are renting by the week, then you will need someone to check tenants in and out, change the sheets and towels and do the cleaning. This could cost 20 per cent or more in fees, but in most cases it is difficult to see how you could do it yourself, especially if you are hundreds of miles away. A cheaper alternative might be to get a neighbour or other local person to do it for you. But you should think carefully before entrusting your newly purchased investment property to a stranger. In most resorts there are agents ready to handle your property. Some may take it over for the season or the year for a lump sum and let it themselves. Any further money they make is theirs. This may ultimately mean a smaller return for you, but at least they are assuming the risk, which can be reassuring if you have mortgage payments to make. Others may merely find tenants for you and take a percentage. It certainly pays to do some good checks in advance on the agency. You are not asking them to find a single tenant for a year or so but rather to provide you with a continuous stream. If you are at a distance, it may be difficult for you to check how well they are marketing your property and to make sure it is not being pushed in the queue behind those belonging to their friends. At the very least, before taking on an agent, it is worth checking how many other similar properties it has on its books and the prices that they are being let at. If the rentals are turning out to be disappointing, then you should also call or e-mail them often to keep them on your toes. Ultimately, you are in their hands, and if they are not doing their work properly you will soon know about it: the voids will start building up and your rental income will drop.

The Internet can be an extremely useful tool, as this is increasingly where potential tenants look for places to rent. Many people set up their own websites to market their property and take bookings. Given the multiplicity of sites out there in cyberspace, though, it is worth consulting people who know what they are doing to make sure that yours is picked up by the search engines and drawn to the attention of the target audience. Remember to include the best pictures you can, not only of the property itself but also of the views from the window (if they are pretty) or of local attractions. To maximise the potential number of tenants, try and provide a version in French, German, Spanish or Italian as well. Brits are not the only people who go on holiday: places such as the Istrian peninsula in Croatia or Egypt's Sharm el-Sheikh are far more popular destinations among Germans and Italians than among British or Irish.

Better still, you could advertise through one of the growing number of websites that specialise in letting holiday flats and villas. Some are specific to particular countries or regions; others are global, such as Holiday Rentals (**www.holiday-rentals.com**), a British-based site which has more than 13,800 properties in 60 countries on its books, and claims an average 360,000 visits a month, or Owners Direct (**www.ownersdirect.co.uk**), which has more than 7,000 holiday homes.

When choosing which site to advertise with, sit at your computer and put yourself in the shoes of a potential tenant as you key your requirements into

Google. Do it a few times, slightly changing the search terms (remember, while Britons will tend to look for 'flats', Americans will search for 'apartments'; those sites that know what they are doing will contain both words). If a few websites keep coming up consistently, then it is worth checking them out in more detail.

Don't forget other more traditional methods, such as newspaper and magazine adverts. A classified advertisement in the travel section of *The Sunday Times* or another newspaper can be very successful, even though your property will be competing with several others. For this reason, also try the classified sections of magazines such as the *Spectator* or *Private Eye*, where your property will stand out more. There is also that good old standby: the card in the local newsagent's window or on the supermarket noticeboard. Although extremely cheap, it can also be highly effective. Friends and relatives may be keen to rent your property once they hear how great it is.

Guaranteed Returns

Many new off-plan developments promise to save you the hassle of letting by finding the tenants themselves and giving you a guaranteed annual return. The numbers are often attractive, with yields of 6 or 7 per cent or even more of your initial purchase price, perhaps just for the first year or maybe for longer. In most cases the developers will have a deal with tour companies, who will block-book a number of apartments for the season. You hand over the property and they do the rest. In a further sweetener, you may also have the possibility of using your property for a couple of weeks or so a year, too. Such arrangements are undoubtedly attractive.

If only for this reason, you should be cautious. It is simple for a developer to jack up the price of flats in a block by 6 per cent and then return that money to the purchaser during the first year in the form of 'guaranteed' rent. Even if the flat lies empty for that year, it hasn't cost him anything. On the contrary, by making the development appear eminently rentable, it has undoubtedly boosted sales. It is not surprising, therefore, that some developers offer discounts to purchasers who say they don't want the rent guarantee. Even if you don't suspect this is the case, look carefully at any guarantee before buying. How binding is it in a legal sense and how easy would it be to enforce in a foreign court if things went wrong? A terrorist attack on a resort, for example, might prompt a tour operator to try to wriggle out of a contract to take a certain number of apartments, leaving the developer with a loss, which they could then try to mitigate. Large developers with reputations to defend are not likely to renege on commitments, but the building business is a perilous one.

Consider also what happens once the guarantee period has elapsed. This is especially the case in places like the Bulgarian Black Sea coast, where a lot of building is going on. Your apartment will be competing with others that have been built subsequently. Since they probably have rent guarantees as well – and are newer than yours – they will be let first, while yours may be relegated to the back of the queue. This is not a problem provided there is sufficient demand in the resort. But if there has been too much building, you may either have to find more imaginative ways of marketing it, drop your price substantially or be prepared for some voids.

Leaseback Deals

Those looking for more certainty should go for a leaseback deal, a formula pioneered in France. It works as follows: you buy an apartment from a developer but then 'lease it back' for a fixed period, typically of 9 to 11 years, to a management company. The idea is to give you all the advantages of investing in property without the hassle. Once you have handed over the apartment, the management company does everything: it finds tenants and looks after the upkeep and maintenance of your property, paying all the bills. Out of the proceeds, it will pay you back a guaranteed rent, normally equivalent to around 5–6 per cent of the purchase price. This annual return will be indexed, increasing periodically in line with the INSEE Cost of Construction Index, which is published by the French government.

Normally speaking, all you will have to cover are accountancy fees and the *taxe foncière* (local rates), typically only a few hundred pounds a year, payable after two years. As a bonus, if you buy a new off-plan apartment, the French government will refund the 19.6 per cent VAT normally levied. A £100,000 apartment, for example, would cost you only £83,613, giving you an instant £16,387 equity. You do have to return a proportion of the VAT if you sell back within 20 years, although the person who buys from you is able to claim it back. In most cases, you will also be allowed some weeks a year in which you can stay in your apartment; some schemes offer more use in return for a slightly lower yield. It is up to you to do the calculations and work out which is best.

Sounds too good to be true? In some cases you might be able to earn more rent if you let the property out directly yourself rather than through the scheme, but then you would also have all the work, too. You wouldn't benefit from the VAT exemption, either, which is worth a few percentage points a year on your yield. It should be remembered that the scheme, which is sponsored by the French government, is part of a deliberate policy of encouraging development of the country's tourism sector, so why not take advantage of it?

Although a French idea, leasebacks are beginning to spread to other countries. Several schemes have recently started in Spain, for example, using a similar formula and offering the same VAT rebate on new builds. The rate, at 7 per cent, is far lower than in France – and so, too, is your discount. Unlike in France, you only need to hold the property for 10 years in order to get all your tax back.

Taxes and Lawyers

06

Anyone who thinks that by buying abroad they will be able to avoid the taxman has another thing coming. By investing in a foreign country you will automatically be drawn into the clutches of the local equivalent of HM Revenue & Customs, which may be just as keen on dipping its fingers into your pocket. Also, unless you leave Britain permanently to go and look after your investments, then the Revenue will also want a share.

As mentioned briefly in Chapter 02, **Location, Location, Location** (see pp.12–18), the nature of a country's tax regime and changes in it can have a significant effect on the real estate market, affecting both the value of your property and the return that you get from it. Given that this book is intended as an overview of investing across the world, it is not possible here to go into detail about the tax regime of every country. At the very least, before even thinking of buying a foreign property, you should read up on the country, either on the Internet or in a specialised guide to buying there (of which Cadogan Guides publishes several). Better still, you should talk to an accountant who either works in that country or is based in Britain and deals regularly with it.

Those Taxing Foreigners

The government of almost every country on earth levies taxes, but the tax regime varies considerably from country to country. One way of judging the weight of taxation in a country is by looking at its government's total tax take relative to GDP. According to figures from the OECD, in 2002 this varied from 25.8 per cent in Japan and 26.4 per cent in United States to 44.0 per cent in France and 50.2 per cent in highly taxed Sweden. Britain, at the time, was in the middle on 35.8 per cent, but has probably gone up a point or two since. Many of the former Communist countries of central and eastern Europe are moving aggressively to cut taxes, with many introducing so-called 'flat' taxes of as little as 18 or 20 per cent. In oil-rich Gulf Emirates, such as Dubai and Ras al-Khaimah, there is no tax at all.

The overall tax burden, although of relevance to the dynamism of a country's economy, is only part of the picture. As a property investor, you will be particularly interested in the relative weight of taxation on real estate, compared to taxation on income, wealth or capital. In some countries, the tax regime will be generally favourable to investors in property; in others it will not, and you will want to take this into account.

So what kind of taxes are we talking about? First of all, there are the local equivalents of what we in Britain call **stamp duty** – the money that you must pay to the state when you buy a property. Most, but not all, countries levy it, although the rate can vary widely. Dubai does not have it; nor, more surprisingly, does Slovakia, which recently proved its free market credentials by abolishing it. In Brussels, by contrast, it is a whacking 12.5 per cent, or 20 per cent in the case of a new property. Once you have added the few percentage points claimed by the **notary**, whose services are compulsory, you will find that your £100,000 flat is costing you well over £120,000. This, in turn, means prices will have to rise substantially before you can break even on the deal.

The level of the tax is normally proportionate to the value of the transaction. In some countries, as in Britain, it can be banded, with a higher rate levied on more expensive properties. Other fees may also be levied, most commonly for inclusion of your property in the land registry. Another cost you may face when you buy – although not a tax as such – is a fee for the **estate agent**. Unlike in Britain, where the seller pays, it is the tradition in many countries for the buyer to pay as well, with the agents typically picking up 3 per cent from each side. Not bad work if you can get it.

Not surprisingly, in countries such as Belgium and Italy, where stamp duty is also in double figures, there is a long and not so honourable tradition of **under-declaring** the value of the transaction to authorities to reduce the tax bill. The same is true in Turkey. A £200,000 flat, for example, might appear to change hands at a bargain £150,000, with the remainder paid in used notes. It may be tempting to go down this route, especially if you are assured by the vendor that 'everyone does it'. They may be right, and it is probably extremely unlikely that you will be caught, but the risk is always there. In some countries, authorities will investigate if a property is sold for a suspiciously low amount. You should also consider the potential risk of walking around with £50,000 or more in your suitcase. If you are buying with a mortgage, it will also reduce the amount you can borrow, since all the documentation will show the bogus purchase price rather than the real one.

Worth considering, too, are the potential implications for your liability to capital gains tax both in the country in which you are buying and at home. By understating the purchase price you will, at a stroke, have increased your taxable 'profit', which could cost you dear when you come to dispose of the property – unless you have gone native to such an extent that you under-state the sale price as well.

This will be only the beginning of your relationship with the foreign taxman. Once you have bought the property, you will find yourself liable for the local equivalent of **council tax**. Again, this varies from country to country, but is generally linked to the value of the property. A few countries, such as France, also levy a **wealth tax**. Even if you are not resident in the country, you will be liable if the value of your property there exceeds a certain amount. In 2005, for example, it kicked in at €732,000 (£493,000), with a tax starting at 0.55 per cent on anything over that, increasing in bands to 1.8 per cent on anything more than €15,255,000 (£10,268,420).

Once you start to let your property, there will be more tax demands. In most cases, **rental income** is treated like earned income and taxed accordingly, although some countries may have different rules. Either way, you will have to fill in a tax form and pay the appropriate amount. As this will probably be your only income in that country, you will come into the lower tax bands and your bill should not be too high. In most cases, you should be able to reduce it by offsetting various costs. The biggest of these will probably be your mortgage payments (although note that only the interest element and not the capital repayments count as a legitimate cost). You should also be able to add in other costs, such as wear and tear and maintenance and maybe even the cost of your trips to the country to inspect the property.

This will not always be the case, however. In both Hungary and Bulgaria, for example, if you buy as a foreign non-resident, then you must pay tax on the gross rent, without the possibility of offsetting your mortgage interest or other costs. Although the headline rates may seem relatively low (25 per cent and 15 per cent, respectively) they can cut substantially into the yield and turn the cash flow negative if you have taken out a large mortgage. The Belgians, whose tax system otherwise has little to commend it, come out surprisingly well here: a flat tax, known as the *précompte immobilier*, is levied on each property according to its *revenue cadastral* (rateable value). Although levied at anything up to 50 per cent or so, depending on the district, it is not as onerous as it seems, since the values used have not kept up with the substantial property inflation in Belgium during the last decade.

Your next contact with the foreign taxman will come when it is time to sell. Most countries, like Britain, levy **capital gains tax** on the proceeds (Italy is an unexpected exception). The rate varies from place to place. The amount you pay will also depend on how long you have owned the property. In order to discourage short-term speculation, most countries levy the full amount on those who sell after only a year or two, but reduce the amount as the years pass. In some place, there is no tax to pay on property held for just three or five years; in France you must wait 15 years for a full exemption. Again, the Belgians have a pleasant surprise in store: three-fifths of the 12.5 per cent stamp duty you were charged when you bought will be refunded if you sell within two years.

You should also consider what would happen if you die while owning the property. **Inheritance tax** regimes differ considerably from country to country. Italy, for example, does not currently impose any inheritance tax at all. Nor do Cyprus or Slovakia. In France and Spain, by contrast, rates can be extremely high. There are other differences, too: while in Britain the amount of tax paid depends on the value of the estate of the deceased, in some others it will depend on the financial situation of the heirs. You should establish how the rules work before you buy, since in some cases it may be more advantageous to buy the property in the name of one partner rather than the other or in the name of children. It is a sobering thought that the amount of money saved (albeit by your heirs) as a result of optimising such arrangements could dwarf the amount of profit made on the property during your lifetime.

Buying as an Individual or as a Company

The above is based on the premise that you have bought the property in your own name or jointly with a spouse or partner. In some countries it may be more advantageous to buy through a specially created local company, which, in most cases, will be treated as if it were native to that country even if it is entirely owned and run by non-resident foreigners. In some countries there is no alternative. In the Czech Republic, for example, foreigners, even from other EU countries such as Britain, remain barred from buying property in their own names and must set up a company to do so instead. (The restriction is due to end in May 2009, but could be dropped earlier.) In Bulgaria, non-residents can buy flats but not yet houses. In a number of countries there are restrictions on buying farmland.

There are also a number of national peculiarities: in Croatia, foreigners buying as individuals must go through the formality of seeking the approval of the foreign ministry for their purchase; this is not required if they buy through a company. The same is true in Turkey, although there it is the military authorities whose permission has to be sought.

In most cases, though, the decision will be purely financial. Buying through a company will, in most cases, allow you to offset more costs against taxable income than if you bought as an individual, while the tax rate levied could well be lower. The treatment of capital gains tax could also be different, although not necessarily more advantageous. There will be other differences, too. When you come to sell, for example, you could sell the company that owns the property rather than the property itself. Your estate could also be treated differently for inheritance tax purposes if you die. Balanced against this are the costs of setting up a company, which could vary from a few hundred pounds to a couple of thousand. The expenses do not stop there. You will also have to file accounts, which will probably mean hiring a local accountant. It could also make it more difficult to obtain finance: some banks may be reluctant to lend on the same terms to a company as they would to an individual, even if you, as an individual, personally guarantee the loan.

Deciding which route to take will require careful consideration, and the decision you make will depend on the country concerned and the precise nature of your investment. It will also be affected by how many properties you buy. It may not be worth setting up a company to acquire one, but could be well worth it if you are spreading the costs across four or five. Any decision should be made only after seeking expert advice.

What about the Inland Revenue?

Your liability does not end there. If you live in Britain (and are not one of the lucky few who enjoy so-called non-domiciled status), then your investments abroad could also mean a tax liability in Britain – irrespective of whether you actually bring any of the proceeds into the country. The authorities in Dubai, for example, will not tax your rental income, but HM Revenue & Customs will, provided that you follow the rules and declare the money you have received on your UK tax form. For this reason, you should not get too carried away by the apparently favourable tax regime of the country in which you are investing. The precise nature of your liability at home will depend on a number of factors – most importantly on whether or not the country in which you are investing has a **double taxation agreement** with Britain.

There are legitimate ways of reducing this liability. The simplest is timing. If you sell your investment property in a year when your income is relatively low – perhaps once you have retired – then your tax bill will be lower. Buying through a company rather than in your own name will also give you greater flexibility in deciding when you receive the proceeds from your investment, which could also be advantageous. As we shall see later in this chapter, it may be possible in certain circumstances to use self-invested personal pensions (SIPPs) to cut your tax bill. There are also far more sophisticated ways of managing your affairs through the creation of offshore companies or trusts, but such schemes are beyond the scope of this book.

I have assumed during the above that you are ordinarily resident in Britain for tax purposes. This may cease to be the case if you go off to tend to your investments and spend less than 183 days a year in the UK. In such a case, your only liabilities would be to the new country in which you live. HM Revenue & Customs can take a lot of convincing that you have really left for good, though: even if you take up residence elsewhere, you will still be considered as 'ordinarily resident' in the UK if you spend an average of 91 or more days in this country over any four-year period.

Some Useful Sources on Foreign Property and Tax

- **HM Revenue & Customs, www.hmrc.gov.uk.**
- **Property Tax Portal, www.property-tax-portal.co.uk.**

Legal Matters

There are not only potential financial pitfalls when it comes to buying abroad; there are legal ones, too. Before handing over your money, you should be confident that you are actually buying what you think you are buying and that there are no associated problems with the transaction that will come back to haunt you some time down the line, perhaps when you decide to sell.

In many respects, the whole process and attendant rituals will probably be unlike what you are used to at home, although the differences will be greater in some countries than in others. In Britain, the transaction for buying property is in two stages: first you exchange contracts and then you complete. Although it is possible to do both simultaneously if you are in a hurry, most people leave a gap of at least a couple of weeks or so between them. There is a similar two-stage process in France, where you first sign a *compromis de vente* (and pay 10 per cent of the price) and then conclude the deal with the *acte de vente*. In France, as in much of the rest of continental Europe, the process is controlled by a *notaire* (notary), who ensures that all the procedures are carried out in accordance with the law and who is paid handsomely in return. In these countries, you will not be required to employ a lawyer separately as well, but you may want to do so – especially in the many parts of central and eastern Europe where there could be problems with legal title to your property. Things can be different in the Middle East or Asia. Procedures also vary when you are buying off-plan and making stage payments.

Although, by definition, all countries in which you would consider buying have some system of **land registration**, these also differ greatly from place to place. Some land registries will be perfectly computerised high-tech institutions, while others are more like relics from the 19th century. For this reason, in some places purchases are registered almost immediately; in others registration can be a long, bureaucratic process that could take months – which could be a problem if you want to sell in the meantime. As mentioned above, the process is further complicated in Croatia and Turkey, for example, by the need for foreign buyers to have their purchases approved by the authorities.

The **quality of title** will also differ. In some countries, it is fairly easy to establish whether everything is in order. In others, where records have not been kept so well, things may be considerably more complicated. This can be exacerbated by **inheritance rules**. If you are buying an old farmhouse in a country where property is traditionally split between all the children, you may find that it has a multiplicity of owners – which can be a problem if it turns out that one of them emigrated to Australia decades ago and can no longer be reached.

Issues relating to inheritance can also be of direct importance to you when buy. Unlike Britain, some countries impose rules on whom you can leave your property to – making it impossible, for example, to disinherit a child even if you have severed relations with him or her years ago. In some places, these rules are binding on you even if you do not live there. In others, there may be an exemption for non-resident foreigners. Such matters will be of particular concern to those with former spouses or otherwise complicated family set-ups. Whatever the situation, it is worth making a **will** in the country in which the property is located – making clear it applies only to immovable property in that country and not to your worldwide assets.

You may come across other problems or obstacles not mentioned above during the buying process; alternatively, the whole procedure may be much simpler and more straightforward than you expected. Either way, there is no substitute for taking good legal advice, either from an English-speaking lawyer in the country in which you are buying or from a British-based firm that has already helped other Britons to buy there.

The Great Pensions Bonanza that Wasn't

When Gordon Brown, the Chancellor of the Exchequer, first announced a major overhaul of the pension system, to come into effect from April 2006, he can scarcely have anticipated the full extent of the excitement – and controversy – that his plans would generate. Pensions, after all, have never been the sexiest of subjects. Admittedly, almost everyone of working age has had it drummed into them by now that the state is not going to look after them in their old age and that they should join an occupational or private scheme. Most of those who have done so acted more out of a sense of duty than enthusiasm; this could be because, quite simply, we do not like to think about getting old, but it may also be because of the way in which our pensions have hitherto been separated from our other savings and investments.

Far from being actively involved in how our pension contributions are invested, most of us sit back passively as the money is deducted from our salaries at source and sent off to anonymous money managers who, despite earning fabulous salaries, seem strangely incapable of even matching the performance of the FTSE 100. And then, to make things worse, once we reach retirement age and try to get our hands on our money, we find ourselves bound by all sorts of rules, including a requirement that, whether we like it or not, we must eventually use a large chunk of it to buy an annuity.

All this, however, was to change on 6 April 2006 – dubbed 'A-Day' – thanks in large part to something called the SIPP, short for Self-Invested Personal Pension, a kind of do-it-yourself financial arrangement that effectively allows people to choose which assets they want to put into a tax-efficient wrapper for their old age. Certain groups had been able to make use of these SIPPs since 1991, but from 'A-Day' everyone was to be allowed to take one out. Equally significant were changes in the kind of investment that could legitimately be put into the wrapper. Brown announced that various restrictions hitherto in force would be swept away, making it possible for SIPPs to be used to buy into a wide range of assets, including residential property.

Egged on by the financial services industry, many people immediately drew up plans to put large chunks of their pensions into buy-to-let properties, both in Britain and abroad. The advantages were obvious: in return for some restrictions on the terms under which the money could be accessed, the government was effectively offering higher-rate taxpayers a 40 per cent discount on the purchase price of their property, coupled with further advantageous tax treatment of the rental income to come. While the main emphasis was on investment property (both at home and abroad), some people considered buying a holiday home through a SIPP or even transferring their main residence into one – even if this meant they would have to pay 'rent' to their own pension fund for the privilege of living there. Taking the Chancellor at his word, a number of investors already signed up during 2005 to buy into off-plan projects that were not due for completion until after 'A-Day' and thus qualified under the scheme.

While many were delighted at the prospect of what looked suspiciously like money for nothing, others, especially on the left, were appalled: in an article on 8 October 2005, entitled 'The great fat cat tax giveaway', *The Guardian* demanded, 'Did Labour really mean to hand billions in property tax relief to the already wealthy?', before going on to portray SIPPs as likely to be responsible for a number of ills, including pushing the prices of the cheapest properties beyond the reach of first-time buyers.

Amid the polemics, there were also questioning voices from within the financial services industry who wondered aloud how suitable an instrument SIPPs were anyway for property investment, given the likely high administration costs and lack of potential for leverage.

Then came the U-turn. In his pre-budget report in December 2005, the Chancellor unexpectedly announced that the government would remove from its 'A-Day' provisions the tax advantages he had promised for investing in residential property and other equally contentious assets such as fine wines, classic cars and art and antiques. The official reason given for the decision to exclude residential property was to prevent people abusing the system by buying holiday homes subsidised by the state. Underlying it, too, was also probably concern that people would be tempted to shift too large a proportion of their pensions into property – which could lead to disaster, and blame for Brown, if the property market crashed.

Despite cries of anguish from the financial services industry, which had ploughed millions of pounds into developing and marketing SIPP-related schemes – and also from those investors who had already taken the plunge – the Chancellor is not for turning. This is not to say, however, that SIPPs cannot be used at all for buying foreign property, providing certain conditions are satisfied. Strangely, though, with only a few weeks to go before the regime was due to come into force, there were still considerable grey areas, which only looked likely to become clear as time went on.

For this reason, much of what follows should be treated with caution, not least because HM Revenue & Customs is expected to enjoy considerable leeway in determining what is allowed and what is not. Before taking such a step, it is also worth considering whether a SIPP is the best vehicle anyway, especially when buying property abroad, where the tax advantages are not as clear-cut as they would be with investing in the UK.

Dos and Don'ts

Commercial Property

So where can you put your money? Taking the Chancellor's words at face value, there is nothing to prevent you from using your SIPP to buy commercial property. Although this is not a subject covered in this book, the commercial property market can be just as attractive as the residential one in a number of countries, especially the rapidly developing economies of central and eastern Europe. Nor need it be any less accessible: few individual investors have anything like the funds to buy an office block, but a small shop, bar or restaurant will not necessarily cost more than an apartment or villa. Commercial properties should benefit just as much from the general economic upswing as residential ones, while leases tend to be longer, with the obligation on the tenant rather than the landlord to maintain the property. Larger properties need not be out of reach, either; individual investors could simply club together and split the ownership of such properties between their SIPPs. The same is true for purchasing **land**.

Before taking the plunge, however, it is worth considering the **drawbacks**, especially when using SIPPs to buy property abroad. The first concerns the **tax benefits** – a fundamental consideration given that this is why people are interested in using the formula at all. Although a SIPP will allow you the initial tax breaks, there is unlikely to be any more favourable treatment of your rental income or eventual capital gains if you buy abroad. With the exception of only a handful of countries, the rest of the world does not recognise the trust structure that underlies SIPPs and will therefore tax your fund's activities as if it were a conventional commercial entity.

Second, as mentioned above, there is the question of **leverage** – or the lack of it. Under the rules, a SIPP will only be able to borrow 50 per cent of the value of its fund, irrespective of the cost of the property in which it invests. As discussed in Chapter 04, **Living on Borrowed Money**, pp.32–4, leverage is at the heart of making money in property and the '50 per cent rule' sharply reduces the possibility for this. Indeed, in markets which are moving quickly upwards, you could make a far larger profit by borrowing heavily, buying in your own name and paying all the tax due rather than doing so through a more lightly leveraged SIPP.

This is also all assuming, of course, that you can find a SIPP provider willing to provide the pension wrapper into which to put your investment – and to do so at a reasonable price. Although most providers will be happy to oblige on a commercial property in the UK, they may be more wary when it comes to buying a shop in Bulgaria or small office block in Poland.

Residential Property

The situation with residential property is more complicated. While the Chancellor made it clear that he would not allow an individual to buy a single flat or house, he carried out a further U-turn days before 'A-Day'. Treasury officials indicated that it would, after all, be possible for people to hold residential property, provided they did so through vehicles such as **real estate investment trusts (REITs**, a new form of investment vehicle to be introduced in 2007), **property unit trusts** or by creating a **syndicate**. Under the new rules, the latter must have a minimum of 10 members and own at least three properties worth a minimum of £1m in total. The different investors must not be related and cannot use the properties personally. In a further restriction, no single asset can be worth 40 per cent or more of the total value of the pension assets. There are other considerations, too, like what happens if your circumstances change and you want to leave the syndicate. Such schemes will be completely illiquid, meaning you would have to find someone else prepared to buy your holding.

If you don't mind all these complications, it could still be an effective way of including property in your pension, especially since it is thought the schemes will be able to borrow money on normal loan-to-value terms, rather than only 50 per cent of the value of net assets, as is the case with pensions. But be ready to be closely policed by HM Revenue & Customs, which will undoubtedly take a dim view of anything it considers an attempt to circumvent the letter or spirit of the law. Ultimately, it may take a test case to decide – with potentially painful consequences for those who have chosen to go down this path. If the tax authorities decide a particular scheme does not satisfy the rules, they could take punitive action against any SIPPs that have invested in them.

Conclusion

Given the pitfalls, the safest course for those determined to go down the SIPP path might simply be to invest in one of the many funds that have been set up to cash in on the global property boom. The nature of such investments may be anathema to the classic fly-to-let investor; as with any other fund, you are giving up control of where your money is invested and leaving the decisions to a fund manager. You may not even be able to choose the country to which it goes. In contrast to direct investment in property, there are also no possibilities for leverage. On the plus side, however, the returns enjoyed by such funds look likely to be good as long as the global property market continues to grow. You will also be able to sleep soundly at night, secure in the knowledge that the taxman is not poised to raid your pension pot.

Where Will It All End?

The Global Property Boom

Will the British love affair with bricks and mortar ever end? In the first years of the new millennium, as first the London property market and then those in the rest of the country began to slow and turn downwards, it seemed as if this might at last be the case. Admittedly, many home-owners, especially in the southeast, were sitting on tens or even hundreds of thousands of pounds of equity thanks to years of steep price rises, while the various television channels were still pumping out hours of property-related programming every week. Yet there was no doubt that property was no longer looking like the one-way bet that it had seemed a year or so earlier.

That old fascination has proved difficult to break, however, even though the object of desire has changed. If the UK housing market is looking old and tired, so growing numbers of people reasoned, then why not look elsewhere instead? And so the foreign property boom began in earnest, as traditional buyers of second and holiday homes were suddenly joined by a new breed of investor in search of good yields and capital returns. Indeed, owning a house or flat abroad is no longer the preserve of the super rich.

To portray this as a solely British phenomenon would be inaccurate. The Irish, for example, are even more avid buyers. Inspired – and financed – by their own domestic property boom, they have been buying in almost industrial quantities, especially in the former Communist countries of central and eastern Europe. During a visit to Kraków, in southern Poland, in spring 2005, a local estate agent told me about an Irish investor with whom she had just been in contact. 'He said first of all that he wanted to buy 10 properties, but he has just sent me an e-mail saying he wants 20,' she said, already salivating at the prospect of the commission to come.

We are clearly talking here about a far broader global phenomenon that goes way beyond the British Isles. On one level, it is all simply part of one of the most controversial and also inexorable trends of the late 20th and early 21st centuries: globalisation. For those who mount noisy – and sometimes violent – demonstrations against it at G8 summits, globalisation is all about ruthless multinationals carving up the world's markets between them, riding roughshod over the impoverished and powerless masses of the developing world. Yet globalisation, in the widest sense of the word, has also been about individuals. In the last couple of decades there have been enormous changes in the way we go on holiday. The invention of the package tour, which democ- ratised foreign travel in the 1960s and '70s, was followed in the late 1990s by the arrival of low-cost airlines, which ushered in a new era of weekend breaks and more adventurous individual travel. Crossing borders has also become much less bureaucratic as growing European integration, coupled with the end of Communism and fall of the Berlin Wall, have drastically reduced the need for visas. Not content with setting out to visit new places, people have become increasingly keen – and able – to buy property there as well. This is not just a function of growing affluence and the growing sophistication of financial markets that have allowed people to withdraw and then spend equity from their homes; globalisation has played its part, too. Just as financial institutions are now free to transfer billions of pounds backwards and forwards across borders, so individuals can do the same with far smaller amounts. We sometimes forget how quickly things have changed; after all, until Margaret Thatcher came to power in 1979, exchange controls still limited the amount of money Britons could take out of the country.

At the same time, other countries have moved to end restrictions that prevent outsiders from buying property there. The European Union, whose members are barred from discriminating against citizens from elsewhere in the EU, has led the way, with the 10 countries that joined in 2004 obliged to bring their rules into line with the existing 15 members. Many other countries have followed, as their governments have realised that the benefits of foreign investment outweigh broader concerns about their countries being 'bought up' by foreigners. As will be seen in the second part of this book, restrictions still remain. This is not just in Communist Vietnam and some of the Gulf states, but also, far closer to home in Switzerland.

Factors that Have Helped the Boom

Other, more specific factors have helped fuel the boom, chief among them the growing perception that houses are not just somewhere to live but also a financial asset like any other, with a capital value that can vary over time like that of a share, and a dividend in the form of rental income. True, property can be an extremely illiquid asset, as anyone who has tried to dispose of a house in a hurry knows only too well. The costs of buying and selling in many countries can also be far higher than with shares. Earning the 'dividend' requires work, too, such as finding a tenant and maintaining the property.

On the other side, though, thanks to mortgages, property offers a degree of leverage not easily available with other forms of investment, which can magnify a gain by as much as a factor of five. In many countries, the taxman also treats investments in property more generously than other financial assets (even though most privileges are usually confined to first homes).

Various other factors have encouraged this trend towards foreign property-buying. One has been timing: the UK economy has been largely out of sync with those of its European partners, with the result that the British property market peaked earlier than those of, say, Spain, France and Italy during the 1990s. This meant that, as things began to cool at home, people looked across the Channel, saw things were still moving there and were encouraged to try their luck. The high levels of property prices, especially in London and the southeast, also helped. Viewed through the eyes of the owner of a modest Victorian semi in

Islington or Wandsworth, almost any other property in the world – with the exception of prime Manhattan – looked cheap.

The expansion of the EU also, at a stroke, added a series of new countries seen as a more or less 'safe' investment. Thanks to aggressive marketing, Bulgaria, an impoverished former Communist country not even due to join the EU until 2007, has been successfully portrayed as the next Spain, prompting growing numbers of people – who would never previously have dreamed even of visiting the place – to invest in off-plan projects. Others have looked to countries like the Czech Republic, Hungary and the Baltic states, dazzled by their stellar economic growth rates. But why stop at the borders of Europe, when the Middle East, Asia and Latin America also appear ripe for the picking?

And so, the process goes on. The property supplements of *The Sunday Times* and other newspapers and television programmes like *A Place in the Sun* are constantly on the outlook for the next Bulgaria or Dubai. So, too, are the small, but growing, number of British-based agencies such as Property Frontiers and Someplace Else, which offer off-plan investments in increasingly exotic destinations. It is no coincidence that this boom has coincided with the growth of the Internet. The web is an extraordinarily important medium for such companies – and others that specialise in individual countries or regimes; the large sums many spend on the targeted online advertising programmes pioneered by Google are proof enough of that. The Internet has also empowered the individual buyer, who, sitting at his or her home computer, can carry out quite detailed research into many of the world's property markets.

What Next?

And so, to return to the question posed at the beginning of this chapter: where will it all end? Clearly, property prices are no more immune to the rules of gravity than anything else and years of double-digit growth cannot go on for ever. As discussed in detail in Chapter 02, the prevailing property prices in a particular place will depend on a number of variables, chief among them the income levels of the end-users – the people who live there. This simple relation may be distorted by the presence of speculators buying property purely in anticipation of future gains. It may also be more complicated in tourist areas, where prices will also reflect the economics of the buyers' home countries.

Despite such distortions, it is nevertheless plausible to point to a broad correlation over time between incomes and house prices, and to draw lessons about the state of a market if prices deviate far in either direction from this trend line. At its most basic, this correlation may simply be the crude ratio between average incomes and average houses. Thus, the fact that house prices in Spain in 2004 had reached a historic high of 5.14 times average income, while the multiple in France was a more modest 3.17, was, on the face of it, a sign that

Spain was overvalued relative to France and a warning sign to anyone entering the Spanish market that it was dangerously near the top.

Although a start, this is clearly an oversimplification: not only do national averages conceal enormous differences between cities and regions, but there may also be reasons why property becomes relatively more expensive over time; this is especially the case with hitherto obscure places in developing countries that are suddenly discovered by foreign second-home buyers.

Even more importantly, such a ratio also omits the effect of interest rates, which are of vital importance in developed economies where property is generally bought not for cash but on credit. The important ratio, therefore, might not be the one between incomes and the absolute level of house prices, but instead between incomes and the level of mortgage repayments required to buy such a property. Such a ratio is necessarily more difficult to calculate with precision, but it helps to explain some movements in prices. For this reason, it is hardly surprising that, as nominal (if not always, real) interest rates have come down in most European countries during the last decade, the value of property has gone up. The ratio may have been further distorted by the growing availability of mortgages and emergence of long-term or interest-only loans, which will also tend to boost affordability.

That being said, there is still little doubt that in early 2006 several property markets were beginning to look distinctly overvalued. As will be discussed in greater detail in Part Two of this book, Spain – or parts of it – is certainly one. So, too, is much of the USA. There are also dangers of more localised bubbles elsewhere, in Dubai, for example, or in Bulgaria, where, in echoes of a pyramid scheme, demand has been driven largely by investors rather than by end-users.

What will happen next remains difficult to predict, however. One, particularly gloomy school of thought was represented by an article in *The Economist*, published on 16 June 2005. Entitled 'In Come the Waves', it was illustrated by a picture of a precarious-looking sandcastle, about to be overwhelmed by water. 'The total value of residential property in developed economies rose by more than $30 trillion over the past five years, to over $70 trillion, an increase equivalent to 100 per cent of those countries' combined GDPs,' the article noted. 'Not only does this dwarf any previous house-price boom, it is larger than the global stockmarket bubble in the late 1990s (an increase over five years of 80 per cent of GDP) or America's stockmarket bubble in the late 1920s (55 per cent of GDP). In other words, it looks like the biggest bubble in history.'

Concentrating on the situation in America, the article's author outlined a gloomy scenario in which property prices would fall sharply, dragging the broader economy down with them, as house-owners who had used equity withdrawn from their houses to fund increased spending drew in their horns. As the magazine points out, the housing market is of vital importance to the overall health of the US economy: in the four years to 2005, consumer spending and residential construction together accounted for 90 per cent of the total growth in GDP, while more than two-fifths of all private-sector jobs created since 2001 were in housing-related sectors, such as construction, real estate and mortgage broking.

Yet maybe one should not be overly depressed by such predictions. While looking for *The Economist* article quoted above, I came across another, published just over two years earlier on 29 May 2003 and written by the magazine's economics editor, Pam Woodall, which made almost exactly the same point. Entitled 'House of cards', it was introduced with the words: 'In many countries the stockmarket bubble has been replaced by a property-price bubble. Sooner or later it will burst.' The author went on, Cassandra-like, to predict 'falls in average real house prices of 15–20 per cent in America and 30 per cent or more elsewhere over the next few years'. Ms Woodall may well eventually be right – just as those who were too early to call the end of the dot-com boom of the late 1990s were proved correct when the bubble finally burst. With every year of double-digit growth that passes, some kind of correction appears more likely. Yet shifts from boom to bust and back again in property markets are notoriously difficult to call. Indeed, if anyone had responded to that May 2003 article by selling their investment property in Paris, Barcelona or Florida and putting the proceeds in the bank, they would probably be kicking themselves.

That said, caution is certainly advised, especially in those markets where prices have been rising especially strongly. Falling yields, although a normal phenomenon as markets mature, should also be watched closely. The value of an asset is ultimately dictated by the value of the income that it generates. If this drops too far below the cost of borrowing, then alarm bells should ring.

Wherever and whatever you buy, you should also bear in mind the amount of time and effort that can be involved in maintaining a property, especially one abroad. It may seem all too painless when you are picking your shiny new off-plan flat from the brochure; but fast-forward a year when the development is completed and you are trying in vain to find a tenant – or a year on from there, when the roof is leaking or maybe, even worse, the tenant has decided to stop paying the rent. A good local management agency should be able to shield you from a lot of the hassle. Ultimately, though, it is your property, and if serious problems do arise, they are going to come back to haunt you.

But enough of the doom and gloom. Provided you watch out for the pitfalls and don't get carried away, there is still considerable money to be made in property in a bewilderingly large number of places, and this is likely to remain the case for several years to come. The only question is where.

In the next part of the book, therefore, I look at the world region by region, focusing on the countries of most interest. If you already know where you want to invest, you could simply turn straight to that section. But why not take a little time to wander through the other parts of the world first? If not, you might never realise what you are missing.

Part Two: Where to Fly to Let?

Emerging Europe

The fall of the Berlin Wall in 1989 and collapse of the Soviet Union two years later changed not just Europe but also the world for good. The artificial division that had existed for more than four decades was gone and, slowly but surely, Europe began to knit itself together again. As well as the enormous political, economic and social changes that have occurred on what used to be the 'wrong' side of the Iron Curtain, aspects of life in the west have changed, too. It seems just as normal these days to go for a long weekend to Prague or Budapest as it does to travel to Paris or Barcelona – or to find a Pole, Lithuanian or Czech making the same trip in the opposite direction, or working in Britain. Buying property in these countries is also becoming commonplace, and prices, although still relatively cheap, are moving rapidly towards western European levels. In some cases, they have even overtaken them. Strange as it may sound, some districts of Prague are already more expensive than parts of Berlin.

Growth of a Market

Foreign property investors – and indeed the creation of what could be called a real estate market in the British or American sense of the term – were some time coming in the eastern European countries. Communism had left the countries' new democratic rulers with a number of problems to resolve. As far as property was concerned, this meant locating and compensating the rightful owners of houses and flats seized by the state in the years after the Second World War. In most cases the problem was complicated further by the question of what to do with property confiscated from Jewish owners by the Nazis during the 1930s and 1940s.

Many of the buildings were also in a deplorable state after decades of neglect. Once-elegant late 19th- and early 20th-century Art Nouveau buildings were shabby, with entrances and staircases badly in need of attention. Even many of the modern prefabricated concrete tower blocks that sprang up across the region during the 1970s and 1980s were already starting to crumble.

Braver investors already recognised the potential of cities such as Prague and Budapest in the early 1990s and took the plunge, buying property there. Some of the more unfortunate ones soon found they did not actually own what they had just paid their hard-earned money for. Others bought at what in retrospect look to be ridiculously cheap prices, and have seen the value of their initial investments increase four- or even fivefold.

Ownership issues in most countries have now been largely resolved, although anyone buying in the region would be advised to pay even more attention to title than they would do in France or Italy. (There are particular problems in Croatia and the Turkish part of Cyprus, which, although not a former Communist country, still belongs under the 'Emerging Europe' heading. I will discuss both in more detail in their respective sections.)

That is not all that has changed. Visit any of the capital cities today and it is difficult to imagine that less than 20 years ago they were still run by authoritarian Communist regimes. The shopping streets today are full of familiar names from McDonald's to Giorgio Armani, while the once ubiquitous statues of Lenin have long since been consigned to museums or theme parks. Even more important, if less immediately visible, is the extent to which these countries' economies have been reformed and reorientated towards the west. In the process they have become some of the fastest-growing and most dynamic countries in the world, with low taxes and rapid growth. Serious structural problems remain, however. Travel a few miles away from the bustling capitals and you will enter a very different and depressing world of grinding poverty and high unemployment.

What Is Meant by 'Emerging Europe'?

To talk of 'emerging Europe' is also an over-generalisation, since the countries in this chapter are at various stages of development. It would be more accurate to divide them into the 'emerged' and the 'yet to emerge' countries of Europe.

The 'emerged' countries are the Czech Republic, Estonia, Hungary, Latvia, Lithuania, Poland, Slovakia and Slovenia, together with Cyprus and Malta. All joined the EU in May 2004, with all the positive implications that this has for the workings of their economies. Their respective levels of affluence vary considerably, as do the economic policies pursued by their governments. Some – chiefly the Baltic states and Slovakia – have turned themselves into highly attractive places for foreign investors by embracing a Thatcherite model of free markets and low 'flat' taxes. Partly as a result – and party because they started from such a low base – their economies have grown twice or three times as fast as those of western European countries. The Czech Republic, Hungary and Poland, by contrast, have not gone for such radical change, perhaps because they were already wealthier; their growth rates, although impressive, have been slightly lower. All the countries are committed to joining the euro, but at different times: at the time of writing (early 2006), Estonia, Lithuania and Slovenia were hoping to adopt the single currency in 2007; Latvia, Cyprus and Malta were planning to follow in 2008; Slovakia in 2009; and the three largest, Poland, Hungary and the Czech Republic, looked likely to wait until 2010.

The property markets of these countries have developed in broadly similar ways, with prices rising strongly in the first few years of the new millennium, as a result of rapidly growing incomes and falling interest rates. Just as important has been the growing availability of mortgage finance, which was unheard of in Communist days. The level of mortgage debt in all the countries remains only a fraction of that in Britain or other western European countries, but has been growing rapidly as people take out loans to buy their first home or trade up. Price rises were especially fevered in the run-up to these countries joining the

EU – in most cases, overshooting and drifting back down afterwards when the expected wall of western money did not materialise. The overall trend remains upward, with annual rises of 10 per cent or so typical across the region, underpinned by rising incomes and the continuing downward trend in interest rates, which must still fall a few more points before the countries can join the euro. All those years of Communism have also created considerable pent-up demand for housing: the amount of living space enjoyed by an average citizen in a central or eastern European capital is far less than that of his or her counterpart in the west. The quality of many apartment blocks is also extremely poor. For this reason, prices will continue to be driven by the growing aspiration of the emerging middle classes, in particular, to move out of old, cramped Communist-era flats into modern blocks, ideally with underground parking.

And then there are the 'emerging' three: Bulgaria, Croatia and Romania. Of the three, Bulgaria is the one that has so far attracted the most attention from British property investors. Thanks to massive marketing campaigns by developers and their agents, thousands of people have bought into off-plan developments on the Black Sea coast and in the mountains, seduced by the prospect of soaring property prices. As we shall see in the section on Bulgaria, there are concerns about the sustainability of the boom, but there is no doubting the considerable efforts made by the Bulgarian government to modernise the economy ahead of the expected entry of the country into the EU in 2007. In this way Bulgaria has proved itself just as keen to adopt free-market, investor-friendly policies as the most advanced of the 'emerged' countries. Romania, although considerably larger, has attracted far less attention, despite having a similar economic system and its own stretch of Black Sea coast. If all goes according to plan, Romania should join the EU at the same time as Bulgaria does, and prices, especially in Bucharest, the capital, are likely to continue rising sharply in the meantime. Croatia, by contrast, does not yet have an EU entry date, but this has not stopped prices shooting up in recent years. As with Bulgaria, foreign interest has been largely concentrated on coastal areas. Here, unusually, the British and Irish are not the pioneers; the Germans have had their towels round the pool for years.

Why stop there? The especially intrepid may want to venture even deeper into the former Soviet Union, to Ukraine or Russia, Moldova, Georgia, Armenia or Azerbaijan, or maybe even into Kazakhstan or Uzbekistan. There is undoubtedly money to be made there – but the risks are also considerable. None of these countries has what we consider a normally functioning real estate market. If you are determined to go there, the best I can do is to wish you luck!

Buying Property in Emerging European Countries

Even if you choose to buy property in one of the 'emerged countries', bear in mind that, despite the remarkable progress made since the fall of Communism, many practices relating to property are still different from those in France or Spain, let alone Britain or Ireland.

Differences begin with the buying process itself. Estates agents did not exist during the Communist years and, although large numbers have become established since, they do not dominate the market in the way they do in Britain. Many properties therefore continue to change hands through classified advertisements in the newspapers or by word of mouth – which can make it more difficult for a buyer to see a wide selection of what is available. Some chains have begun to emerge, but most agencies are small and not very professional. Even in a country as relatively sophisticated as the Czech Republic, agents do not have any certification, are not controlled by or answerable to a governing body and do not even need to be an incorporated company. All a budding agent must do is pay a licence fee of around £50 and, hey presto, they are in business. As a foreigner buying in a country that you do not know well, this can make you extremely vulnerable. In rare cases, agents can be downright dishonest, talking you into buying an unsuitable or overpriced property and perhaps recommending a lawyer or tax adviser who is also not licensed. More commonly, they will simply not be as efficient as you would like and may waste your time by failing to show you the kind of property that you really want.

Unlike in Britain, most properties will normally be on sale with several agencies rather than just one. In some respects this makes things easier, especially if you have a limited amount of time in the country for your search: all you have to do is give your requirements to the agent and he or she will have access to a considerable proportion of what is on the market. Owners will often fail to notify all the agents once they have sold their property, however, which means some of the properties you are being offered may no longer be available. Viewings can be complicated by the fact that your agent will not necessarily hold keys to all the properties on his or her books. If you decide to consult a second agent, you will probably be invited to look at some of the properties you have already seen with the first agent all over again.

You may prefer to use one of the many British-based agents that market property in the region in which you are interested. They will speak English and probably grasp more easily the kind of property that you are looking for. In most cases, they will also understand the peculiarities of buying there and help you navigate them. The good agents, which specialise in one particular country, will also have built up a good relationship with local agents. In many cases, though – especially with those web-based agencies that deal with a number of countries – there will only be a limited selection of properties, most of them off-plan, as these are the easiest for them to obtain and sell at a distance. Such developments will not necessarily be the best deals around. The agents will also probably charge you a commission of as much as 3 per cent, which you could avoid by buying straight from the developer. (This is not so difficult to do as it sounds: just tap the name of a development in which you are interested into

Google and you should be able to find the developer's website, which may well be in English as well as the local language.)

There are other potential pitfalls. It is common sense when buying in an existing building that you should have a survey to make sure there are no hidden structural problems. You should also try as far as possible to establish how the building is run and maintained and the cost implications of buying it. Many buildings in central and eastern Europe are still in extremely poor shape, with crumbling façades and common parts in need of expensive renovation. As these countries become more affluent, this renovation is beginning to happen, but someone has to organise and pay for it. The way in which ownership is organised varies from country to country, but the problems are common – and solutions rarely rapid.

Take the example of a prestigious late 19th-century building in the heart of one of the capitals – the kind of place where a foreign investor is likely to buy a splendid 100-square-metre apartment with big windows and high ceilings. I know the situation well, since this is the precisely the kind of apartment that I bought in Bratislava and with which I started this book. The flat itself was in a fairly good state, but the common parts, although once beautiful, were a disaster. I was encouraged, however, by signs that work was under way: building materials were stored in the central courtyard and a cement mixer was positioned near the entrance. In a curious arrangement that one comes across quite often in the region, I was told the repairs were being organised and paid for by one of the tenants in return for being allowed to make a flat in the attic. A lift was also supposedly being installed as part of the deal.

As anyone who has driven past a motorway partially closed for repairs knows, the mere presence of such equipment does not guarantee that the work is going to be done any time soon. And so it is that almost a year later, despite the occasional cameo appearance by a builder, the works have still not been finished, and my tenant still has to pick her way in through a dirty entrance. My only consolation is the knowledge of how splendid it will be when it is finished.

In theory, at least, new builds should avoid such problems. This may be the case when you are buying an apartment in a recently completed building, but if you are doing so off-plan then, as discussed in the first part of the book (*see* pp.25–8), a whole series of other factors come into consideration, among them the extent to which you can rely on the developer to come up with the goods. Developers in central and eastern Europe are not necessarily any less honest than those elsewhere, but regulatory controls may not be as strong and it is far better to be safe than sorry. Considering the amount of your money at stake in this venture, it is worth taking time to carry out at least the minimum of checks.

That being said, there is no denying that this part of the world is probably one of the most exciting and easily accessible for the British- or Irish-based property investor. So let us now look in more detail at the various countries and the pros and cons of each.

Bulgaria

Bulgaria is one of the most talked about of the 'emerging market' destinations. Go to any foreign property show and a substantial proportion of the exhibitors will be selling Bulgaria. The Internet is also full of companies trying to sell houses and apartments there. Try typing 'property' and 'Bulgaria' into a search engine; when I did so on Google, it came up with a staggering 8,130,000 entries, including two pages of sponsored links. It is also the country that provokes the most polarised opinions among those in the know.

For some people, and not only for agents selling there, Bulgaria is the 'New Spain' and the best thing since sliced bread. The sharp rise in property prices since the market first began attracting international attention in 2002 has reflected that: although starting from an extremely low base, they shot up by an average of 45 per cent in 2004 and, according to Bulgaria's National Association of Real Estate Agencies, were expected to rise another 14–24 per cent in 2005. Of the 204,000 property deals made during that year, 37 per cent involved foreigners, many of them British. This growth has been underpinned by the Bulgarian economy's impressive performance: GDP was expected to have grown 5.7 per cent in 2005 and to remain above 4 per cent in 2006 and 2007. The prospect of EU membership, likely in 2007, appears to provide another incentive to buy. Others are deeply suspicious and see the whole business as little more than a get-rich-quick scheme that will inevitably end in disaster.

Generalisations are dangerous, though. From an investment point of view, there are four Bulgarias: the Black Sea coast, the ski resorts, Sofia, the capital, and the countryside.

The Black Sea Coast

The hype begins already on the plane from Britain: pick up a copy of the in-flight magazine of Bulgaria Air, and almost every other page carries an advertisement for the latest Black Sea apartment complex, each apparently more glittering, splendid and above all profitable than the last. Pitch up in Sunny Beach, the brash heart of the coast, and the streets are full of estate agents peddling luxury flats and seaside villas. People go on holiday to Bulgaria these days, it seems, as much to snap up property bargains as to lie on the sand.

'There must be 40 or 50 agents here now, but very few of them have any experience or know what they are doing,' I was told during during a visit in summer 2005 by Mihail Chobanov, age 30, co-founder of Bulgarian Properties, one of the country's best-established agents, whose little office in the resort is already surrounded by several clones. 'You get one kiosk selling clothes, the next one selling hamburgers and the one in the middle selling property.'

The Bulgarian property market is booming. Old-style Communist resorts that were once the summer playgrounds of Russian, Czech and Polish workers are being demolished and replaced by a Balkan version of the Costa del Sol. In scenes familiar from the Spain of the 1970s and 1980s, virgin coast is filling rapidly with apartment blocks and prices are climbing steadily. The price of land, meanwhile, is going through the roof: plots five or 10 miles inland are being snapped up even if the sea views are so distant that you need a telescope. Many of the developments are being bought by the British and the Irish: at any property show, a substantial proportion of stands will be for Bulgarian property.

The Bulgarian coast, stretching for more than 100 miles between the Romanian and Turkish borders, certainly has much to offer, even if it lacks much of the charm of the Mediterranean. Those seeking sun, cheap beer and a noisy nightlife will make for **Sunny Beach**, near **Burgas**, or the slightly leafier **Golden Sands**, further north; known respectively as Slanchev Bryag and Zlatni Pyasatsi to Bulgarians, they have been rebranded under English names for the British market. Other, more upmarket resorts are springing up in quieter coastal locations. And in the ancient city of **Nessebar**, about a mile south of Sunny Beach, the Bulgarian coast can boast a UNESCO World Heritage site that was already a Greek colony in the 6th century BC. Worth considering, too, is **Varna**, which, as Bulgaria's third largest city, has a commercial life of its own and is not exclusively dependent on tourism.

Golf, the great motor behind much Spanish property development, is also on its way. It would be an understatement to say that Bulgaria cannot boast a great golfing tradition. The Communists who ran the country until 1989 frowned on such bourgeois leisure pursuits, preferring athletics or weight-lifting (even if the generous use of hormones meant there were often doubts about the sex of some of the competitors). Even by late 2005, the country had just three 18-hole courses and one nine-hole course. That is all changing rapidly. Gary Player, the South African veteran, is involved in two courses, north of Varna on the Black Sea coast. Ian Woosnam, the leading British professional, is developing two others, one in nearby Balchik and another close to the ski resort of Bansko. Others are planned, with a mixture of foreign and Bulgarian backers. There is also talk of exploiting the traditional spas and exotic mud treatments.

Despite annual increases of 40–50 per cent or so, property remains remarkably cheap by Spanish, let alone British, standards. It is still possible to buy a studio in Sunny Beach for as little as £400 per square metre, although the view from your window will be of concrete rather than sea or sand. Remember to check out the soundproofing: at the height of the season, the music in the open-air bars is still pounding at 3am. The nearer you get to the coast, the higher the prices, but even frontline property close to the beach with uninterrupted sea views can still be bought for well under £1,000 per square metre.

With prices this low, many investors buy in cash, perhaps by remortgaging at home. It is now possible to obtain mortgages for property in Bulgaria, although there are relatively few lenders and borrowing in the country is not especially cheap or attractive – around 7 per cent in euros was the prevailing rate in early

2006 – with a maximum loan-to-value of around 70 per cent. For some time, the only lender was Greece's Piraeus Bank, which did not fund off-plan properties, obliging buyers to find some other interim financing solution until the development was completed and signed off. Bulgaria's DSK Bank, which has since entered the market, is more flexible. Given the amount of interest from Britons and other foreigners, more banks are likely to move in as time goes on.

Matters are more promising on the taxation side. Bulgaria has embraced the 'flat tax' revolution that is sweeping Eastern Europe and looks likely to continue on this path. If you let your property, you are liable to a flat 15 per cent tax on the proceeds. Although this is low, it is not possible, as in other countries, to reduce your liability by offsetting mortgage interest and other costs against income. The local equivalent of stamp duty and other purchase costs amounts to around 3 per cent. Even though Bulgaria is not yet in the EU, it is possible to buy apartments in your name. If you wish to buy a house or just land (which can be an extremely profitable investment), you must first form a company. This is relatively straightforward and should cost around £500 or so.

Before getting too carried away with all the hype, you should ask a couple of important questions: who is going to rent your shiny new off-plan apartment from you, and how easy is it going to be for you to sell it to realise your profit?

Let us deal first with the rental issue. The most striking thing about these developments is that most foreigners – and indeed Bulgarians – buying into them are doing so purely as an investment and not because they are looking for a holiday home for their own use. Their hope is that they will be able to let them to tourists. Bulgaria's tourism figures are indeed impressive. As you can see from the table below, the number of people visiting Bulgaria grew from 2.76 million in 2001 to 4.01 million in 2004 and is likely to have gone on rising in 2005. The growth in the number of Britons has been particularly dramatic: more than 250,000 of us went on holiday there in 2004, 62 per cent more than the previous year and more than three times as many as in 2001. The overall number of visitors in 2004 was up 13.6 per cent on the previous year.

Number of Tourist Arrivals from Key Feeder Countries (2001–04)

Country	2001	2002	2003	2004	Percentage year-on-year increase 2003–04
Greece	344,677	391,386	547,700	707,453	29.2
Macedonia	643,092	621,875	672,385	655,974	−2.4
Serbia & Montenegro	359,475	534,822	591,781	576,965	−2.5
Germany	374,321	480,460	534,582	565,337	5.8
United Kingdom	69,192	110,902	159,341	259,092	62.6
Others	964,960	853,145	1,025,778	1,245,505	21.4
Total	2,755,717	2,992,590	3,531,567	4,010,326	13.6

Source: Bulgarian National Statistical Institute

Some of the British visitors might actually have been potential property investors, but they too needed somewhere to stay during their search.

Agents selling property cite such figures. Many of them claim to have deals with tour operators, who dominate the tourism business, which remains largely package-tour-based. This is likely to continue to be the case until low-cost airlines such as Ryanair or easyJet start to serve the country. Under such arrangements, the tour operators take on whole buildings for the season for use by their holiday-makers and pay a flat fee in return. To make such deals more attractive, some developers have started offering a guaranteed return for an initial period of, say, two or three years.

It would be foolish to base a long-term investment strategy on rent guarantees that are limited in time and difficult to enforce if things go wrong. The more fundamental question over the longer term is whether the growth in tourist numbers will keep pace with the amount of construction going on: you may be able to let your new flat in Sunny Beach or Golden Sands this year or next, but what will the situation look like five years from now? Tourists can be extremely fickle and places can move rapidly in and out of fashion. Many of those who holiday on the Black Sea do so not because they particularly like it, but because it is cheap. According to the scenario favoured by the doom-mongers, the bargain prices for food, drink and entertainment which are currently the country's main selling point will gradually rise towards European levels, especially once the country joins the EU. If this, in turn, dampens the growth in tourist numbers, they warn, then the tour operators will cut the amount they pay to rent flats, squeezing yields. Not every tourist wants to stay in an apartment, either; many will prefer a hotel, and if they build too many of those it will be more difficult to let your flat.

While we are being negative, it is worth noting that the Black Sea coast has a relatively short summer, at least compared with Spain or the south of France. The Bulgarian season lasts a maximum of 120 days. Beaches that seemed so welcoming in July and August can be dusted with snow in January and February. Therefore the country is not suitable for 'snowbirds', the increasing numbers of affluent retired northern Europeans who choose to winter in southern climes. Having property that is empty for just a few weeks during the season can cut quite sharply into your return.

Equally important is your exit strategy: will you be able to sell your property when you want to do so, and at what price? Those trying to persuade you to buy will point out how prices have been rising in recent years at 20 per cent or more per annum. But as any property investor knows, a profit you make is only a paper one until you actually find someone willing to purchase your flat or house. Thus there is not yet a genuine real estate market of the sort one would find in London, Paris or Prague based on existing properties changing hands between private buyers and sellers. On the Black Sea coast we are talking instead about developers putting up their prices with every new development that is

Case Study: Buying Property in Bulgaria

Jeremy Leach, 34, an IT specialist from Reading, has discovered there is money to be made in Bulgaria. Since spotting the country's potential relatively early, in 2003, he invested more than £110,000 in two flats on the coast, a village house in Nikolaevka, 14 miles inland, and some land – and reckons to have doubled his money already.

Whether this will continue to be the case remains to be seen. After selling on the first flat, in Varna, in April 2005, for a healthy profit after just over a year, he has tried to repeat the trick with a second apartment he bought for £46,000 in the Fort Knox development in Sunny Beach. Three months later, it was still on the market. 'In the past year, so many builders have been flooding Sunny Beach with new off-plan apartments that the level of competition has gone up drastically,' says Leach, who was asking £55,000 – about £3,000 less than the developers wanted for finished units. 'It seems easier for people to sell off-plan apartments than real ones, because they have huge marketing campaigns for them and everybody is trying to grab them before they go. But if they do have some flats left over once the building is finished, the development companies don't have so much to spend on the marketing.'

Although Leach remains bullish, the difficulty he is having in disposing of his latest apartment is seen by some experts as a warning sign of trouble ahead.

completed; far from being deterred by the rises, many investors are encouraged by them as an indicator of further hikes to come. Until now, the number of completed properties that have changed hands has been relatively small. As long as development continues at such a hectic pace and prices keep rising, you may well have trouble when you come to sell your apartment unless you are prepared to drop the price substantially. After all, why should another investor want to buy a second-hand property from you when they could put down a small amount of money and buy off-plan straight from the developer? And by definition the developers are only going to stop building once the market is oversupplied – in which case it will be even more difficult to shift your flat.

The same issue underlies the question of rentals and eventual sales: the domination of the market by investors rather than end-users gives the whole thing the air of a pyramid scheme. This will tend to change over time as Bulgarians become more affluent and have the money to buy a second home on the coast. But don't hold your breath. Bulgaria is one of the poorest countries in Europe, with GDP per head of around £4,400 – only just over half the level of even Hungary or the Czech Republic – which translates into an average monthly wage of just £100. Although there are a number of extremely wealthy people, most Bulgarians are more concerned with buying or renting a decent main home. And even those that are will not necessarily want a flat in Sunny Beach.

Patrick Berger, who has analysed the Black Sea property market for CA-IB, an investment bank that specialises in emerging Europe, is concerned at the sheer size of the flood of British and other western money pouring into Bulgaria in search of investment projects. He fears the result could be the kind of overbuilding that has blighted much of the *costas*. 'If you want to make a profit, then invest now, but you need to monitor developments and time your exit from the market carefully,' he told me. 'It's not something where you can invest and then just go to sleep at night, because overnight they might start building a mega-complex next to you.'

All the above may be unduly negative. Jonty Crossick, co-founder of Brighton-based Ready 2 Rent, which has already sold more than 130 flats off-plan in Bulgaria for other developers and is developing three complexes on the coast at Kranevo, Obzor and Akutino, has little time for such doom-mongering. As Crossick sees it, high economic growth and foreign investment, rising tourist numbers, a stable currency and political system and impending EU membership make for an irresistible combination. A further boost is likely to come from the eventual arrival of low-cost airlines that will bring in individual tourists alongside those on packages. 'Once Ryanair and easyJet get in there, it will be a whole different ball game,' he said. 'We wouldn't let our investors go into these off-plans unless we felt there was real demand. There has actually been a flattening off in the supply of developments, while tourist numbers are still going up. It's like Spain just before it joined the EU.' Anyone investing on the Black Sea coast today will have to hope that he is right.

The Ski Resorts

While much of the attention has been devoted to the Black Sea coast, there has also been an enormous marketing machine behind the selling of flats in the principal ski resorts of Bansko, Borovets and Pamporovo. The pattern has been the same: developers put up new blocks en masse and then sell them off-plan to foreign investors. The main selling point again is price – a flat in a Bulgarian resort will cost a fraction of one in France, Switzerland or Austria.

Bansko, situated within a two-hour drive of Sofia, is the fastest-growing of the three. At the heart of the town is a UNESCO World Heritage site with cobbled streets, *mehanas* (taverns) and restaurants and an Orthodox church dating from the mid-1800s. It is still possible to buy old houses and flats in or near the resort, but the main action is in off-plan developments, with a number of developments under way. In early 2006 apartments in the most luxurious new buildings in Bansko, within a few minutes of the gondola, were selling at £650–700 per square metre. Often they offer spa and sports centres, with gyms, Jacuzzis and saunas, pools and other such facilities. Flats in more modest developments are appreciably cheaper.

The Manhattan Loft Corporation, well known for its developments in New York and London, is working on an apartment complex due to be completed in 2007. Prices start at £31,000 for a studio and rise to £84,000 for penthouses. Lending the resort a touch of class, Kempinski, operator of such exclusive hotels as the

Grand Hôtel des Bains in St-Moritz, has opened the 158-room Grand Hôtel Arena, one of a series of new luxury hotels going up there.

The skiing is fairly good, although not up to the standards of the best Alpine resorts. Bansko has 65km of pistes and a ski season running from mid-December to mid-May. At present, the runs are served by a lift which can carry 2,500 skiers an hour, but the resort is spending heavily on infrastructure and a second gondola should be completed by the 2006–2007 season. A further boost is likely to come from Bansko's bid to host the 2014 Winter Olympics, even though it is so far just that – a bid. The resort has signed up Mark Girardelli, one of the most successful all-round skiing champions of all time, to promote it.

Bansko's two rivals are struggling to keep up: **Pamporovo**, although the largest and reputedly the sunniest of the three resorts, does not have a lot to offer expert skiers. **Borovets** is smaller, but is more convenient, just 70km from Sofia.

As discussed earlier in the book, rental returns are likely to be higher in the mountains than on the coast. This is not least because people have accepted that skiing is an expensive activity and so are prepared to pay more to rent an apartment for a week in a ski resort in February than they would for the equivalent property by the sea in July or August. The season is also slightly longer, although things quieten down outside the peak Christmas, New Year and February half-term weeks. It may be possible to let in summer to mountain walkers or to golfers using the new courses being developed near the resorts.

The same caveats apply as when buying property by the sea: Can you really be sure that the rental demand will be there, and how easy will it be to sell when you decide to realise your investment? Equally important is the quality of the infrastructure and whether the construction of new ski lifts will keep pace with the building of new apartments. As one contributor to an online property forum put it, 'Who cares about cheap apartments if they are standing in the middle of queue hell trying to get up the mountain?'

Sofia

The market in the capital city, which has 1.5 million people, is very different from that by the coast or in the mountains, and buying here is much more akin to investing in Prague, Warsaw or Budapest. Prices are still lower than in other eastern European capitals, but are rising strongly – and look likely to continue to do so in the run-up to EU membership. Joining Europe is also likely to help the rental market, as more diplomats and other expatriates are posted to the city.

Most promising from a rental point of view are studios and one- and two-bedroom apartments in the town centre in the area around the Sheraton Hotel, Parliament, National Palace of Culture and in or around the main shopping street, Vitosha Boulevard. An area called the Doctor's Garden is also popular. Apartments here are suitable both for letting to expats and also as short-term serviced apartments to tourists. Few have parking places, but there are a number of car parks where it is possible to rent a place by the month. Also attractive are some of the better residential parts of the city such as Lozenets, Ivan Vazov, Strelbishte, Lagera, Iztok, Geo Milev, Pirogov and VMA.

Prices vary according to location and the state of the building, but could be as low as £700–750 per square metre, or less. The general quality of the housing stock is not great; even if the apartment that you buy has itself been renovated, the common parts may not have been. Dealing with this problem may involve considerable hassle. Bulgarian blocks of flats are typically owned jointly by the owners of the individual apartments, who must make such decisions collectively.

An alternative is to buy into one of the off-plan developments being built in the city. Some may actually be cheaper than buying in existing buildings, with prices as low as £600 per square metre. Prices in others, such as the Embassy Suites, a substantial gated development about 10 minutes from the city centre, are closer to £900 per square metre, although this is for a luxurious complex aimed at diplomats and expat businessmen.

The Countryside

Many Britons have also bought houses in the countryside, where it is still possible to pick up properties for as little as £3,000–5,000. At this price, they are unlikely to have inside bathrooms and will need to have time and money spent on them to bring them up to a habitable level. Strictly speaking, these do not belong in a book on fly-to-let, since there is not really a rental market for them. Those in good locations, especially near the Black Sea resorts, could be a good investment, and the prices of some have gone up considerably in percentage terms in recent years. Before getting too carried away by the low prices, bear in mind that there is a huge potential stock of them: since the end of Communism in Bulgaria, young people have been moving from the countryside into the towns, often taking their parents or grandparents with them and leaving empty unwanted houses behind them. (Sometimes, though, the elderly do not quite realise what is going on. I was both amused and saddened during one visit to the Bulgarian countryside to hear from a British couple who had bought a village house only to find that the elderly woman who had lived there was convinced that she could stay on – and even tried to climb back in again over the wall after they had gently asked her to leave!)

Estate Agents

- **Address Bulgaria, www.escapetobulgaria.com, t** 0800 389 7543.
A selection of off-plan flats in ski resorts and on the coast, together with some useful information and news.

- **Barrasford and Bird, www.barrasfordandbird.co.uk, t** 0845 600 1871.
A selection of off-plan developments on the coast and in ski resorts.

- **Best Bulgarian Properties, www.bestbgproperties.com, t** + 359 887 594 680. Bulgarian agency with a wide selection of properties across the country.

- **Bulgari Dom, www.bulgaridom.com, t** (01279) 778 999. Agency with a variety of new and used properties.

- **Bulgaria Revealed, www.bulgariarevealed.com, t** 0845 054 8697. Manchester-based agency with a selection of properties and some information.

- **Bulgarian Dreams, www.bulgariandreams.com, t** 0800 011 2750. British-based agency with wide range of new and second-hand properties.

- **Bulgarian Properties, www.bulgarianproperties.com, t** + 359 2 868 1188. Bulgarian-based agency with very wide range of properties of all sorts for sale and rent, together with lots of useful information. Associated sites handle letting, car hire and other useful services.

- **Bulgarian-Properties Ltd, www.bulgarian-properties.co.uk, t** (020) 8801 1008. Bulgarian-British agency with a wide range of properties of all sorts.

- **Buy & Sell Bulgaria, www.buy-sell-bulgaria.com, t** + 359 899 145 454. Bulgarian-based agency offering off-plan developments, existing properties and land.

- **Buy in Bulgaria, www.buyinbulgaria.com, t** 0845 056 8629. Irish agency with property listings and some information.

- **My Bulgaria, www.mybulgaria.info.** Property portal featuring private sales and offerings from dozens of agents, with forums and chat-rooms.

Croatia and Montenegro

Croatia

Croatia has emerged in recent years as one of Europe's fastest-growing holiday destinations, boasting a number of attractions from the Istrian peninsula in the north, down through the Dalmatian coast with its 1,185 islands, islets and reefs, to the splendid medieval city of Dubrovnik in the south. Nearly 10 million people visited in 2005 – more than double the permanent population of just 4.5 million. The Croatian authorities are determined to preserve the very thing that makes their country so popular, namely its glorious coastline. It has not entirely been spared the attention of the developers or individual house-builders, but at least attempts are being made to curb their worst excesses.

Once part of the former Yugoslavia, Croatia declared independence in 1991, but then had to endure four to five years of sporadic and often bitter fighting both with the Yugoslav People's Army and the forces of the self-proclaimed breakaway Republic of Serbian Krajina. Croatian offensives in 1995 defeated the separatists and ended the war, but it was several years before normality returned, while President Franjo Tudjman, who led the country to independence, continued to rule in an authoritarian manner until his death in December 1999. Under Tudjman's successors, the country has pursued a more western style of politics, and EU membership – frozen for several years because of the failure of Croatian authorities to co-operate fully with the UN War Crimes Tribunal – is now back on the agenda. It was agreed in October 2005 to open entry talks, but Croatia remains behind Bulgaria and Romania in the queue and, realistically, is unlikely to join before 2009. The mere prospect of membership has had a salutary effect on the government, which has improved the workings of the legal system and westernised the economy, which grew at a very respectable, if not spectacular 4 per cent in 2005 and is expected to repeat this rate in 2006. Inflation has been low at well under 3 per cent, and the kuna, the national currency, has been fairly stable against the euro, typically moving up in the summer as all the foreign tourist money comes in and slipping back down again in the autumn. There is investment in the road network, with a major new motorway now linking Zagreb, the capital, with Istria and with Split, the country's second city halfway down the Dalmatian coast. It is being extended further south and should reach Dubrovnik by 2008. Air links with Britain, in particular, were slow to improve, but Croatia has signed the so-called Open Skies agreement with the European Union, and easyjet will start flying to Rijeka and Split in June 2006. Other airlines have also joined in, including Wizz Air and Flyglobespan. Construction of a number of golf courses is also under way.

To the property investor, Croatia is interesting primarily for holiday lets, although there may be a long-term rental market in Zagreb and other larger cities. The tourist industry, strong during the 1970s and '80s, was hit badly during the Balkan wars of the 1990s, but has been recovering strongly in the last few years. Tourism generated around £6 billion in revenue in 2005, with the World Travel and Tourism Council predicting annual growth of around 6.4 per cent over the next decade.

A real estate market, which did not really exist before in any meaningful sense, has also sprung into existence, and prices have increased rapidly. According to a study by international property consultants Bradmore King Sturge, published in summer 2005, prices of residential real estate on the coast have risen an average 200 per cent in the last decade – the bulk of the rises have been since the beginning of the millennium, with average growth of 20–30 per cent a year. Land prices have grown even more strongly, putting on 300 per cent in the same period. The upward trend is likely to continue, with existing properties enjoying frontline positions near the sea likely to benefit from new environmental protection laws which went into force in September 2004 preventing any new building within 70 metres of the shore line. Prices in Dubrovnik, in particular, and some other places on the coast and islands, have grown so rapidly that they are already close to French or Italian levels, which may put something of a lid on future growth. Agents who work in Croatia have complained to me that many sellers are over-optimistic about the prices that their properties will fetch – meaning you should prepare yourself for a substantial bout of haggling if you decide to buy. There is also an increasing number of off-plan properties on sale. Some could be attractive, but this is not Bulgaria: the main attraction of Croatia lies in its old stone-built houses, available in a variety of finishes from beautifully restored down to do-it-yourself wrecks.

Whatever you buy, as discussed earlier in the book, do not underestimate the amount of work involved in handling holiday lets, or overestimate the number of weeks a year that your property will be let. Realistically, the rental season in Croatia extends from May to September, limiting you to a maximum of 16 or so weeks – during only half of which will you be able to let at top prices – so you should err on the side of caution when estimating how much income your property will generate. Buying in Croatia could be an ideal solution, though, for someone who is already looking for a holiday home for their own use and who would be happy to let it for a few weeks a year to help cover costs.

In deciding which part of the country to go for, you should approach the question as if you were a tourist: if a particular part of the country appeals to you, then, provided you don't have bizarre or idiosyncratic taste, it should also appeal to someone looking for a holiday let. The same goes for the choice of property: if you fall in love at first sight with an old stone-built house, then so will other people. Ease of access is important, though: if you plump for an inaccessible island a long way from the coast, don't be surprised if few holiday-makers are ready to make the long trek out to rent it from you.

There are two ways for non-resident foreigners to buy. Buying in your own name is probably the most straightforward route, although you must obtain a permit (a *suglasnost*) from the Ministry of Foreign Affairs, which could take six months or maybe even longer. This should be a formality provided you haven't somehow fallen foul of Croatian authorities, and you are able to go ahead and complete the purchase in the meantime. (In their report, Bradmore King Sturge estimated that a mere 3,500 such permits had been issued to foreigners since 1995, the majority of them from Germany and Austria – a tiny number if you compare it with the 3.6 million properties in Spain believed to be owned by foreigners.) You are not permitted to make changes to the outside of the building during this period – which can mean annoying delays if you have bought a wreck that you intend to do up. You are also not allowed to sell it on until your *suglasnost* comes through.

One way around this to is to set up a Croatian company and buy through that. In this case you do not require any permission from the authorities. Many agents will arrange this for you, although watch out for the cost: while some claim to be able to do everything for under £1,000, others will charge up to £3,000 – although this should include the 20,000 kuna (around £1,835) of start-up capital, which you are effectively refunded once the company is up and running. If the company's turnover is expected to exceed 85,000 kuna (around £7,800) in a calendar year, then you must register for *PDV* (VAT), currently levied at 22 per cent. This would have to be paid on the transfer of any property built after 31 December 1997, but can be deducted from the company's next VAT obligation. The company's profits are taxed at 20 per cent. Private buyers, by contrast, must pay a 35 per cent capital gains tax if they sell on their property within three years. Both individual and companies buying must also pay a 5 per cent property transfer tax, which is levied on the market value rather than the sale price to prevent deliberate under-declaration of property values. Communes and cities charge a holiday house tax, varying from 50p to £1.50 per square metre per year; therefore a 100-square-metre flat would carry an annual tax liability of up to £150 or so. Most agents will also charge buyers 3 per cent commission.

However you choose to buy, there can be serious problems with existing buildings over the validity of title. Croatian properties effectively have two separate sets of paperwork. Each has an entry both in the land registry and in the *cadastre*, and you must make sure that they tally with each other. Here, even more than elsewhere in eastern Europe, it is very important to take good, impartial legal advice to make sure you are actually buying what you think you are. This is especially the case with older properties, which may have been inherited by an extended family, all of whose members must agree to a sale. Many a deal has been held up by the inability of the lawyers to track down an heir who has long since gone off to work in Australia or Canada. Help is on its way: the land register is under revision and is to be digitised by the end of 2008, which should improve matters to some extent.

Croatian banks have long been reluctant to lend to non-residents. Things are now improving and rates, until recently as high as 9 per cent, had dropped to 6 per cent at the time of writing (early 2006). The maximum loan-to-value may be as low as 50–60 per cent. At least one bank, however, Hypo-Alpe-Adria, has begun offering foreigners a pioneering leasing system, which works, in practice, much like a mortgage but with an effective loan-to-value of 78 per cent.

There is also another peculiarity as far as letting your property is concerned. If you have bought as a private person, you must first obtain a rental licence and then formally register your flat or house as available for rent. To do this you must first secure the approval of the Ministry of Foreign Affairs. You must also open a Croatian business bank account that has been set up to take rental deposits. In theory, failure to comply with this can lay you open to prosecution. A way around it is to set up and let the property through a company.

Istria

Located at the head of the Adriatic between the Gulf of Trieste and the Kvarner Gulf, the Istrian peninsula is easily accessible from Italy, Austria, Germany and the rest of western Europe and has the most developed holiday home market in the country. Istria also has a distinctly Italian feel; for several centuries it was run by the Venetian Republic, and although the Venetians were later pushed out by the Austrians, almost as many Italians as Croats and Slovenians lived there in the first years of the 20th century. Their numbers grew further when Istria was taken from the Austro-Hungarian empire and given to Italy after the First World War. It was transferred to socialist Yugoslavia after the Second World War, and in the years that followed most of the Italian population fled. A few thousand were killed. The cultural links remain, and Italian is still an official language alongside Croatian; as a result, most cities have two names, one in each language. The food, too, shows strong Italian influences.

The Istrian countryside is beautiful, with a number of attractive stone-built houses, prompting some fans to describe it as the 'new Tuscany'. The western coast, which tends to be the more expensive part, is largely flat, with beaches, while the east is more mountainous. **Medulin**, and the surrounding area in the south, is popular with divers. The peninsula also boasts some delightful towns. My favourite is **Rovinj** (or Rovigno to the Italians), although **Poreč** (Parenzo), **Pula** (Pola), **Labin** and several others are noteworthy. Because of its location close to the northeastern Italian city of Trieste, Istria is a popular weekend destination for Italians. It is a manageable drive from Germany and Austria, as well, although there can still be long queues on the border between Croatia and Slovenia at peak times. Istria has not so far featured much on the British tourist radar, perhaps because its airport, Pula, is not very well served from Britain. This will change, though, once the low-cost airlines arrive.

A flat in Rovinj or one of the other towns could make a good holiday let. To maximise your yield, you would have to find a way of marketing it to Italians and Germans rather than just relying on Britons and other English-speakers. Apartments in old buildings in Rovinj go for around £1,200–1,500 per square metre, depending on the quality of the building, many of which are fairly run-down. Prices elsewhere on the coast can vary widely; a number of new-build developments have been going up recently, with prices ranging from as little as £700 or so per square metre to more than £2,000–3,000 in the swishest new buildings with frontline sea positions. Be careful when buying anything with a view, though: such is the construction boom that it could soon be blocked by a new building. Prices fall sharply outside the towns, with a wide range of properties on offer from houses in need of complete renovation for as little as £20,000 or so up to new-build luxury villas for £500,000 or more.

The Dalmatian Coast and Islands

The Dalmatian coast stretches more than 3,600 miles from **Rijeka** (Fiume), in the north, down to Dubrovnik in the south, and is what most people understand by Croatia. With its hidden bays and sparkling seas, the Croatian Adriatic is a must for beach-lovers, island-hoppers and sailors. The crystal-clear water is perfect for swimming and wind-surfing, swimming, snorkelling and diving. The **Kvarner** area, especially the parts close to **Opatija** and the island of **Krk**, are popular tourist destinations and cheaper than Istria, with some apartments going for as little as £1,200 per square metre. **Zadar**, around 150 miles down the coast, and its archipelago of around 300 islands, is also relatively cheap. Many of them are comparatively undeveloped, but **Vir** is an exception. Connected to the coast by a bridge, it is covered with dozens of new tacky apartment blocks, many of them built only a few yards from the shore, in an apparent complete disregard of planning rules.

Things become more expensive as you continue down the coast. Prices in **Split**, Croatia's second largest city, which lies around 100 miles south of Zadar, are considerably higher. So, too, are those on its islands. Properties on those further out from the coast generally cost less than on those just a short hop from the mainland. One of the most popular and consequently most expensive islands is **Hvar**, where a restored stone-built house with grounds and a sea view could easily cost £300,000 or more. **Brač**, to the north, is also expensive, but nearby **Šolta** is substantially cheaper, for reasons that are not easy to fathom.

If you are buying somewhere as a holiday let, then the best way to start is to imagine yourself in the role of a potential tenant: flick through travel agents' brochures and surf the net to find the most heavily promoted and beautiful places. Transport links are also important; if you are primarily going to target Britons and other foreigners, then it would help to be within easy reach of Dubrovnik airport, from which British Airways and Croatia Airlines fly directly to London. There are also airports in Zadar, Split and on Brač. The relative fortunes of the different parts of the coast may depend on which ones the low-cost airlines plump for.

Dubrovnik

Some 1,300 years old, Dubrovnik in southern Dalmatia, near the border with Montenegro, is undoubtedly one of the Mediterranean's most beautiful cities, with an old walled town, steep cobbled streets, splendid squares, and churches and palaces, earning it a designation as a UNESCO World Heritage site. Thanks to its extremely sunny climate, it also enjoys luxuriant subtropical vegetation. This is not a place for bargains: Dubrovnik has already been well and truly discovered. Mention it to estate agents elsewhere in Croatia and prepare for sharp intakes of breath and much rolling of eyes.

New-build apartments in the Old City, for example, can go for more than £2,700 per square metre, even without a sea view, which means a spacious two-bedroom flat could cost well over £250,000. Grander properties are also available. In early 2006 one agent was selling an unmodernised, four-storey, eight-bedroom palace for just over £1.2 million and another six-bedroom villa overlooking the sea and the Old City for a cool £1.7 million. Although the season is relatively long, it may be difficult with prices like these to make a house or apartment in one of the best locations pay for itself. Prices drop substantially when you leave the city, which could make buying somewhere a few miles away a more realistic proposition.

Estate Agents

- **Broker, www.croatia-info.net, t** + 385 21 541 000. Agency with wide selection of properties across the country and some useful information.

- **Croatia-apart, www.croatia-apart.com, t** + 385 98 904 6254. Agency offering property management and lettings in Istria, and also some sales.

- **Croatia Blue, www.croatiablue.com, t** (020) 8566 3182. A wide selection of property in Istria, with maps and other useful information.

- **Croatia Coast Property, www.croatia-coast-property.co.uk, t** + 385 21 717 497. British-run agency specialising in property on the island of Brač.

- **Dubrovnik.com, www.dubrovnik.com, t** + 385 20 357 307. A reasonable selection of properties across the coast, with some useful information.

- **Istra Nekretnine, www.istra-nekretnine.com, t** + 385 52 841 585. A small selection of property in Istria, mostly in and around Rovinj.

- **J.E.M. Trade, www.croatia-istria.com, t** + 385 52 575 593. A small selection of property in Istria only.

- **Letterstone, www.letterstone.com, t** (020) 7384 7488. Agency that sells off-plan property in several countries. Also some analysis of the market.

- **Pent-a Split, www.penta-nekretnine.hr, t** + 385 21 314 852. Split-based agency with a small selection of properties.

Montenegro

Worried that you may have left it too late to buy in Croatia? Then why not move further down the coast to Montenegro? This southwestern part of the former Yugoslavia is being heavily promoted by British agents as a new and hitherto undiscovered version of its more illustrious northern neighbour. With more than 180 miles of stunning Adriatic coast, steep mountains and lush national parks, Montenegro certainly has a huge amount of natural beauty to offer. There are many attractive properties to be found on the coast, in its pretty walled towns and villages inland or on the Gulf of Kotor, the largest fjord in southern Europe.

To describe Montenegro as undiscovered is not the whole story. Its coast was widely appreciated by foreign visitors during the 19th century, among them Lord Byron, who was a particular fan. 'At the birth of our planet, the most beautiful encounter between the land and the sea must have happened at the coast of Montenegro,' the poet wrote. 'When the pearls of nature were sown, handfuls of them were cast on this soil.' Later, during the Yugoslavia years, its resorts were popular with celebrities like Elizabeth Taylor, Richard Burton and Sophia Loren. Even though Montenegro escaped relatively unscathed, the Balkan wars of the 1990s effectively killed its tourist industry, but Montenegro's government has since realised the enormous potential of the business and has been pushing it hard – and with some success. Numbers in 2005 rose by 50 per cent, albeit from a low base. The property market is also coming to life, and more than 1,000 Britons are believed already to have bought there.

The spectacular **Gulf of Kotor** is undoubtedly the main attraction; the medieval town of **Kotor**, itself, although badly damaged by an earthquake in 1979, has been painstakingly reconstructed. The pretty town of **Budva**, with cobbled streets, bars and boutiques, is a popular spot, as is the beach resort of **Petrovac**, while the resort island of **Sveti Stefan** is spectacular.

Montenegro is not quite as cheap as you might expect, however, and prices are moving rapidly towards Croatian levels. Although it is possible to find very cheap, unrestored rural houses in the hills of the south for £30,000–40,000, you could pay £300,000 for a classic villa with sea view near the Croatian border or overlooking the fjord. There is plenty of choice in between, though, and £150,000 should buy an attractive stone house near the water.

Tourism – and with it the rental market – is relatively undeveloped, which means the motivation is less current yields and more future capital gain. There should still be plenty of the latter, with prices expected to continue registering annual double-digit growth, at least for a few years. An improvement in air links would help: although Montenegro has its own airports, the easiest way of reaching the country from Britain currently is to fly to Dubrovnik and then set off on a long drive southwards.

Perhaps even more than in Croatia, there can be problems with legal title, so before putting down a deposit you should get all the documentation checked out by a reliable and independent lawyer. Although there is a formal land registry, it has not been compulsory to log land or property details, and disputes can arise. Buying costs are low, with a tax of just 2 per cent on second-hand properties. (New builds, by contrast, are liable to 17 per cent.) Mortgages are not yet available, meaning you cannot leverage your investment.

There are also broader questions about Montenegro. The government is pushing hard to take the country on a western path and is slowly privatising state firms. In a sign that it sees its (eventual) future in the EU, it also adopted the euro as its currency in 2003 (although it is not, of course, a member of the eurozone as such). In early 2006, however, Montenegro was still locked into a political confederation with Serbia, which, although no longer ruled by Slobodan Milošević, the late former Communist president, has still not broken entirely free of the shackles of its dark past. That looked set to change in May 2006, however, with a referendum on declaring independence from Serbia. A clean, amicable break with its larger neighbour would give an enormous boost to Montenegro's image – and also its property market – and set it firmly on the long path towards EU membership. As the experiences of Bosnia, Croatia and Kosovo have shown, such divorces can be extraordinarily acrimonious – and bloody – and there have been fears that Serb nationalists opposed to the break-up of the confederation could use the referendum as an excuse for stirring up unrest.

Estate Agents

- **Dream Montenegro, www.dreammontenegro.com, t** (01753) 831 182. A variety of modernised and unmodernised properties for sale.

- **Montenegro Living, www.montenegro-living.com, t** + 381 88 350 485. A selection of apartments, houses and land for sale.

- **Montenegro Real Estate, www.montenegrorealestate.org, t** + 381 82 308 000. A wide range of property and land for sale in Montenegro.

- **Monteprop, www.monteprop.com, t** + 381 85 303 308. British-owned agency with offices in Montenegro and a wide selection of property.

Cyprus

The Republic of Cyprus

Britons have been holidaying on Cyprus for years, attracted by the climate, beautiful scenery and wealth of cultural links with home. Following its entry into the European Union in May 2004, the island has turned into a highly popular destination for property-buyers as well. Most purchasers are looking for holiday or retirement homes for themselves at prices substantially below the equivalent spots in Mallorca, the Costa del Sol or the Côte d'Azur. The island, the third biggest in the Mediterranean after Sardinia and Sicily, is also increasingly being pitched as an attractive place for fly-to-let investments. A number of developers have got in on the act, offering off-plan flats and villas, some of which come with annual rental guarantees of up to three years.

Cyprus's most obvious attraction is its 300-plus sunny days a year. Situated at the eastern end of the Mediterranean, it enjoys predictably warm summers but also, unlike Bulgaria or Croatia, extremely mild winters. This considerably prolongs the season and, with it, the potential rental returns. Even in December or January, the temperature is an average 15°C, making the island an ideal destination for the growing ranks of the 'snowbirds', retirees from northern Europe who head south for the winter. As many as 60,000 British expats currently live on Cyprus and English is widely spoken by the locals, making complicated discussions with the estate agent, bank or builder that much easier. As in the UK, which ran the place from 1878 to 1960, you drive on the left and, in another taste of home, they even use the same chunky electrical plugs. Britain still maintains two military bases on the island. The Germans and Scandinavians are keen visitors, too, as are a growing number of affluent Russians, many of whom have taken advantage of Cyprus's favourable tax regime to form companies there.

Tourists and, to a lesser extent, retirees therefore form the most obvious and attractive rental market. Numbers have been rising steadily in the last few years and look set to continue to do so. A growing trend towards individual tourism and away from the packaged variety should also boost rental demand. Golf is another draw: although Cyprus is still a long way behind Spain and Portugal, courses are springing up all over the country. It is moving into the conference business, too.

Underpinning this is the favourable broader economic picture – which is similar to that in some of the more advanced former Communist countries that joined the EU with Cyprus in 2004. The economy is growing steadily at around 4 per cent a year and interest rates have been falling; the base rate in early 2006 was 4.25 per cent. Inflation, at 2.5 per cent, is under control and public finances are in good order, with a government deficit of around 3 per cent. All this means the country is on target to join the euro as early as 2008, which will bring a further drop in interest rates down to eurozone levels (and which will tend to push up prices). The tax regime is also favourable. Income is taxed in bands from 20 per cent to 30 per cent, while companies pay corporation tax of just 10 per cent. Retirees who spend more than half the year on the island can become Cyprus tax residents, which means their foreign pension is taxed at just 5 per cent. In a further bonus, property law is based on English Common Law, which makes it easier for British buyers. Mortgages, too, are relatively easy to obtain, with lenders ready to lend as much as 80 per cent loan-to-value over up to 30 years at rates only a percentage point or so above those in the eurozone countries. Off-plan developments can also be attractive, provided the payments are staged in an advantageous way. It should be possible to find one where only a 20 per cent deposit is required, with the remainder due on completion. Some developers also offer rental agreements with hotel chains, with yields of as much as 7 per cent a year and some own use.

Cyprus has its minuses, too. When buying, you must pay a property transfer tax which in early 2006 started at 3 per cent and rose to 8 per cent on anything more than CYP100,000 (around £120,000), as well as a more modest stamp duty of 0.15–0.2 per cent. Capital gains are taxed at 20 per cent, although the first CYP10,000 is free. In early 2006 foreigners were still allowed to buy only one property each, but this restriction is expected to be abolished by 2009, at the latest, under the rules governing Cyprus's accession to the EU. Those who want to purchase more than one property at present can do so by buying through a company. These can be set up relatively cheaply and easily and allow you to take advantage of lower corporate taxes.

Given all the above, it is not surprising that property prices have been rising, although the exact extent of this increase has been a matter of contention. While some less scrupulous agents have been claiming annual rises of 15–20 per cent, the BuySell Home Price Index, based on actual transactions, found a 7.2 per cent increase in 2004 and a modest 2.5 per cent the following year. Gross rental yields can be as high as 7–8 per cent, but look likely to fall back.

There are nevertheless causes of concern for the future, not just because of the sheer scale of the building but also because, as in Bulgaria, many of those buying into new developments have been investors rather than end-users. Fears of oversupply were undoubtedly partly behind the slowdown in 2005. There may also be a negative knock-on effect from the surprise decision in December 2005 by Gordon Brown, the Chancellor of the Exchequer, to reverse plans to allow people to buy residential property with their self-invested personal pensions or SIPPs (*see* pp.54–8)). Cyprus is one of the few countries outside Britain which recognises trusts, the basis of SIPPs, and so had expected a sizeable amount of this pension money to flow into its property market.

Land prices have continued to surge ahead, though: while Britons and other foreigners have been sinking their savings into bricks and mortar, most Cypriot investors prefer to buy plots and sit on them. A favourite trick is to buy up land adjacent to building zones cheaply in the hope that development area permits will be extended and its value will soar.

The Coast

Cyprus is a relatively small island, so regional variations in weather are not great. Different areas will nevertheless appeal to different kinds of visitors. Some resorts are dead in the winter; others are open for business for 12 months a year, making for greater overall yields.

Paphos, in the southwest, is one of the best known and most popular places in Cyprus, but also one of the most expensive. An average detached three-bedroom house cost just over £200,000 in early 2006, while a two-bedroom apartment was £72,000. Rents, though, are only marginally higher than in other resorts, which could keep yields down to a modest 4 per cent. Once divided into two separate areas, Kato (lower) Paphos and Ktima or Pano (upper) Paphos, it is now one big town. The two parts remain distinct from each other: Kato Paphos is the beach, harbour and tourist resort, while Ktima is the retail and commercial area.

Continuing anticlockwise around the coast, you come to **Pissouri** and **Limassol**. Nearby is the **Aphrodite Hills** complex. Situated close to the spot where the ancient Greeks believed the goddess of beauty appeared from the sea, it describes itself as 'the first ever fully integrated golf, leisure and real estate development in Cyprus'. A 98-square-metre apartment there would cost around £190,000; the most expensive four-bedroom villas, with their own grounds, go for over £800,000. By contrast, properties in **Larnaca**, which lies south of Nicosia, are relatively cheap, with flats at around £1,000 per square metre, but the rental market is good and yields can be closer to 6–7 per cent. In the southeast of island lies the pulsating resort of **Ayia Napa**, with white sandy beaches, theme parks and lively clubs and bars.

Looking long-term, the stretch of coast that runs northwards from here up towards **Famagusta** – which lies on the Turkish side of the border – has considerable potential. Values here have been depressed because of the division: expect them to go up if and when the island's division ends, though, and Famagusta is reunited with what would be its natural suburbs.

Location is important, but so too is choosing the right kind of property. To some extent, this choice will be linked with your choice of resort. If it is a family-friendly place, then it might make more sense to go for villas with gardens. If your clients are more likely to be singles or young couples attracted by the nightlife, then a one or two bedroom flat might be a better bet. Whatever you choose, always think water: whether sea or swimming pool, the closer to it you are, the better. However beautiful the villa you buy, not having a pool will count against it. The same goes for flats: wherever possible, make sure that the block you buy in has a communal pool – and check it is large enough to accommodate the number of people likely to use it during high season.

Nicosia

The capital of Cyprus for more than 1,000 years, Nicosia is a lively, cosmopolitan city; since the fall of the Berlin Wall, it also enjoys the dubious distinction of being the only militarily divided capital in Europe. Property is reasonably priced, with apartments in new developments at around £1,000–1,500 per square metre, depending on location and quality. Rental yields should be among the highest on the island; as well as shops and offices, the city also has a number of universities and colleges, which should ensure there is a steady flow of potential tenants.

Estate Agents

- **Buy Sell Cyprus, www.buysellcyprus.com.** Listings site with thousands of properties for sale and rent.

- **Canterburys, www.canterburys.com, t** (020) 7371 0777. A wide range of properties for sale, together with maps and useful information.

- **Cyprus Ideal, www.cyprus-ideal.com, t** 0870 446 0010. British-based company with property and land in the Paphos, Larnaca, Limassol, Polis and Agia Napa areas.

- **Cyprus Online, www.cyprus-online.com, t** + 357 7777 7067. A wide range of properties, news and other information.

- **Cyprus Prop, www.cyprusprop.com, t** + 357 2557 1715. British-run agency with new-build and existing property.

- **Cyprus Realtor,** www.cyprusrealtor.com, **t** + 357 2682 2320. Land and property for sale, largely in the Paphos area.

- **Fitzgerald, www.fitzgeraldcyprus.com, t** + 357 2693 0345. A selection of new and resale properties in the Paphos region.

- **Invest in Cyprus, www.investincyprus.com, t** (0151) 482 5526. Liverpool-based company offering various off-plan investment properties.

- **Sold on Cyprus, www.soldoncyprus.com, t** + 357 9982 8963. Properties to buy and rent across Cyprus.

Northern Cyprus

All the above refers to the Republic of Cyprus, the Greek-speaking southern two-thirds of the island. There is, of course, another Cyprus, the self-proclaimed Turkish Republic of Northern Cyprus (TRNC), which was created after the Turkish invasion in 1974, but which is still not recognised by any other country apart from Turkey. The two are separated from each other by the so-called Green Line, which runs east–west across the country, dividing Nicosia, the capital of both parts of the island, into two.

Various attempts have been made by the international community to reunify the island, most recently in 2004, when a plan was put to a referendum. But although the north voted overwhelmingly in favour, the south did not. Although, formally speaking, the entire island joined the EU that May, European laws apply only to the south, leaving the Turkish area in a legal limbo. Further attempts will undoubtedly be made to bring the two together; the decision by Brussels in November 2005 to start membership talks with Turkey should also improve the atmosphere.

If and when reunification finally happens, it will obviously bring an enormous economic boost to the whole island, with hundreds of millions of pounds in European Union aid certain to come pouring in. Those areas near the border will benefit in particular, with property prices likely to surge. Given the political uncertainties, though, this should be treated as a potential bonus, rather than something to be factored into your short-term calculations. In the meantime, it should be noted that the property market in the Turkish-controlled part of the island is completely separate from that in the south and should be treated accordingly.

Northern Cyprus contains some of the most beautiful parts of the island and the authorities have been happy to see a real estate market developing. The developers have moved in and as many as 10,000 Europeans – many of them Britons – are believed to have invested. Prices, although initially substantially below those in the south, have risen far more quickly, encouraging other buyers to follow. A study released in November 2005 found the price of flats and houses in northern Cyprus had risen 36 per cent from the first half of 2003 to the first half of 2005, while land prices rocketed by 172 per cent – against 10 per cent and 14 per cent respectively in the south.

However, the events of 1974 left behind a bitter legacy which is of direct relevance not only to the two communities but also to anyone else buying property in the north. More than 75 per cent of the land there was officially owned by Greeks expelled after the invasion. Greek Cypriot authorities consider those who buy and sell properties abandoned by the Greeks as effectively dealing in stolen goods, putting any foreign purchaser into a potentially difficult situation. In what looked certain to be a test case, Cyprus's court of appeal in April 2005 upheld a judgment under which Linda and David Orams, from Hove, Sussex, were ordered to demolish their house in Lapithos, return the plot of land and pay the original Greek owner £10,000 in damages. The couple, who invested an estimated £160,000 in the property, insisted they bought in good faith, but, in a test of EU law, lawyers planned to move to secure compensation in British courts. The outcome of the case was still not certain in early 2006; what is clear, though, is that anyone buying property previously owned by Greeks could, at best, face a long legal battle and, at worst, the prospect of losing it completely.

All too conscious of this problem, many agents active in the north have made great play of selling flats and houses only with pre-1974 Turkish title – that is property that was always Turkish- rather than Greek-owned. This will reduce the danger of an irate former owner suddenly turning up and claiming back your house, but such a purchase is not risk-free either, given the reluctance of the Greek Cypriot authorities to recognise the legality of any actions carried out under the auspices of the Turkish Cypriot authorities.

Much, of course, depends on whether the two halves of the island are ever reunited and the precise conditions under which this happens. But, given the number of other possible places in the world in which to invest, it is worth thinking long and hard before plumping for Northern Cyprus.

Estate Agents

- **Anglo-Cyprus Homes, www.anglocyprushomes.co.uk, t** (020) 8808 0025. Properties for sale in Northern Cyprus.

- **First Homes Worldwide, www.firsthomesww.co.uk, t** 0870 043 4401. Property for sale in Northern Cyprus.

- **Green Paradise Estates, www.greenparadisecyprus.com, t** + 90 392 8211 850. Property for sale with pre-1974 Turkish title.

The Czech Republic

Think of the Czech Republic and you will immediately think of Prague, probably the best known and certainly the most attractive of the central and eastern European capitals. This was one of the first cities in the region to be discovered by the backpackers and the long-weekend crowd, and then by property investors. For this reason, this is a market which can properly be considered as 'emerged' rather than emerging. Even though property prices in the best parts of Prague are on a par with some western European capitals, however, there is still money to be made provided you choose carefully.

With a population of just over 10 million people, the Czech Republic is one of the most advanced and westward-looking of the EU's newest member states. It also has the advantage of a stable political system. The economy is growing at around 4 per cent – fast by western European standards, but below that of most of its neighbours – and is predicted to stay at those levels, or even pick up slightly, in the years ahead. Significantly, much of the growth is service-driven – a sign that, unlike many of its less developed neighbours to the east, it has put the old days of Communist central planning behind it. Services now account for more than 60 per cent of the economy, which is approaching western European levels. A number of big international companies have set up in the country, among them DHL, the courier company, which chose Prague as the site for a European service and logistics centre. The Czech Republic is also a centre for car manufacturing (no Skoda jokes here, please). The picture is not entirely rosy, though. The government budget deficit is relatively high, while unemployment has been nudging double figures.

Property prices, especially in the more prestigious parts of Prague, have soared since 1989, with the largest gains made by the predominantly Italian, Israeli and Irish investors who moved in during the early 1990s. As elsewhere, there was a lot of hype in the run-up to EU membership in May 2004, but in reality little happened – supply dried up as many owners looking to sell held back in anticipation of higher prices. In reality, this did not happen, and those prices which had been marked up too optimistically began to drift back. Prices are rising again and look likely to continue to do so, thanks to rising incomes (real wages are going up roughly 6 per cent a year) and to the greater availability of mortgages. While earlier generations of young Czechs would stay living with their parents, today's affluent 20-somethings will take out a mortgage to buy a home of their own.

The Czech Republic lags behind its neighbours in one important respect: foreign buyers are not able to buy property directly, but must do so by forming a company, as part of a government policy to prevent the country being bought up by foreigners. This involves setting up either a limited or a joint stock company. The process can be quick (if you choose an off-the-shelf company) and also relatively cheap (some £600–1,200), but is still an extra inconvenience.

Such restrictions are not normally allowed by the EU and the Czechs have been given until May 2009 to open the market completely to other Europeans. One way around this would be to apply for a Czech residence permit, for a minimum of five years, but it may be difficult unless you are actually employed in the country. The main advantage of this is when you come to sell: those who buy in their own name are not liable for capital gains tax if they have held the property for five years or more (or two years if they actually lived in it). Companies, by contrast, are liable for corporate tax (due to be cut from 28 per cent to 24 per cent in 2006) on the profits when they sell.

Even if you buy through a company, it is possible to obtain a mortgage, typically for up to around 85 per cent, although repayment terms tend to be restricted to 15 years. Rates in early 2006 were 5–6 per cent. With yields on most property 6–7 per cent and the only mortgages repayment ones, you should not borrow more than 60–70 per cent if you want to keep monthly cash flow positive.

There are two forms of property ownership in the Czech Republic: *osobni vlastnictvi* (private ownership) and *družstevni vlastnictvi* (co-operative ownership). The first is much as it says: whether as a company or a private individual, you buy an apartment or a house and your name is entered in the land registry as the owner. Many flats in blocks, however, are still co-operatively owned. Under this system, the entire building belongs to a co-operative and you buy the right to be a member of it and to use a particular flat. Consequently, there is no record in the land registry of a particular member's ownership of the flat in which he or she lives. The overwhelming majority of co-operatives restrict ownership to Czech citizens and do not allow them to be bought by companies either. It is also extremely difficult to obtain a mortgage.

There has been a craze in recent years for acquiring the loft space of buildings from co-operatives and converting them into privately owned flats. Often the buyer does not pay in money, but instead puts in a lift and carries out a general renovation of the common parts. This can be extremely profitable, but usually involves considerable hassle. You should only embark on it after having the building inspected by a structural engineer and the project properly costed.

You should also take care before letting your property. The country's landlord–tenant laws are confusing, ill-administered and impossible to enforce, and, if tenants decide not to pay, there is little the owner can do to evict them. Absentee-owned properties are common targets for non-paying tenants and also for property management companies, which routinely place these problem tenants in properties owned by foreign-based investors. Watch out for rent-controlled buildings, for which landlords can charge only approximately 20 per cent of what would be the market rent. Maintenance requirements for such buildings are also extremely strict. Politicians have been talking for years about phasing out rental controls. There could be substantial capital gains on such properties if they finally press ahead with this.

Prague

The most obviously attractive part of the city is the centre (otherwise known as Prague 1), with the 13th-century Charles Bridge, Old Town Square, Prague Castle and other historic buildings. As well as being the historic and commercial centre, it is also the most romantic part of Prague. At its centre is the Old Town (Staré Město). The architecture dating as far back as the 11th century has been almost completely preserved, giving it a lively and magical atmosphere, with many restaurants, pavement cafés, shops and businesses, even if its narrow lanes are almost permanently clogged with tourists. Just to its north is the Jewish quarter (Josefov), with beautifully ornamented buildings almost entirely rebuilt from the ground upwards in the 19th century. The main thoroughfare running through the district is Parizka, an Art Nouveau-influenced boulevard that is now lined with chic shops and restaurants. Its Jewish heritage lives on in the shape of several synagogues and the Old Jewish Cemetery. To the south is Nové Město (New Town), which despite its name is several hundred years old. Situated partly in Prague 1 and largely in Prague 2, the quieter, greener and more residential part of the centre, it has beautiful architecture from the late 19th and early 20th century.

Across the Charles Bridge from the Old Town is Malá Strana (the 'Small Side' or 'Lesser Quarter'), a romantic neighbourhood nestling just below the castle, with picturesque buildings crowded along twisting cobbled lanes. The central square, Malostranské Namesti, is dominated by the spectacular church of St Nicholas. None of this splendour comes cheap: at £2,000–2,500 per square metre and upwards, prices here are already at similar levels to those in major western European cities.

Vinohrady, a residential district in Prague straddling Prague 2 and Prague 3 on the hill just above Václavské Namesti (Wenceslas Square), is popular with expat tenants. The name means 'vineyards' in Czech and it was once the site of royal vineyards; a few still remain on its southern slopes. It boasts impressive classical apartment buildings, with high ceilings and ornate façades as well as stylish restaurants, bars and clubs. The city centre is a short distance away by tram or metro. Prices per square metre in early 2006 were around £1,800. Those in search of capital gain should consider nearby Vrsovice, to the southeast, in Prague 10, which is fast becoming a hip place to live, with an expanding expat community, quiet tree-lined streets and great local bars and restaurants. Also worth a look is Žižkov, which borders Vinohrady. Long one of the poorest districts in Prague and with a large Roma (Gypsy) population, it traditionally had a less than salubrious reputation. It has good transport links and two universities and something of a counter culture feel – making it ripe for the kind of gentrification that has taken place in parts of London.

Attractive, too, are Prague 4 (a large district in the southern part of the city extending from the lower edge of the centre to the city limits), Prague 5 (which stretches from the bank of the Vltava (or Moldau) River to the western edge of the city) and Prague 6 (which covers the area from the castle to the north-western edge of the city). The latter is the site of a number of embassies as well as the International School of Prague, and its detached houses and villas with gardens are popular with affluent expats. Houses here can start at around £300,000–400,000, with the most luxurious worth well over £1 million. Other good long-term bets are Prague 12 and some parts of the southern outskirts of the city, hitherto largely ignored by property developers. Prague 9, a former industrial factory area east of the centre, has many new developments, but the rental prospects may not be so good.

Generally, property prices in Prague rose an average 12 per cent in 2004 and an estimated 8–10 per cent in 2005, and are expected to continue going up, ensuring good capital gains. Rents have been falling back in recent years, though, cutting sharply into yields. This has been particularly the case at the top end of the market. During the boom years of the 1990s, Americans and other expat managers on lucrative packages flocked to the city, providing massive returns for anyone with a half-decent flat to let. Tenants of rent-controlled apartments would sublet them to foreigners for up to 10 times what they paid, while older couples would leave for the countryside to make way for an expat tenant who would finance their retirement. That all changed at the beginning of the new millennium after 9/11 and the end of the dotcom boom: many of the foreigners went home and were replaced by Czech managers, who not only had far lower salaries but also were more inclined to buy than to rent. The result has been falls of anything from 20–70 per cent in rents and frequent voids.

A better strategy therefore might be to aim to buy properties that would be attractive to average middle-class Czechs. This essentially means small and relatively inexpensive one- and two-bedroom flats of 50–70 square metres that would let for 10,000–20,000 Czech crowns (£230–460) a month. Also of potential interest are former office buildings that are being converted for residential use because of the glut of commercial property, which will be especially attractive to young Czechs and expats wanting a taste of loft living. It may also be worth looking at the *panelaki*, the Communist-era prefab blocks; despite their bad reputation, some of those in Prague are actually quite pleasant, well-managed blocks, which are being renovated. Bear in mind, though, that the size of the rental market will be limited by the fact that 55 per cent or so of Czechs still live in rent-controlled properties, where they are paying something like only 20 per cent of market rates. Of the remainder, many will be owner-occupiers or those on low incomes of £5,000 or less a year.

Brno

If you feel you have missed the boat in Prague, it may be worth looking at Brno, the country's second city. It certainly does not have the cachet of the capital, but prices here are substantially lower and expectations of capital growth greater.

Property Secrets, which analyses eastern European property, has described it as the 'equivalent of Leeds in the UK – but Leeds ten years ago'. You can see their point: during the Communist days it was a centre for heavy industry but has since begun to transform itself, developing a flourishing service industry and becoming a trading centre. Like Leeds, it also has a large student population, which in turn makes for a highly skilled workforce.

Not surprisingly, perhaps, the city is also short of good accommodation. As far as the rental market is concerned, you cannot rely on the expats that you find in Prague; short-term holiday lets are also not likely to be much of a factor despite there being daily direct flights to Brno from Stansted.

Estate Agents

- **Atrium Real Estate, www.atriumrealestate.cz, t** + 420 224 911 071. Agency with property to buy and let in Prague and surrounding area.

- **Continental Realty, www.continental.cz, t** + 420 222 517 105. Agency with property for sale and rental in Prague.

- **Expats.cz, http://realestate.expats.cz**. Real estate portal with flats and houses for sale and rent in Prague, Brno and elsewhere in the country.

- **Prague 101, www.czechpoint101.com**. Property-finding service, with lots of useful information about buying in the Czech Republic.

- **Prague Real Estate, www.praguerealestate.cz**. Real estate portal with properties for sale and rental in Prague. Has links to mortgage-providers.

- **Prague Real Estate Agents, www.real-estate-prague-agents.com, t** + 420 257 328 281. A comprehensive listing of flats and houses to buy and rent, together with a map and useful information.

- **Prague TV, http://prague.tv/realestate**. Listings of flats and houses for sale and rent.

- **S Reality, www.sreality.cz**. A comprehensive listing of flats and houses to buy and rent.

- **Sorent, www.sorent.cz, t** + 420 261 214 795. Czech-run agency with a selection of properties to buy and rent.

Estonia

Mention Tallinn and the chances are that people will immediately think of stag weekends. Every Friday evening the streets of Europe's newest party capital fill with crowds of young British men – and a few women – drawn not so much by the glorious medieval architecture as by the more predictable pleasures of cheap booze and the wild nightlife. Yet there is far more to the Estonian capital which makes it of considerable interest to the foreign investor.

The northernmost of the three Baltic states, Estonia is one of the most dynamic and investor-friendly of the 10 new members that joined the European Union in May 2004. Linked closely ethnically and linguistically with the Finns, whose country lies just 50 miles away across the Gulf of Finland, the Estonians have always had a Nordic air of efficiency about them – even during the half-century after they were forcibly annexed by Stalin's Soviet Union. The smallest of the then 15 Soviet republics, Estonia was always one of the most affluent and well run. I was always amazed by what I found whenever I visited the city while based as a foreign correspondent in Moscow in the late 1980s, before the fall of Communism. Not surprisingly, since winning independence in 1991, the Estonians have quickly swept away the last remaining vestiges of their Soviet past, embracing liberal, free market ideals with gusto.

The results speak for themselves. Estonia was badly hit by the Russian economic crisis in 1998, but has since reorientated its economy more firmly to the west, and for the last few years has notched up impressive annual growth rates of more than 6 per cent. Although it cannot continue growing indefinitely at such a speed, there are no immediate signs of a slow-down, giving the country a well-deserved reputation as a Baltic Tiger. Inflation, which dropped below 2 per cent in 2003, moved back up towards 5 per cent in 2005, but should be brought back under control, while salaries are rising at around 10 per cent a year. Interest rates have tumbled from double figures in the mid-1990s down to eurozone levels. The currency, the kroon, first fixed to the deutschmark in 1992, is currently pegged to the euro at the rate of one to 15.6466 (don't ask me why they didn't go for a slightly rounder number!). Estonia is hoping to be among the first wave of new EU members to join the single currency in 2007.

Much of this success is due to the bold decision in 1994 of the country's then prime minister, Mart Laar, to introduce a flat tax of just 26 per cent on incomes. The International Monetary Fund warned against it, but Laar, aged 34 at the time, pressed on regardless, laying the groundwork for the rapid growth and prosperity that his country has enjoyed for much of the time since. A number of other countries in the region have since introduced flat taxes of their own – albeit with lower rates – and the Estonians have responded by announcing their intention to cut their rate to 20 per cent in 2007.

In a sign of the openness and transparency of its economy, Estonia ranks fourth in the world, behind Hong Kong, Singapore and Luxembourg (and well ahead of Britain and America) in the US Heritage Foundation's so-called Index of Economic Freedom. The legal system is commendably efficient, while when it comes to indicators of modernity such as mobile phone and Internet usage the country is well ahead of most of its eastern European neighbours and almost up to western European levels. Although their native language is almost completely impenetrable, a gratifyingly large number of people in Tallinn and other large cities are able to speak good English (and Finnish, German and Russian).

The real estate market, needless to say, has been surging in the last few years. Prices have in most cases doubled since 2000, with especially sharp rises in the run-up to EU membership in 2004. The reason is not just the rapid increase in incomes, but also the fall in interest rates. As recently as 2002, an average mortgage cost 9 per cent; it can now be as little as 4 per cent. Estonians are consequently rapidly acquiring an appetite for debt. The economy had been expected to grow a little more slowly in 2005, cooling the housing market in the process. In the event, prices in Tallinn and the surrounding area grew an impressive 11 per cent in the first half of the year and perhaps even faster in the second six months, with many new developments selling out within weeks of coming on the market.

All this makes Estonia an interesting place for investors in search of capital gains. Mortgages are readily available for foreigners, with banks typically offering 75 per cent loan-to-value on old buildings and 85 per cent on anything built within the last five years. They are also cheap at around 1.5 per cent over six-month Euribor (Euro Interbank Offered Rate), which in early 2006 was equivalent to a rate of just over 4 per cent. The tax system is fairly advantageous, too. When you come to buy, you will be pleased to see that stamp duty as such does not exist, while land registry registration fees and other administrative charges could come to as little as £100. Rental income and capital gains are taxed at 26 per cent.

Tallinn

A good place to start a tour of the city is Raekoja plats, the main square. The glorious Old Town (or Vanalinn in Estonian) around it has been transformed since the Estonians kicked out the Soviets in 1991, and has been smartened up with chic cafés, bars and restaurants. Towering above it is Toompea Hill, the birthplace of the city, where the Knights of the Sword first built a fortress in 1229. This is the site both of Toompea Castle, the seat of the Estonian government, and the Alexander Nevsky Cathedral, the giant 19th-century symbol of the Russian tsar's power over the country.

The narrow, winding streets are full of wonderful apartments in medieval buildings; while most of the façades have now been restored to their former glories, many boast highly modern, loft-style interiors, with high-tech kitchens and bathrooms. In a nice touch, mini-saunas are also *de rigueur*. The Old Town Real Estate Agency (*see* estate agent contact details), which specialises in selling in the historic heart of the city, has produced a handy street plan, which not only lists each property individually, but also tells you in which year it was built. You can pick one up from their office in Suur Karja 2, just south of Raekoja plats.

Don't be fooled by the narrowness of the streets. Some of the apartments inside are extremely large. During a visit to the city in spring 2005, I came across the ultimate bachelor pad in one of the narrow streets radiating out from the square towards Toompea. Tucked up under the eaves of a 15th-century building, it offered 168 square metres of space, high ceilings, exposed beams and, of course, a mini-sauna. The flavour was distinctly medieval: you would almost expect a knight to come in and start loosening his armour. The price of £255,000 worked out at a very 21st-century £1,520 per square metre. In some parts of the Old Town, you could pay even double that.

The problem with a trophy apartment like this is that it is so gorgeous that you would want to live in it yourself or show it off to your friends, rather than let it. One compromise solution, if you can bear strangers sleeping in your flat, might be to let it by the day or week to the growing number of tourists who visit the city. Even so, something smaller and cheaper would give you a better return. Letting long-term might be trickier, since the pool of potential tenants – almost exclusively foreigners – looking for this kind of property is not very large. While the Old Town is undoubtedly the ideal place to stay during a long weekend, its charms may wear a little thin if you live there permanently. The narrow streets can be extremely noisy when they fill with drunken revellers late into the night during the summer months, and parking is a nightmare. The likely yield would realistically be around 4–5 per cent, barely enough to cover the mortgage and other costs.

Indeed, the rental market as a whole in Tallinn is not large, and is getting smaller as a result of the growing availability of mortgages. Besides foreigners, the only other substantial group of potential tenants is students and others on low incomes willing to pay a maximum of £200 a month. According to the agent Pindi Kinnisvara, which conducts detailed and very impressive analyses of the Estonian property market, potential salvation may come from short-term lets of three to six months or so, largely to people working temporarily in the city or to those who have sold one home and are waiting for another to be completed. Potential rents here could be £350–450, and there are several agencies that specialise in this part of the market. The yield, again, is not great since such a flat could now cost well over £100,000.

The main reason to buy in Tallinn, anyway, is not so much yield as capital gain. Opinions differ, however, on whether the largest future rises will come in the Old Town itself or in the nearby modern city centre, where most of the offices, shops and hotels are located and a large number of new residential blocks have either been built or are under construction. Pindi Kinnisvara predicts that the prices will continue to rise particularly sharply in the Old Town. By definition, the supply of medieval buildings is finite and, although property in this area remains the most expensive in the city, the gap in price between flats there and those in some of the new city centre blocks is falling. To have a vision of Tallinn 10 years hence, look at the enormous premiums that the swankiest districts of London, Paris or New York command over other parts of their respective cities.

Others disagree. Darren Goodson, founder of property consultants Tallinn Property, and a serial investor in the city, suggests looking instead at new builds in the city centre inside the Ring Road, within a 10-minute walk of the Old Town.

(Goodson has certainly put his money where his mouth is: in early 2006 he already had eight apartments in his portfolio and was in the process of buying another four, all of them off-plans in the city centre.) Here, he argues, you have all the advantages of being close to the centre's bars, restaurants and other attractions, but without any of the disadvantages. In these parts of town you can still pick up restored or new-build flats starting at around £900 or so per square metre, some with parking and the kinds of panoramic views of the Old Town that you don't get when you are inside it. As long as prices keep rising, then by buying into such projects off-plan you should also be able to make a handsome profit even before they are finished.

One of the most interesting of the latter is the Fahle residential and office development, a bold reconstruction of a former cellulose factory a 20-minute walk from the Old Town. Prices in the development, due to be completed by late 2006, were as high as £2,000 per square metre for the flats on the 14th floor, which offer a spectacular view across the city, but a more modest £1,000 or so on the lower floors. An equally dramatic addition to the cityscape is the Tornimae development, a 30-storey residential tower and interlinked 28-storey Swissotel, which have inevitably been dubbed the Twin Towers. This has the advantage of being closer to the Old Town as well, an important consideration if you are letting to tourists.

Those looking for a more modest investment could take a look at the outskirts of Tallinn, where apartment blocks are springing up along the shores of the Baltic Sea. Some British companies have started marketing flats in off-plan developments in Viimsi, for example, which lies about 15 minutes' drive from the capital. Prices here are appreciably lower than in the heart of the capital and there is undoubtedly potential for capital gains. But before buying, you should ask how easy they will be to let. Few resident foreigners would want to live this far from the centre, while many of the locals will take advantage of the ease of obtaining mortgages to buy rather than rent. It is far from ideal for holiday rentals either: those coming on weekend breaks will want to be much closer to the heart of things, rather than stuck out in the suburbs.

Parnu

Although most interest is concentrated on Tallinn, some British companies have started marketing apartments and houses in Parnu, the 'summer capital'. Among the more unusual properties on offer are seafront log cabins. Take a look on a map at the city's location and you will see that the climate, although mild by Estonian standards, is far from balmy or Mediterranean. Summer is short and in some years does not come at all. However, the area is undoubtedly beautiful and provides a cut-price alternative to equivalent spots in Norway, Sweden or Finland. Prices are also likely to rise as Estonians become more affluent, but the rental prospects are not so obvious.

Estate Agents

- **Admiral Apartments, www.admiralapartments.ee, t** + 372 5100 936. Apartment rental service.
- **Arc Property, www.arc-property.co.uk, t** (020) 7371 7633. British-based company aimed at investors offering a limited selection of off-plan properties, but has some useful information.
- **Arco Vara, www.arcovara.ee, t** + 372 6144 600. A wide range of properties, both existing and off-plan, with lots of useful information and market analysis.
- **Churchill Properties Overseas, www.churchilloverseas.com, t** 0800 085 6565. Agency that sells property in several countries. A selection of existing and off-plan property for sale, primarily in Tallinn and Parnu.
- **Ober-Haus, www.ober-haus.ee, t** + 372 665 9700. One of the biggest agencies in Estonia, with a good choice of property in Tallinn and elsewhere, and some useful market analysis.
- **Old Town Real Estate Agency, www.vanalinn-tallinn.ee, t** + 372 6414 440. Properties for sale and rental in Tallinn Old Town.
- **Pindi Kinnisvara, www.pindi.ee, t** + 372 6103 900. A wide selection of properties for sale across Estonia and some useful market analysis.
- **Safe Property Investments, www.safepropertyinvestments.co.uk, t** (01442) 384 987. Company that helps you buy off-plan property in several countries, including Estonia.
- **Tallinn Property, www.tallinnproperty.com, t** (07956) 256 434. Offers a consultancy service for those wanting to buy property in Tallinn.

Hungary

There is no doubt about it, Hungary is one of central Europe's great economic success stories. After enjoying one of the more liberal of the region's Communist regimes (Goulash Communism, as it was known) in the years before the fall of the Berlin Wall in 1989, the country has established itself as one of the leading new members of the expanded European Union. Annual inflation, as high as 17 per cent in 1989, had fallen to a mere 4 per cent by 2005, while the economy has been growing at around 4 per cent a year since 2001. In a sign of international confidence, a number of blue chip companies such as General Electric, Coca-Cola, Siemens and IBM have set up factories and regional headquarters in Hungary. Tourism is also growing strongly, with low-cost airlines such as easyJet and the splendidly named Wizz Air bringing in growing numbers of people; over 2.3 million people visited in 2004, 16 per cent more than in the previous year, with further growth in 2005.

All this has already had its effect on the property market. According to the Hungarian Central Statistics Office, house prices in Hungary rose on average 63 per cent between 1999 and 2003, with a 60 per cent rise in the capital, Budapest, home to 2 million people – or one in five Hungarians – and the main focus of interest for the foreign property investor. The market notched up further gains in the run-up to EU entry in May 2004, but things have since begun to slow, or even grind to a halt, with no immediate signs of upward movement. The villain is oversupply: in the first years of the new millennium, a series of financial incentives sparked a construction boom. Many Hungarians with no experience of the real estate business got in on the act, borrowing heavily to build apartment buildings of their own, with varying degrees of success. Then the foreign buyers, many of them Irish or Israeli, moved in; the bigger players built or renovated blocks of their own, while smaller investors bought individual flats, many of them top-of-the-range 100-square-metre properties in luxurious new buildings.

This oversupply has had an impact on the rental market, too. Most of the investors who bought into these new projects did so in the hope of letting their flats to expats, but there have not been sufficient potential foreign tenants to fill them. Most expats, in any case, prefer to live in newly renovated 'classic apartments' in turn-of-the-last-century Austro-Hungarian-style buildings. Nor can the locals be expected to step into the breach: with the average Hungarian in Budapest earning around £100 a month, few could afford the £600 or more monthly rent that their owners would like to charge. And those who do have enough money will probably want to buy anyway. Like their British counterparts, most Hungarians would prefer to own their own home; indeed, rates of owner-occupation are among the highest in the world.

Matters will undoubtedly sort themselves out over time. But if you want to make money in the short term, it is not as simple as putting down a deposit on any off-plan development you find on the Internet and letting a rising market take care of the rest.

The first rule is to select your area carefully. As with any other large city, Budapest's property market is not a single market, but rather a series of inter-connected ones. A slow average rate of price growth can mask the fact that the cost of property in some districts is appreciating quickly while prices in other districts are moving up much more slowly or perhaps even decreasing. For this reason, you should act as if you were buying in London or any other mature market: do that little bit more research to try and determine which areas look as if they are becoming more fashionable and trendier, and buy there. It isn't easy, but the extra effort can certainly pay dividends.

Those with sufficient time and energy can turn themselves into mini-property developers. One well-proven method is to buy an unmodernised apartment in one of the period blocks, renovate it in a fairly economical manner and then sell it on and reinvest the proceeds. If you choose well, you might easily make 20–25 per cent per deal. Here, as elsewhere in central and eastern Europe, you should pay careful attention to the entrance and common parts. While it can be easy and cheap for you to do up your own apartment, sorting out the communal spaces can be a longer, more time-consuming job. In most cases, the state is prepared to match money raised by owners for major works like repairing the roof. But persuading the other tenants to put up the money can be a long process, especially if a good proportion of them are elderly and poor.

The financial side of things also poses potential problems. Hungarian banks have long been reluctant to lend to non-residents. Although some are now willing to do so, they are unlikely to offer loan-to-value of more than 70 per cent. The tax system also has its drawbacks: if you buy as an individual, then count on adding close to 6 per cent to the price in purchase tax (only the first 4 million forints – just over £10,000 in early 2006 – is taxed at a lower rate of 2 per cent). If you do everything by the book, you will also have to pay 25 per cent of your rental income in tax, without the possibility of offsetting mortgage interest or other costs against it, which will make it that much harder to make your investment self-financing. On the positive side, capital gains tax when you come to sell is 16 per cent and may be cut further. Hold on to the property for more than five years and the rate starts to reduce, with a total exemption if you sell after 15 years.

Many people prefer to set up their own Hungarian company and buy through that instead. It will only cost around £400–500 and will more than pay for itself through the tax saved, but there will also be an annual administration charge. As a company, you can offset repairs, renovation, mortgage interest and other costs against rental income, which will cut the tax bill. It may be difficult to obtain a mortgage unless your company has been operating for more than a year and can show a certified income.

Budapest

Budapest is not really one city, but two: hilly Buda, on the west of the Danube, which is divided into six districts (I, II, III, XI, XII and XXII) and has a population of around 500,000, and Pest, to the east, home to 1.3 million people spread over the city's remaining 17 districts.

Most foreign buying interest – especially from those intrepid Irish investors – has so far been concentrated on Pest. Some of the most expensive properties are in District V, a sliver of land along the eastern bank of the river, which includes the parliament and government buildings as well as the city's main financial district. Prices can be at least £1,300 per square metre here; properties with a view over the Danube or the parliament building command a premium. The three districts immediately to its east (VI, VII and VIII) are also of interest and slightly cheaper. The northernmost of the three, District VI, is the main cultural area, boasting Andrássy út (Budapest's Champs-Elysées), the Opera

House and the Liszt Music Academy. It is crossed by Nagymezo utca, another busy street with numerous cafés and bars that spill onto the pavement at the height of summer. District VII is the historic Jewish quarter, with several synagogues, bakeries, restaurants and hotels. It has recently seen tremendous investment, with buildings renovated rapidly and parks cleaned up beautifully. The part which lies within the ring road is of interest to those buying properties to let to students at the Veterinary School or Medical University.

Some of the best chance of capital gain could be in District VIII, the southern-most and also the cheapest of the three. Many Hungarians have long looked askance at the area, which was traditionally poor and had a large Roma (Gypsy) population. This is where the well-to-do once lived, and its buildings, although run-down, have impressive architecture that speaks of past glories. The government is spending considerably on restoration, holding out the prospect of gentrification and substantial future prices rises. This is probably one for the medium and long term, rather than a place to make a quick killing.

Two other riverside areas of Pest are of interest: District IX, which lies south of District V and is emerging as an up-and-coming area with new trendy bars and cafés and heavy public investment in a new development area; and District XIII, which lies north of District V, and contains some elegant and exclusive areas as well as the Westend City Center, Budapest's largest shopping mall. Properties with a view over Margit island are especially attractive. This is the site of the city's largest new development, Marina Part. In three phases, the last of which is due to be completed in December 2006, it will comprise 1,500–2,000 units around a natural lagoon on the banks of the Danube. Spread over 75 acres, it boasts a sports centre and its own purpose-built marina.

Although most of the new building has been in Pest, Buda is the place to which Hungarians aspire to move when they have made a little money. A haunt of the nobility, artists, academics and diplomats before the Second World War, it is worth a look now, not least because the foreign buyers who have driven up prices so relentlessly in Pest have not been so active here. As a result, some of what were traditionally the city's more prestigious addresses have begun to seem relatively more affordable. Rental yields tend to be higher, too, since this is where the majority of the city's 50,000-strong expat population lives. The international schools are in Buda, parking is easier on its leafy hills and the air is more breathable than in Pest.

Property prices rise as you go up the hill; flats near the castle looking down on the river and the winter smog of Pest are the most expensive. Indeed, District I, which incorporates the castle, the northern end of Gellert Hill and Naphegy (Sun Hill), boasts the highest average property prices in the country. The district nevertheless offers the best of both worlds: proximity to the fleshpots of Pest, many good bars and restaurants, combined with the comforts and tranquillity of a more suburban location. As a rule, old apartments here have also been better looked after than those in Pest. Foreign investors may only now be discovering

Buda, but prices in the Naphegy area in particular have already been boosted by the arrival of Hungarian media and software companies and their well-heeled employees. Because of the shortage of building land, there have been very few new projects here. One of the few is the Anjou residence, a luxurious complex near the castle with a commanding view of the city, where flats cost anything from £2,400 to £3,700 a square metre. It has been calculated that the price of the cheapest unit is equivalent to 15 years' wages of the average Budapest-dweller.

Also worth a look is District II, which lies immediately to the north. Parts of it have been spoiled by ugly 1960s developments, but a number of old villas have survived unscathed. Rozsadomb (Rose Hill) and Pasaret are among the areas most favoured by the *nouveaux riches*. To the south of District I lies District XI, where a new metro line under construction is likely to push up prices, especially around Gellert Hill and the Technical University by the Danube.

Further out, west of Districts I and II lies District XII, which boasts the highest hills in the city and is popular with diplomats and expat executives. Property available here is mostly houses costing more than £200,000, but the yields are also impressive, with monthly rents of £1,500 or more for the best properties. The roads into the city are increasingly clogged with traffic, though, and the consensus among the locals is that the area is on the way down rather than up.

Those who are feeling adventurous might also venture out into the Buda suburbs. The most interesting include Diosd, Budaors, Torokbalint, Nagykovacsi, Budakeszi and Solymar.

Estate Agents

- **Avatar, www.avatar-hungary.com, t** 08707 282 827. British-based agency offering a small selection of off-plan developments, together with useful information about Budapest and some of its districts.

- **Casaro Hungary, www.casaro-hungary.com.** Agency offering an extensive range of off-plan and 'classic' apartments.

- **Filolog, www.filolog.com.** Hungarian agency offering a wide choice of property and lots of useful information.

- **First Homes Worldwide, www.first-budapest.co.uk.** British-based agency offering a small selection of off-plan developments.

- **Gateway Properties, www.gatewayproperties.co.uk, t** + 36 1 374 0782/3. Well-organised site, with good selection of off-plan and 'classic' apartments and plenty of pictures.

- **Hungarian Investments, www.hungarianinvestments.com, t** (01787) 463 774. British-based agency offering a small selection of off-plan developments.

- **Letterstone, www.letterstone.com, t** (020) 7384 7488. Agency that sells off-plan property in several countries. Also provides some analysis.

• **Otthon Centrum, www.property.hu, t** + 36 1 487 3309. A good selection of off-plan and other new-build properties, with some basic information about Budapest.

Latvia

Sandwiched between Estonia to the north and Lithuania to the south, Latvia lies at the geographical heart of the Baltic states. Its capital, Riga, a traditional hub for international trade and business, is also one of the largest cities in northern Europe, with a population of more than 700,000, and is *de facto* business capital of the region – and a bridge between Russia and the west. Over the last few years, the city has also seen some of the most spectacular rises in property prices in central and eastern Europe, of up to 30 per cent a year, with many British and Irish buyers flocking into the market.

Some analysts have characterised the market as a bubble threatening to burst. For others the rapid rise in prices has been caused by Latvia's impressive economic performance. One of the richest and most sophisticated parts of the former Soviet Union (into which it was forcibly incorporated along with Estonia and Lithuania in 1940), Latvia has developed rapidly since winning independence in 1991. The tensions with Moscow over treatment of the large ethnic Russian minority (who actually form the majority in Riga and several other cities), which cast a shadow over the early years of the newly independent state's existence, have more or less dissipated – even though many who moved to Latvia from elsewhere in the Soviet Union during the Communist years have not been given citizenship in independent Latvia and are still not allowed to vote.

The economy, meanwhile, has been powering ahead, with GDP growth in 2004 a blistering 8.5 per cent – the highest in the EU – with almost as impressive a performance the following year. (This, admittedly, has been from a low base: wages, at an average of £250 a month, are the lowest in the EU.) Although the country has been governed by a succession of short-lived, predominantly centre-right coalitions, there has been a broad consensus in favour of free market, business-friendly policies, which have included tax cuts, an ambitious privatisation programme and a series of measures to encourage foreign investment (including the creation of four special economic zones). In another important indicator of the level of economic sophistication, services account for more than 70 per cent of GDP.

It has not all been smooth: the Latvian economy was hit hard by the Russian financial crisis of 1998 and did not grow at all the following year. It has been back on track since 2000 and the government has followed a deliberate policy of reducing its economic links with Russia and orientating business more towards western Europe – a process that has been intensified since Latvia joined the European Union in May 2004. (Surprisingly, perhaps, Britain is now its largest export market.) The local currency, the lat, has been pegged to the euro since January 2005 (one lat is worth €1.42), making it close to parity with the pound. Full membership of the single currency is possible as early as 2008. This will partly depend on the government's ability to bring down inflation, which at 7 per cent is several points above the level permitted for eurozone countries. The government deficit, however, is well within acceptable levels, and unemployment, although still (just) in double figures, is falling. It is unevenly distributed and, as elsewhere in the region, there are considerable pockets of poverty outside the capital. Mortgage rates, too, have been falling dramatically, from 11–13 per cent in 1998 to below 4 per cent in early 2006. The tax situation is fairly favourable: income tax on rent is 25 per cent, while the same rate of capital gains tax is levied if you sell; you are exempt if you hold the property for more than a year. A combination of such positive factors has helped underpin the dramatic surge in property prices, with average values in Riga's Old Town and city centre increasing two- to threefold between 2000 and 2004, with slightly smaller rises in the suburbs. The banks' determined efforts to expand the mortgage market have played an important role. Unusually for central and eastern Europe, they have been ready to lend to the locals for terms of up to 30 or even 40 years. This can make repayments low, even with a possible loan-to-value of as much as 95 per cent. Foreign investors can also obtain loans, although the maximum loan-to-value could be slightly lower. They are free to buy flats and houses in their own name, but may have to set up a Latvian company to buy land.

Speculation – both by developers and by domestic and foreign investors – has played a part, especially in Riga. Whether it will all end in tears remains to be seen. Some fear prices will crash, leaving those who entered the market too late looking at substantial losses – but this seems unlikely given the strong underlying demand among the locals for new property. Alternatively, the rate of increase may slow or prices just glide gently to a halt as they have done in recent years in Britain, for example. Either way, they are unlikely to continue rising indefinitely at such a ferocious rate. For that reason, before investing in Latvia, in particular, it is imperative to do even more research than usual – and be wary of any developer or agent who holds out the prospect of prices continuing to increase by 20 per cent or more a year on into the distant future.

Another word of warning: before buying, be sure of exactly what you are getting. New-build flats in Latvia are typically sold as 'grey', which means the floors, walls and ceilings must be decorated, and inner doors, windowsills, a kitchen and a bathroom installed. Depending on finish, this could cost as much as £250 or so per square metre, adding up to 20 per cent to the total cost.

Riga

Riga has at its heart a fine medieval Old Town (Vecriga), featuring sights such as the castle, built in 1330 as a residence for the master of the Livonian order, the

Dom Cathedral and square, and a host of other medieval churches and guild houses spreading out along the cobbled streets and squares that lead down to the Daugava river. Far larger than Tallinn and Vilnius, it is the only one of the three Baltic capitals to boast a genuine big city buzz, with growing numbers of tourists coming to stroll around its gleaming, newly renovated buildings and enjoy the ambience of the bars and cafés springing up all over the place.

Riga, which celebrated its 800th anniversary earlier this decade, was an important member of the Hanseatic League, deriving its prosperity during the 13th to 15th centuries from trade with central and eastern Europe. Much of the urban fabric of the medieval centre reflects this prosperity, even though most of the earliest buildings were destroyed by fire or war. It became an important economic centre in the 19th century, when the suburbs surrounding the medieval town were laid out, first with imposing wooden buildings in neoclassical style and then in Jugendstil. According to UNESCO, the United Nations cultural organisation, which has added the Old Town to its World Heritage list, Riga's collection of Art Nouveau buildings is the finest in Europe. The city has had a turbulent history and was routinely sacked over the centuries by the Teutonic knights and the Swedes, followed by the French and the Polish. Then, in the 20th century, came the Nazis followed by Stalin. As elsewhere in the former Communist bloc, the Soviets left behind eyesore housing estates on the periphery of the city, many built to accommodate Russian workers brought in after the war to work in industry. But their traces are gradually being paved over.

The Old Town is the focus of attention for tourists and full of the kind of splendid apartments that every self-respecting property investor would love to get their hands on. Sadly, if you are buying now you are probably several years too late to get a bargain. This is where some of the steepest price rises have been, and renovated apartments in the most picturesque streets in the area between Kalku iela and the cathedral can cost from £2,500 to £3,400 per square metre. Prices fall as you move northwards from there along the river towards the docks to an area known by the locals as the 'quiet centre'; a reasonable apartment there should cost from around £1,400 to more than £2,000.

Going away from the river from the Old Town on the other side of Bastekalns park lies the city centre (or Centrs in Latvian), with its broad avenues and grid-like streets. This is where you can find most of Riga's glorious Art Nouveau buildings, which date from the mid-1890s until the First World War. Many of the finest were the work of Michael Eisenstein, whose son Sergei later found fame as the director of the classic Soviet film, *Battleship Potemkin*. Prices in the best buildings will be more than £2,000 per square metre, although you could pick up a flat in a good central location in need of renovation for as little as £1,000–1,200 per square metre.

Many foreign investors have been attracted to the growing number of off-plan developments that have been going up, especially on the south side of the river known as the Pardaugava. The attractions are obvious, at least as long as you get in early enough and prices are continuing to rise. You put down a deposit of anything between 10 and 20 per cent, wait for nine or 10 months for the flat to be completed and then, all going well, take a substantial profit. Thanks to the leverage, even a relatively modest 10 per cent rise in prices will have increased your original stake by 50–100 per cent, depending on the deposit, if you sell on. Alternatively, you can take out a mortgage at that point, ideally based on the higher valuation. Watch out for the location. Most people work on the north side of the river, and the three road bridges can become very busy during the rush hour, which can make some people reluctant to move out too far south. One good bet is the Kipsala district, which lies on the bank and is within walking distance of the Old Town. Flats in off-plan developments there have been selling for around £1,200 per square metre.

The rental picture is not so promising. Given the sharp recent increases in prices, yields may be lower than in other parts of central and eastern Europe, not least because many Latvians will take advantage of many of the great mortgage deals on offer to buy their own homes. There will always be some who want to rent: those who have just arrived in the city from elsewhere in Latvia, for example, or young people saving up the deposit to buy. Salaries are still low, which means that any rentals costing much more than £250–300 a week will be beyond the reach of most locals. Expats may be a solution, but, as elsewhere, there may not be as many of them as you hope for. An alternative might be to tap into the growing tourist market. While the number of visitors has been rising sharply (thanks in part to the arrival of the low-cost airlines), provision of hotels has not been keeping pace, making it attractive to let by the day or week. This is obviously much more hassle than letting long-term, but should give a better return provided you choose your property carefully.

Estate Agents

- **Arc Property, www.arc-property.co.uk, t** (020) 7371 7633. British-based company aimed at investors, offering a limited selection of off-plan properties, but some useful information.

- **Arco Real Estate, www.arcoreal.lv, t** + 371 736 5555. A wide choice of properties, both existing and off-plan, with lots of useful information and market analysis.

- **City24, www.city24.lv.** Extensive real estate portal with property from a number of agents.

- **Ober-Haus, www.ober-haus.pl, t** + 371 728 4544. One of the biggest agencies in Latvia, with a good selection of property in Riga and elsewhere and some useful market analysis.

- **Realia, www.realia.lv, t** + 371 7 111 111. Agency offering a selection largely of off-plan properties.

- **Safe Property Investments, www.safepropertyinvestments.co.uk**, **t** (01442) 384 987. Company that helps you buy off-plan property in several countries, including Latvia.

Lithuania

The largest of the three Baltic states, Lithuania is also the least well known to British property investors. While many British-based agents have been enthusiastically punting off-plan developments in Latvia and individual buyers have been discovering Estonia for themselves, relatively few foreign buyers (with the exception of the usual intrepid Irish) have been travelling to Lithuania. This is despite the fact that this country of 3.6 million people is just as deserving of the title of 'Baltic Tiger' as its two northern neighbours.

Since 1995, the economy has been growing at more than 5 per cent a year, while average salaries (although a modest £270 a month) are currently surging ahead at an annual 9 per cent. Inflation was projected to be around 2.7 per cent in 2005, probably falling back slightly in 2006, while the government deficit was below 3 per cent. Lithuania is likely to be in the first wave of euro entrants in 2007. Property prices in the capital, Vilnius, a city of around 600,000 people situated in the east of the country, are considerably lower than in Riga and just about equal to those in Tallinn. But they are moving very fast: in some districts of Vilnius, they shot up by more than 30 per cent in 2005 alone.

Such rises are being driven in part by a shortage of decent modern housing that is typical of much of the former Communist world. As elsewhere, it is also being fuelled by the growing availability and low cost of finance for the locals. As recently as the late 1990s, mortgages were difficult to obtain and interest rates were as high as 14 per cent. Although levels of mortgage debt, at around 5 per cent of GDP, are still tiny by western European standards, banks now offer loan-to-value of up to 80 per cent on well-restored old buildings and as much as 95 per cent on new buildings. Interest rates, meanwhile, have dropped to an all-time low of 3–4 per cent. Foreigners will enjoy the same rates, but will probably be restricted to a maximum of 50–70 per cent on a first property, although they can borrow a greater proportion of a second.

The tax situation is also favourable. In keeping with the country's low-tax philosophy, transaction costs are low: paying the notary and other legal charges will probably add around 3 per cent, but the local equivalent of stamp duty is only a few hundred pounds. Any rental income (minus mortgage interest and other costs) is taxed at 15 per cent, with the same rate of capital gains tax levied on profits made by those who sell on their property within three years. Real estate held for longer is exempt.

Vilnius

Any tour of Vilnius begins in the 14th-century Old Town, known as Senamiestis, which lies to the south of the geographical centre near the railway lines. One of the largest in eastern Europe, it boats some 1,500 historic buildings in a mixture of Gothic, Renaissance and other styles, spread over some 360 hectares. In a reflection of its unique character, it has been inscribed on the UNESCO World Heritage list. Among the principal sights are Gediminas Castle and Cathedral Square. Prices have been rising sharply here, perhaps as much doubling between 2002 and 2005, and the cost of flats has broken through the £2,000 per square metre barrier. Back in 2000, you could easily have bought one for a quarter of that. Many of the buildings have been renovated by large Lithuanian firms, often on behalf of foreign investment companies, which have then sold on the individual apartments. Prices of flats in buildings that have not been so well modernised are correspondingly lower. In a peculiarity, most buildings in the Old Town still belong to the city council, with flats effectively owned on a 99-year lease. Don't worry: it is not like Britain. The lease is automatically renewed at no cost, so it effectively makes little difference.

The rental market can be difficult, especially for larger properties. While it should still be relatively easy to let a reasonably priced one-bedroom apartment to a foreigner on a short-term or even daily contract to tourists, there is less demand for two- and three-bedroom properties. Despite the obvious charms of the Old Town, living there is not always that convenient: parking is difficult, while the trappings of everyday life such as shopping malls, cinemas, supermarkets and so on are all elsewhere. Some Lithuanians nevertheless want to live in the Old Town, but people able to afford £700 or more a month in rent will probably choose to buy instead. As a result, rents of larger apartments have actually fallen, meaning that anyone buying now can expect to earn a modest gross yield of 4–6 per cent (about half what you could have got in 2002).

Going north of the Old Town towards the river brings you to the more modern city centre. The main street, Gedimino Avenue, is Vilnius's answer to London's Oxford Street or the Champs-Elysées in Paris. Prices here are lower than in the Old Town, although not that much lower in the smarter streets. Most of the properties are existing period ones, but there are a few new developments as well. On the northern side of the river lies Konstitucijos Avenue, which is growing into an American-style downtown with new office, commercial and residential developments. Prices here are 10 per cent or so lower than in the Old Town, at around £1,800 per square metre. This is where much of the off-plan buying is going on. Such modern buildings are popular with Lithuanians keen on contemporary living, but, as in the Old Town, many of those able to afford the rent you would want to charge will be buying instead. More expensive, but worth a look, is Zverynas, which lies in a river valley with low rise buildings, and is the site of a number of embassies and diplomatic residences. Another popular residential area is Antakalnis.

If you want higher yields then you must leave the city centre, moving out northwards and eastwards. The most flourishing market is probably for smallish one-bedroom apartments that can be let to young couples or students who do not yet have the money to buy. Around £50,000–60,000 should get you a 50-square-metre one-bedroom flat in a new block, which, decorated and furnished simply, should yield around £300 a month. There is also demand for studios, which are correspondingly cheaper.

The main attraction of buying in Vilnius now is future capital gain rather than yield, with a lack of supply likely to keep prices increasing by as much as 15–20 per cent or so a year. One solution would be to buy into an off-plan development with nine months to a year to completion. Much of the development has been in the so-called 'dormitory' districts such as Zirmunai, Pasilaiciai, Fabijoniskes and Karoliniskes. A one-bedroom flat of 50–60 square metres, which is easily affordable for many locals, could be a good bet. There has been significantly less building in greener, upmarket Zverynas and Antakalnis, though, which should help push up prices there.

With deposits on some projects still as low as 10–15 per cent with nothing more to pay before completion, it should easily be possible to double your initial stake by the time the building is finished. Indeed, such has been the degree of this kind of speculative buying – by Lithuanians as well as foreigners – that there is talk of raising the deposit on future projects. In calculating the cost, bear in mind that most apartments, as in Riga (but unlike in Tallinn), are sold in a raw state without full interior decoration. Count on completion costs of around £100–150 per square metre.

Another possibility might be to sit back and wait for possible repossessions. According to one analyst, some locals have mortgaged themselves so heavily that they may be forced to sell their properties because they cannot keep up the repayments. 'Everyone is so excited that they can get a mortgage rather than rent, but some people are not very realistic with their income and how much they can spend,' he said. 'They forget that they still have to eat, buy clothes and go on holiday and cannot just put all their wages into an apartment.'

Estate Agents

- **Arco Real Estate, www.arcoreal.lt, t** + 370 5 248 7231. A wide selection of properties, both existing and off-plan, with market analysis.

- **Gijoneda, www.gijoneda.lt, t** + 370 46 252 320. A small choice of property in the port city of Klaipėda.

- **Imbiana, www.imbiana.lt, t** + 370 5 273 5111. A range of property for sale and rent in Vilnius and elsewhere in the country.

- **Ober-Haus, www.ober-haus.lt, t** + 370 5 210 9700. One of the biggest agencies in Lithuania, with a good selection of property in Vilnius and some useful market analysis.

- **Optarem, www.optarem.lt, t** + 370 5 273 0771. Lithuanian-based agency with a small selection of property for sale and rental.
- **Re&Solution, www.resolution.lt, t** + 370 5 252 6444. Agency with a good choice of properties and some analysis.
- **Vilo, www.vilo.lt, t** + 370 5 211 3332. Agency with property for sale and rent in Vilnius and elsewhere.

Poland

You may never have been to Poland, but the chances are that you have already met a good number of Poles. Go out for a drink or meal in Britain, especially in London, and the barmaid or waitress could well be Polish. So could that useful handyman who does everything from plumbing in radiators to sanding floors. The good news for the fly-to-let investor is that there are still plenty of Poles left in Poland – more than 38 million of them to be precise – many of whom are looking for somewhere to live.

By far the largest of the 10 countries that joined the European Union in 2004, Poland is becoming an increasingly important player both politically and economically. The economy has been growing well, inflation has been falling and the currency, the zloty, has been one of the strongest in the world in recent years. There has been considerable foreign investment, both in the car industry and in the financial sector. Given the size of the Polish market, a number of multinationals naturally choose Warsaw for their regional headquarters.

As always, there are downsides, such as unemployment, which remains in double figures – although falling – and government debt, which is high. The country has not embraced wholeheartedly the dynamic, free-market policies seen elsewhere in the region, and corruption remains a serious problem. The government of Kazimierz Marcinkiewicz, who was sworn in as prime minister in November 2005, also initially unsettled some investors with its populist rhetoric, including a bizarre claim by his finance minister that foreign hypermarkets such as Tesco were 'not welcome'.

None of this seems to have dented the upward movement of property prices (or, indeed, of the zloty). After surging in the run-up to EU entry in May 2004, they have been increasing more modestly since – but an annual 10 per cent looks achievable for the near future. There is still potential for quite substantial gains if you leverage your investment; both Polish banks and the Polish subsidiaries of foreign finance houses are happy to lend to foreigners, offering as much as 80 per cent loan-to-value, even though you cannot enjoy the 100 per cent available to the locals. The growth of the mortgage market, albeit from a very low base, will give a further boost to prices.

In early 2006, rates in zloty, at 7 per cent, looked daunting – and certainly high enough to wipe out your rental income. There is a way around this: the banks are willing to lend in other currencies, such as dollars, euros and Swiss francs, at substantially lower rates. Dollar or euro rates will probably work out a couple of percentage points lower than in zloty, but Swiss franc mortgages in early 2006 were as low as 2–2.5 per cent. The usual rule of property-investing is to keep your repayments and income in the same currency in order to avoid exchange rate risk. With such a differential, however, the risk looks attractive. There is a danger, however, that the zloty could fall, plunging you into negative equity.

While we are on the peculiarities of the Polish market, another one is that new-build apartments are usually supplied 'black' – that is, undecorated and without kitchen and bathroom – leaving it up to the purchaser to complete them. Although the choice of finish is welcome, this means more hassle and will add several thousands of pounds to the purchase price. There can be exceptions, so read the small print on the contract.

Warsaw

The Polish capital is not one of the most beautiful cities in central Europe – indeed, some might consider it downright ugly – but it is proving an increasingly attractive destination for investors. Demographics are the key. Warsaw is simply too small for Poland. Look around Europe – or indeed the world – and you will find that the capitals of most countries are home to around 10–20 per cent of the population. Warsaw's 2 million people are equivalent to just 5 per cent.

This is largely because of the effect of 40 years of Communism; while the rural populations of, say, France and Italy shrank considerably during the 1950s, '60s and '70s, their Polish counterparts just stayed on the farm. That has changed since 1989 and the trend is expected to continue now Poland has joined the European Union. Warsaw, with its high-paying jobs in finance, marketing and other dynamic growth sectors, is acting as a magnet, especially for ambitious young people. A 2005 survey by Tabelaofert (**www.tabelaofert.pl**), a mine of information on the Warsaw property market, found that 60 per cent of new apartments in the city were bought by people who had not been born there. Add in the fact that the average Warsaw dweller has just 17 square metres of living space and it is easy to see the appeal.

So where is the best place to start? In most central and Eastern European cities, you might head for the historic Old Town – no doubt with a castle in the centre of it. Warsaw is different. Much of the heart of the city, including the old Jewish ghetto, was destroyed during the Second World War. There is an Old Town known as Stare Miasto, but it is small and slightly to the northeast of the centre (and also fake since it, too, was destroyed during the war and painstakingly reconstructed afterwards). You can buy a flat there, but prices, at as much as £3,500 per square metre, are extremely high by Warsaw standards and it could be difficult to let the flat at a high enough price to make it worth it. Stare Miasto boasts large numbers of cafés and other night spots, but potential tenants might be put off by all the tourists and the extremely difficult car access.

The city centre (Śródmieście), which spreads around the Palace of Culture and Science (Palac Kultury I Nauki), the neo-Gothic pile which Stalin gave the city, is still a good bet. Most of Warsaw's economic activity is concentrated here and apartments are always sought after. Some streets are noisy and lined with ugly Communist-era tower blocks, but there are some beautiful old pre-war buildings in the streets to the south of Al. Jerozolimskie, the main east–west road through the centre. The Powisle district running eastwards towards the river is also very attractive and surprisingly green. Prices are relatively high by Warsaw standards, averaging £1,500–1,600 per square metre in 2005. A typical 50–60-square-metre flat would probably set you back around £75,000. You could probably let it at around £400–450 a month, giving a reasonable yield of 6–7 per cent. Also attractive are the districts of Żoliborz, immediately to the north, and Mokotów, to the south, which both lie along the metro line. Indeed, Mokotów is frequently cited in surveys as the part of the city in which most Warsawites would like to live. The prices in the most attractive pockets of both are therefore not much lower than in the centre. Wilanów, a leafy area to the south where the British and American schools are located, can also be pricey.

Property becomes cheaper as you move further outwards, with prices lower on the north (and some would say 'wrong') side of the Vistula river. As in any city, previously fashionable districts can fall out of favour, while those hitherto considered beyond the pale can be 'yuppified'. Those taking a long view – 10 years or more – may consider Praga district (formally divided into two parts, Praga Poludinie and Praga Północ), which lies just across the river from the city centre. The area survived the Second World War largely intact because this was where the Soviet army parked its tanks and watched the 1944 Warsaw Uprising being crushed by the Nazis. There is a serious crime problem here and it may be difficult finding tenants. Others see parallels with Shoreditch, a hitherto rundown and dangerous district of east London at the start of the loft boom. A planned metro line running east–west through Praga could also help.

There are other candidates: in a report in October 2005, Property Secrets, a web-based eastern European intelligence service, tipped two areas: Bialoleka, in the far north of the city, and old Mokotów. Although an attractive and green area, Bialoleka is relatively cheap at the moment. Average prices are around £400–700 per square metre because transport links to the centre are poor. However, prices could be boosted substantially when a new tram route and the Pólnocny Bridge and expressway are completed, likely by around mid-2008. Old Mokotów, although closer to the centre and on the 'right' side of the river, has plenty of parks and other green areas, and is the site of a number of villas, embassies and consulates. The predicted boost this time will come from the construction of Marina Mokotów, a landmark development of 1,511 flats and villas being built around a landscaped environment centred on a large lake. Property Secrets likens the development to London's Chelsea Harbour, and predicts a 'ripple effect' in surrounding areas once it is completed.

So much for the area, but what kind of property should you be going for? The temptation, as usual, is to splash out on a large two-bedroom flat that would be attractive to an expat working in one of the many multinationals that have set up in town. The obvious is not always the best choice: as Poland's economy and society develop, the number of expats will not actually grow that fast or may actually start to go down in absolute terms. While many top management jobs will still be filled by foreigners, the next level will be taken by smart, well-educated locals. Given the ready availability of cheap mortgages, they will increasingly want to buy their own homes rather than 'waste' £600 or more a month on rent. There will always be people who want to rent, of course, but they will generally want cheaper places. A more profitable alternative might to look far further down the market: for around £30,000 you could pick up a 27–30-square-metre studio, with separate kitchen, close to public transport. It may look cramped to you, but it could be a dream come true for a young Polish professional who has just moved to Warsaw to take up a job in an ad agency or a bank. He or she would be happy to pay you £250 a month for the privilege of living there – which would just about take your yield into double figures.

It is your choice whether you go for a new build or an older building, although the 1970s prefabricated Communist-era blocks – known here as *bloki* – are probably the least attractive. Old buildings, especially in the centre, can be charming, with big windows and high ceilings, but they can suffer from shabby common parts, which always seem about to be done up. Many Polish tenants prefer newer blocks, especially if they boast parking and other amenities. Few are in the centre, because of the lack of suitable sites; they are concentrated instead in Mokotów, further south in Urysnów and Wilanów, and in Bielany and Bemowo in the west.

There are a lot of them, however – more than 50 were at the planning stage at the end of 2004 – raising the spectre of possible oversupply. Before buying, check the transport links carefully – the nearer the metro or a tram route, the better. As a rule, it makes sense to be wary of developments that are too large or which are being marketed by British, Irish or other non-Polish companies primarily at foreign investment buyers. Once the development is completed, you will find your flat competing against dozens or perhaps hundreds of other flats for tenants. Far better to buy into a development primarily marketed at the Polish owner-occupier. This will, of course, be more difficult at a distance, but Tabelaofert, in particular (and other websites listed under 'Estate Agents', to a lesser extent), has details of dozens of different projects.

Kraków

No one would ever accuse Kraków (sometimes also spelt Cracow in English), the Polish capital during the medieval period, of being ugly. This city of 800,000 people, around 180 miles south of Warsaw, is one of the most beautiful in central Europe, with at its heart the enormous Rynek Główny (market square), dating back to 1257. Dubbed by enthusiasts as the 'New Prague', Kraków boasts a variety of attractions, including the Royal Castle, home to several generations of kings, and the cathedral, with its 18 chapels, where many members of the royal family are buried. Around 20 minutes' walk from the centre is Kazimierz, the spiritual and cultural heart of Polish Jewry from the 14th century until the Second World War, which was once a town in its own right. Irish investors have been buying in the city for the past few years, and prices in the most picturesque parts of the centre are not far below Warsaw levels. They drop back substantially as you move further out. This was where Pope John Paul II first served as a parish priest; some predict the city could increasingly become a place of pilgrimage if, as expected, the late pontiff is eventually made a saint, giving a further boost to the local economy.

Case Study: Buying a Flat in Kraków

Caspar Gibilaro, 37, and his Polish-born wife, Monika, from Buckinghamshire, had always wanted to buy a flat in Kraków, and in 2004 they fulfilled their dream. For £32,000 they purchased a 65-square-metre, third-floor attic flat in the Krowodrza district of town. The property, which is a pleasant 10–15 minutes' stroll from the centre, was in a poor state and they spent at least £10,000 on a new kitchen and bathroom and general refurbishment.

Although they bought the flat primarily for their own use, the Gibilaros decided to take advantage of the growing interest in long weekend breaks in the city and let it. They do so primarily through Holiday Rentals (**www.holiday-rentals.com**), a holiday letting Internet portal that charges a flat fee for advertising properties across the world. Gibilaro, who works in IT, reckons he will be able to let the flat for the equivalent of a couple of long weekends a month at around £45–65 a night, which is just about enough to pay the mortgage and other costs. The flat has already appreciated significantly, and in November 2005 the couple bought a second one nearby, which they were planning to let long-term to students rather than tourists.

Gibilaro believes the secret of a good holiday let lies in good-quality fixtures and fittings and, above all, in making sure the building has a clean, well-lit entrance and common parts – often not the case in the former Communist countries. 'Our flat is in a very nice block, which is very important,' he says. 'You don't want people thinking they have walked into a war zone.' Although happy with his purchase, Gibilaro warns there is a lot of administration involved, ranging from taking bookings and handing out the keys to monitoring feedback. He also employs a cleaner to go in to tidy up after each set of guests. 'If your only aim were making money, then it would be probably easier to get somewhere in the sun that you let for two weeks at a time rather than weekends, since the amount of work involved is the same,' he says.

Although tourist numbers are still relatively small, Kraków is joining cities like Barcelona, Prague and Tallinn on the stag and long weekend circuit and is well served by both cut-price and full-cost airlines. Choose carefully and team up with a reputable agent, and it might be possible to make a go of a flat in central Kraków or perhaps Kazimierz as a holiday let – which you, your friends and family could use when it is not let. There is also potential for long-term lettings. The city's reputation as a pleasant place in which to live – coupled with its respected university – has made it an attractive location for the multinationals, ensuring a supply of ideal tenants. Or, if you are feeling brave, you might consider letting to students, although you would need a reliable local agent to manage your property for you.

Most of the housing stock in central areas is old, although there are several new developments, some of them fairly near the heart of the city. Prices, at £1,000 or more per square metre, are not cheap. As in Warsaw, beware if buying a flat in a project that is being sold primarily to foreign investors rather than Polish owner-occupiers, since you could have problems when you try to let it.

Other Cities

The port city of **Gdansk**, which became known across the world as the cradle of Solidarity, the trade union that helped overthrow Communism, could also be attractive. Prices here are lower than in Warsaw, although it is worth testing the rental market in advance. Those with a real pioneering spirit might consider heading for **Poznan, Katowice** or **Ddynia**.

Estate Agents

- **Firma Kontrakty Nieruchomošci, www.fk-nieruchomosci.pl, t + 48 12 631 1255.** Agency specialising in Kraków and southern Poland.

- **Letterstone, www.letterstone.com, t (020) 7384 7488.** Agency that sells off-plan property in several countries. Also provides some analysis.

- **Locumnet, www.locumnet.pl.** Real estate portal with offerings from across the country.

- **Magnat, www.magnat.informer.pl, t + 48 12 292 0265.** Agency specialising in Kraków, especially Kazimierz.

- **Maxon Nieruchomošci, www.maxon.pl, t + 48 22 530 6000.** A large agency with a wide selection of property in Warsaw.

- **Ober-Haus, www.ober-haus.pl, t + 48 22 829 1212.** One of the biggest agencies in Poland, with a good selection of property in Warsaw and elsewhere and some useful market analysis.

- **Property Investment Services, www.property-investment-services.com, t + 48 22 624 7077.** Agency that helps find you property.

- **Real Estate, www.realestate.com.pl.** A wide range of largely off-plan developments in Warsaw and elsewhere.

- **Tabelaofert, www.tabelaofert.pl.** Real estate portal with thousands of properties across the country for sale and lots of useful market analysis.

Romania

Spare a thought for poor Romania, home of Vlad Tepes (aka Vlad the Impaler), tennis aces Ilie Nastase and Ion Tiriac, and the late dictator Nicolae Ceaușescu. All going well, the country should join the European Union in 2007 or maybe 2008, but while the name of Bulgaria, due to become a member at the same time, is on the lips of every British property investor, its far larger neighbour to the north gets barely a look-in. Indeed, a quick trawl through the Internet produces only a handful of entries for property for sale there. That has not prevented prices from rising steeply in the first half of the new millennium, even though the motor has been domestic rather than international demand.

With a population of 22 million people, Romania is the second largest country in the region after Poland. The capital, Bucharest, a grandiose city of 2 million people, is the largest city in southeastern Europe, with wide boulevards and more than its fair share of neoclassical public buildings and ornate private villas. The country also has considerable tourist potential, thanks to the stretch of Black Sea coast south of the second city of Constanța and the ski resorts of the Prahova Valley, hitherto little known outside the country.

The transition from Communism under Ceaușescu to a more western-orientated political and economic system has been a long and difficult one – starting with the bloody fall of Ceaușescu himself, ousted and then killed in Christmas 1989, together with his wife, Elena, as a result not of genuine popular uprising but rather by what is now widely believed to have been a palace coup orchestrated by elements of the ruling Communist Party. Ion Iliescu, a former Communist functionary who became president the following year and served until 1996, was reluctant to break completely with the political ways of the past. He also found it difficult to turn around the old command economy, which was dominated by state-owned heavy industrial plants making products that no one wanted any more. Emil Constantinescu, the pro-western president who succeeded him in 1996, appointed a government committed to turning Romania into a market economy, but faced resistance, especially from the powerful coal miners. The low point came with the economic crisis of the late 1990s, when the economy was shrinking 7 per cent a year, unemployment went into double figures and inflation hit a staggering 155 per cent.

Matters have improved substantially since the start of the new millennium and the decision in 2002 by the EU to set 2007 as target date for Romanian membership. Unemployment has been brought down to single figures, government debt is a mere 1 per cent of GDP and the economy has been growing at a respectable 4–5 per cent a year. The privatisation and restructuring of the country's banks – some of which are now foreign-owned – has been continuing apace, while foreign direct investment has been pouring into the IT sector, one of Romania's traditional strengths, as well as into telecommunications, biotechnology and manufacturing. Judging by the experience of other recent EU entrants, even larger amounts of investment and aid from Brussels are likely to flow in after Romania becomes a member.

The government has, nevertheless, been caught between the International Monetary Fund, which has been calling for rapid and often painful reforms, and the trade unions, which are resisting change. Inflation, although down from levels of the late 1990s, was close to 9 per cent in 2005 – high by western European standards. The liberalisation of bank credit has triggered a frenzied consumer boom that may yet end in tears, with a balance-of-payments crisis and the need by the government to step in and rein back growth. Corruption, still extending into the highest political levels, remains a serious problem.

So much for the negative stuff. As in the rest of the region, the Romanian property market is booming. Prices in Bucharest and many regional towns rose by around 30–35 per cent in 2004 and again in 2005. (Land is a potentially interesting investment, as prices have been rising even more sharply.) The reasons are the same as those elsewhere in central and eastern Europe: rising incomes and the need for more living space. The average Romanian has just 15 square metres for him or herself, against 25 for his or her Polish counterpart and 89 for the average Briton. A further boost has come from the creation of the domestic mortgage market in the first years of the millennium. Although the total number of outstanding loans is still a tiny fraction of GDP, it is growing rapidly as more banks move in, offering loan-to-value of 75 per cent and longer repayment periods. By early 2006, mortgage rates had dipped to around 9 per cent, with more falls likely as EU membership comes closer.

A further psychological boost came from the July 2005 currency reform, which removed four zeros from the currency, in a symbolic break with the high inflation of the past. (The immediate effect, though, has been one of confusion: just as after decimalisation in Britain, people look set to continue for a long time talking in terms of 'old money', while the cash machines have continued dispensing the old notes alongside the new ones.)

While the locals have been mortgaging themselves up to the ears, Romanian banks have hitherto been reluctant to lend to foreigners. This may change, but it means that if you want to buy in Romania you must raise the money elsewhere, removing the benefits of leverage, which can cut into potential profits. This has not deterred the bigger players: Israeli investors have been especially active; so too have Italians, French and Britons. The lack of finance has tended to hold back many buyers, however, which means that if you do get in now you can be fairly confident of being ahead of much of the pack – and can always remortgage later, ideally at a higher price, once finance becomes available. The high interest rates still charged to the locals can also work in your favour: as they fall further, so property prices will rise.

The buying procedure is relatively straightforward. Buyers can deal directly with the seller, rather than through a lawyer, if they wish (although it is not advisable), but either way the purchase contract (*contractul de vanzare-cumparare*) must be signed in front of an authorised notary, who will endorse the document. His or her fee, together with the local equivalent of stamp duty, will add around 2 per cent to the purchase price. It can take up to six months for final registration of ownership (only a few weeks in Transylvania, where the old but far more efficient Austro-Hungarian land registration system is used). Rental income is taxed at 16 per cent; so are capital gains when you come to sell, although there is no liability if you have held the property for more than three years. New-build apartments also attract VAT at the same 16 per cent. Before entering any transaction, it is worth bearing in mind that Romania remains a very bureaucratic place.

If you want to buy land or a house with land, then you must set up a Romanian company – a relatively easy process that will cost a few hundred pounds. You can buy an apartment as an individual, but you might be better off putting the flat into a company as well. This could prove advantageous from a taxation point of view – especially with a new-build, where you will be able to defer the VAT on grounds that you are not the end-user.

Bucharest

First mentioned in 1495 as the residence of Vlad Tepes, the ruler of Wallachia (southern Romania) and inspiration for Dracula, Bucharest began to develop during the 1860s after the formation of the modern state of Romania into an elegant capital that became known as the Paris of the Balkans. The French influence is apparent, not just in the design of its broad, tree-lined avenues radiating out from a number of *piate*, or squares (including, of course, the Piata Charles de Gaulle), but also in the style of architecture. The city even has its own Arc de Triomphe (Arcul de Triumf in Romanian). During the 1970s and '80s, though, parts of Bucharest began to look more like North Korea under a policy of 'systemisation' pursued by the increasingly authoritarian Ceaușescu. The most visible monument to the former dictator's megalomania is the gargantuan 12-storey Palace of the People, now known as the Palatul Parlamentului. With more than 1,000 halls and rooms, a lobby stretching 300ft, over 4,500 chandeliers (of the 11,000 originally planned) and its own nuclear bunker, it is said to be the second largest building on the planet after the Pentagon. Some 26 churches and more than 7,000 homes were razed to make way for it, destroying a large swath of the city's historic centre.

This Romanian love of the grandiose is reflected in the housing stock. The northern parts of Cotroceni (the city centre) around Piata Victoriei boast a

Case Study: Buying Property in Romania

James Emmett, age 32, a surveyor from Berkshire, first saw the potential of the Romanian property when he was working in the country on a construction contract. 'I saw the market, I saw the opportunity and I plunged in,' he says. He bought his first property in Bucharest in 2004, paying £70,000 for a 130-square-metre duplex in one of the showpiece Communist blocks in Ceauşescu's Bulevardul Unirii. After spending another £7,000 on fees and decorating, he has been letting his flat on a 24-month contract to the branch office of a Greek shipping company for £890 a month – a very impressive gross rental yield of 16 per cent. A year after James bought the property, it was valued at £102,000, and he thinks it grew another £7,000–10,000 in the 12 months that followed.

Encouraged by his success, Emmett has gone on to buy three other flats: the next one, in a 1950s building near Piata Revolutiei, required complete renovation, including moving the walls to enlarge the bathroom. Measuring 50 square metres, it cost £30,000, and yields around 15 per cent after renovation costs are taken into account. He earns around 12.5 per cent on another 75 square metre flat, near Bulevardul Unirii, which he bought for £50,000, also in 2004. 'I bought that one with a sitting tenant, fully furnished right down to the silver cutlery in the drawer,' he says. Its value has since risen to £79,000. He also has another 65-square-metre flat near the Arcul de Triumf, which he has renovated. He finds tenants either by advertising himself or going through agents, 'badgering them until they find someone'.

With prices per square metre behind those in Bucharest or in neighbouring Bulgaria, Emmett thinks the market has still some way to go – even if Romania has an image problem with many Britons. 'There are a lot of Spanish and Israeli investors, some Greeks, Germans and Dutch, but for some reason it's some-where the English are still steering away from,' he says. 'When I tell my friends, the first thing they ask is "Where's that?" And when I tell them, they say, "What did you do with all the orphans?"'

Like many other foreign investors, Emmett has also moved into land. He has been buying up fields from farmers a few miles northeast of Bucharest with the aim of assembling a 16-hectare plot, which he will then have reclassified as building land. He intends either to sell it as individual plots or in its entirety to a developer. He reckons he should at least double or triple his money and maybe do even better. 'We see similar areas where housing land is being sold at the moment at upwards of 10 times what I am paying,' he says. 'It's our target to be able to get that kind of return in three to five years.'

number of exquisitely ornate villas, dating back to the golden age of Romanian architecture during the late 19th century and between the wars. Some of the most splendid are around Calea Dorobantilor, an avenue running through the upmarket Primaverii and Floreasca districts north of the square, where Ceauşescu and his former Communist cronies used to live. The price tags – at anything from £300,000 to well over £1 million – may appear stiff, but are modest considering the size of the properties; some of the more substantial ones offer more than 300 square metres of living space and have garages and even swimming pools. Long-term, as the country becomes more affluent, their value looks set to rise further, especially as their central position makes them suitable for use as offices. Some of those on sale are in a poor state, though, and it could be expensive to return them to their former glory.

These properties have their modern equivalents in the gated communities of luxury villas and apartments that began to spring up in the early years of the new millennium further north in the Herastrau, Baneasa and Aviatiei districts near a series of lakes. Convenient both for the city centre and for the airport (an important consideration given the city's appalling traffic problems), these are home not just to rich Romanians, but also to many of the expat managers based in the country. Many of the multinationals for which the latter work have their offices on this side of the city, while the American International School of Bucharest is a little further out, in Pipera. Prices for the most luxurious properties here can also pass £1 million, but £200,000–300,000 should buy a two- to three-bedroom villa with pools, gym, sauna and the all-important 24-hour security, suitable for letting to an expat family. Rental yields, still 15–20 per cent or so early in 2001 and 2002, have fallen back to high single figures, as sales prices have risen and more properties have been completed. Indeed, the sheer volume of building may also put a cap on future capital gains.

Rental yields will undoubtedly continue to soften in the future. As the Romanian economy develops, then, as elsewhere in central and eastern Europe, the highly paid foreigners on their generous expat packages and hardship allowances will ultimately leave and be replaced by local staff, who will be less inclined to rent and more likely to buy. Romania lags several years behind existing EU members such as Poland or the Czech Republic, however, which should ensure that the expat market in Bucharest will continue to be an important one for several years to come.

More modest apartments in tower blocks in the centre can also be an attractive proposition. Around £70,000–80,000 should buy a large one- or two-bedroom 1980s flat in Bulevardul Unirii, the showpiece avenue that Ceauşescu built up to his palace. Let to a Romanian professional, it could offer a more attractive yield than on more expensive properties. New-builds are worth considering, too. After initially concentrating on meeting the demands of the rich, developers have begun building more modest complexes aimed at the emerging middle classes, priced at around £600–800 per square metre, depending on proximity to the centre. Capital growth should be good, although the stage payment terms are not always that attractive: buyers will find themselves advancing a substantial amount of the total cost long before the building is finished.

The Black Sea

While the attention of British and Irish buyers has hitherto been focused largely on Bulgaria's Black Sea resorts, it is worth bearing in mind that Romania shares the same coastline, even though the climate is not quite so good and the scenery less picturesque. The stretch of about 60 miles south of **Constanţa** was developed for tourism during the Communist years. But visitor numbers declined after the fall of the Berlin Wall in 1989 allowed people from the former Soviet bloc countries who had once holidayed there to travel to the west instead. The same was true for the Romanians themselves. The resorts and health spas are therefore rather past their best. Something of a revival has got under way in the past few years, and hotels are being upgraded, giving an opportunity for property investors to jump on the bandwagon. Constanţa itself might be worth looking at, as might nearby **Mamaia**, the oldest resort, the elegant **Neptun** and **Olimp**, and the city of **Costinesti**, which boasts film, music, theatre and cultural festivals. The architectural legacy left by Communism is a fairly grim one, though.

Given the poor job that Romania has so far done of selling itself abroad, it remains to be seen whether the resorts will succeed in pulling in foreign visitors, let alone property-buyers, even though some agencies finally began marketing developments to British buyers in 2006. Much will also depend on whether low-cost airlines start to fly directly to Constanţa airport or instead confine themselves to the capital. Prices will undoubtedly continue to rise here, although, with these uncertainties, it remains to be seen how the coast will perform relative to the capital.

Transylvania and the West

Located in the centre of the country and surrounded by the Carpathian Mountains, Transylvania is home to Romania's favourite son. Bran (or Dracula's) Castle, the 14th-century home of Prince Vlad Tepes, is already an important tourist destination, and there are plans to build a Dracula theme park. An international airport is also expected to open in **Brasov**, the third largest city in Romania, which is in the heart of the area, giving a further boost. Farmhouses, including stables and land requiring work, can still be found for under £30,000, and look certain to increase in value, although these are more suitable as unusual holiday homes rather than as fly-to-let investments.

Brasov is important also as the gateway to **Prahova Valley**, Romania's ski area. Like the Romanian coast, it barely has an international profile, but **Poiana Brasov**, the principal resort, is increasingly popular with the smart set of Bucharest, who have been buying up villas there or purchasing land and building their own. Other resorts in the area include **Sinaia**, **Azuga** and **Predeal**. As with the coast, the market here remains far more difficult to read than in Bucharest, making research and good impartial advice especially important.

Moving westwards, other secondary cities such as **Timisoara**, **Arad** and **Oradea**, near the Hungarian border, have benefited from the latter's EU entry in 2004. They are likely to receive a further boost when Romania joins the Union and border controls between the countries are eased and eventually abolished.

Estate Agents

- **Chindia Estates, www.chindiaestates.com, t** (01794) 521 356. British-run agency offering property- and land-buying services, together with useful information about the Romanian market.

- **Coriax, www.coriax.ro, t** + 40 241 546 260. Agency offering property for sale and rent in Constanţa and along the Black Sea coast.

- **Esop, www.e-realtors.ro, t** + 40 21 317 1414. Agency with residential and commercial property to buy and let in Bucharest.

- **Eurisko, www.eurisko.ro, t** + 40 21 313 1020. Large agency offering a wide selection of new-build and second-hand property and useful market analysis.

- **Homes in Romania, www.homesinromania.co.uk, t** + 40 723 774 738. British-run company offering a selection of property throughout the country.

- **Imobiliar Expert Grup, www.real-estate-bucharest.com, t** + 40 21 316 8152. A wide selection of new-build and existing property in Bucharest.

- **Realtors.ro, www.realtors.ro.** A comprehensive real estate portal with property across the country from a variety of agents.

- **Regatta, www.regatta.ro, t** + 232 9012/9013. Large Romanian agency with extensive listings of property to buy and rent.

- **Romauction, www.romauction.ro, t** (01296) 623 682. British-run agency with wide selection of property in Bucharest and across the country.

Slovakia

The people of Slovakia could be forgiven for having something of an inferiority complex. For decades their country was the back end of Czechoslovakia, and Bratislava, their capital, was overshadowed by the more glamorous Prague. Then, when Czechoslovakia split into two parts on 1 January 1993, after the so-called 'Velvet Divorce' of the previous year, Slovakia had the misfortune to be run by Vladimir Meciar, an increasingly autocratic and eccentric figure who steered the country away from the west until his defeat in 1998.

Despite initial fears that it would miss the boat, Slovakia joined the European Union with its neighbours in May 2004 and, under the stewardship of Mikuláš

Dzurinda, who replaced Meciar as prime minister, has become one of the most dynamic and fastest-developing countries in central and eastern Europe. The figures speak for themselves: the economy has been growing at more than 5 per cent a year, inflation has fallen back below 3 per cent, while unemployment, although still well into double figures, is gradually coming down. Slovakia is hoping to adopt the euro in 2009, ahead of the Czech Republic, Hungary or Poland. Making the country especially attractive for investors, there is a flat tax of just 19 per cent on income, with a similar rate of VAT. It is also turning into an attractive base for foreign car makers: PSA Peugeot-Citroën is building a $800 million plant in Trnava, 25 miles from Bratislava, while Kia, the Korean car manufacturer, is setting up in Zilina, in the centre of the country. In a further bonus, the national currency, the koruna, has been appreciating, making for currency gains too.

All this makes Slovakia an extremely attractive place for the property investor. Rental income is taxed, like almost everything else, at 19 per cent, but you can deduct mortgage interest, depreciation, repairs and other costs. Since the first £2,000 or so is tax-free, if you are buying with a mortgage you will probably not have to pay anything. You are also exempt from capital gains tax, levied at the same rate, provided you keep your property for at least five years (or two years if you have lived in it). Stamp duty, already low, was abolished in January 2005. There are no inheritance or gift taxes and the annual property tax for a large two-bedroom flat could be as little as £25. Slovak banks are efficient and ready to offer 70 per cent or more loan-to-value. Expect to pay around 5 per cent or so in euros.

As elsewhere in the region, prices in Slovakia rose sharply in the run-up to EU entry, but then drifted back. The market in Bratislava, and elsewhere in the west of the country, grew around 18 per cent during 2005, with rises of as much as 23 per cent in and around the historic centre of the capital. Ian Brodie, of Bratislava Business Services, expected prices to grow at a faster pace in 2006, driven by the strong economy and Slovakia's growing name recognition among foreign investors. Tourism has also been given a boost by Ryanair's decision to begin twice-daily flights from Stansted in 2005, joining easyJet and Sky Europe, which already served the city. Sky Europe also flies direct from Dublin.

Bratislava enthusiasts point out that property in Vienna, which lies just 40 miles away, costs 250 per cent more than in the Slovak capital. Prices will not automatically converge, but the process should be helped by the removal of all border controls when Slovakia signs the EU's Schengen Agreement, likely at the beginning of 2007. A further boost will come from the opening of a motorway between the two cities, bringing them within an easy commute of each other. It remains to be seen how many Austrians will actually choose to live in Bratislava and travel to work in Vienna; a number are already rumoured to have established formal residences in Slovakia in order to benefit from its low-tax regime and escape their country's own high-tax one.

Bratislava

Home to just 450,000 people, Bratislava is a sleepy but pleasant place, which lies at the southern foothills of the Little Carpathian chain, in the far southwestern corner of the country, close to the Austrian and Hungarian borders. First proclaimed a town in 1291, it was the capital of Hungary from 1536 until 1784, but became part of Czechoslovakia when the country was created in 1918. The city boasts a picturesque pedestrian zone (*pesia zona*) at its heart, full of a growing number of bars, restaurants and designer shops, and has a fine Baroque fortress (which was actually burnt down in the 19th century and rebuilt in original style in 1953). Strangely, one of the best known reference points is the giant Tesco store, located just opposite the main SNP Square.

Bratislava is divided into five districts, the first four of which are on the north side of the Danube and the fifth of which lies to the south. Bratislava I, which takes in the pedestrian zone and the other surrounding parts of the Staré Město (Old Town), is the smallest and most exclusive. The best streets are Panska, site of the British embassy, Laurinska, Venturska and Hlavne Namestie (the main square), where most of Bratislava's concerts and cultural programmes are staged. If you are targeting young childless expats then this is where most will want to live, especially if they work in one of the embassies located in the centre. The streets, although bustling, are not overwhelmed with tourists like those in Prague or Tallinn. Many of the buildings are stylish period ones, with high ceilings and ornate façades, but their communal areas can be tired and in need of renovation. Despite the central location, flats which look out onto the many internal courtyards can be surprisingly quiet. Access by car is a problem, although it should be possible to rent a long-term space in one of the multistorey car parks a short walk away. Property here comes on the market relatively rarely and can cost more than £1,300 per square metre.

Although yields are unlikely to be more than 6 per cent – and may be lower than that – the main attraction, as with the historic centres of other capitals in central and eastern Europe, is that the supply of property is limited. The pedestrian zone spans only a few streets. The premiums that apartments here command over those elsewhere in the city look certain to grow over time as local property-buyers become more affluent and sophisticated.

The surrounding parts of Staré Město are also attractive to investors and tenants and are distinctly more car-friendly. Prices are lower, and it should still be possible to pick up places in a reasonable condition and location for £800–1,000 per square metre. This translates into a decent-sized two-bedroom flat for £75,000. Expect to pay more in Palisady, an attractive residential area beneath the castle, which is home to many diplomats with families. There have been a number of new developments, too, which are especially popular with Slovak home-buyers. A property anywhere in the city centre would be suitable to let short-term to the growing number of visitors coming to Bratislava from Britain and elsewhere in Europe on long weekends.

Moving eastwards to Bratislava II, Nivy, which borders the centre, and Ružinov are also relatively expensive, but prices drop further out towards areas like Vrakuna, Podunajské Biskupice, Dolne Hony and Trnavka. Also reasonable are the Nové Město (new town), to the north of the centre in Bratislava III, and much of IV to the west – with the exception of Zahorska Bystrica, a village situated within its boundaries which is almost as expensive as the centre.

Those looking for the authentic Communist experience will cross the Danube to Petržalka, in Bratislava V, a warren of prefabricated concrete blocks put up in the 1970s and '80s to house peasants brought in from the countryside to work in the giant Slovnaft oil refinery. Such buildings, known locally as *panelaky*, are best avoided. Prices start as low as £20,000 for a tiny studio flat, but despite good yields you are unlikely to see much capital gain. In fact, with the exception of those near the city centre, the price of *panelaky* has been falling.

For a city bisected by the Danube, there is surprisingly little on offer with a river view. That is expected to change, however, thanks to Ballymore Properties, the Irish developers. They are the driving force behind Eurovea, billed as central Europe's largest mixed-use riverside development. It will create a whole new urban district, with over 200,000 square metres of office, retail and apartment space, complete with a casino, a 200-bedroom five-star hotel and an eight-screen multiplex cinema on the banks of the Danube near the Old Town. Planning permission for the first phase was granted in November 2005.

Estate Agents

- **Arc Property, www.arc-property.co.uk**, t (020) 7371 7633. British-based company aimed at investors offering a limited selection of off-plan properties, but some useful information.

- **Letterstone, www.letterstone.com**, t (020) 7384 7488. Agency that sells off-plan property in several countries. Also provides some analysis.

- **Norco, www.properties.sk**, t + 421 905 333 427. Irish-run, Bratislava-based agency with a small selection of 'second-hand' properties.

- **Real Estate Slovakia, www.realestate.sk**. A few property listings.

- **Slovak Real Estate, www.slovakrealestate.sk**, t + 421 2 5910 3236. A few property listings, together with some useful market information.

- **Slovakia Investment Property, www.slovakiainvestmentproperty.com**, t (020) 7152 4014. London-based agency that sells primarily off-plan and also publishes an informative newsletter on the Slovak market.

- **Slovakian Properties, www.slovakianproperties.ie**, t + 353 1 495 4327. Irish-based company with some properties for sale and useful information.

- **Slovakia Property, www.slovakia-property.com**, t (01603) 444 865. An agent with a good selection of properties in Bratislava, Košice and elsewhere in the country.

Slovenia

Home to just 2 million people spread over an area the size of Wales, Slovenia is one of the smallest but also the most affluent of the 10 countries that joined the European Union in 2004. Squeezed between Italy, Croatia, Austria and Hungary, it boasts an interior with spectacular mountains and lakes, a tiny sliver of Adriatic coast and a small but picturesque capital, Ljubljana. Unlike the other central and eastern European entrants, Slovenia was part not of the Soviet bloc but of the former Yugoslavia, which meant that it was subjected to a kind of 'Communism-lite', which has left its economy saddled with far fewer problems. Unlike their Croat, Bosnian or Kosovan cousins, the Slovenians even managed to leave Yugoslavia with relative ease, suffering a mere nine days of Serbian military occupation in 1991 before they were allowed to break free and make their own way.

Often referred to as the Switzerland of the Balkans (even though, technically speaking, it is not in the Balkans), Slovenia has made substantial progress in its transformation from Yugoslav-style socialism to a market economy. Growth, at 4–5 per cent, has been around double western European levels for the past decade, and GDP per head is now more than three-quarters of the EU average. Interest rates, as high as 10 per cent at the end of 2002, had fallen to half that by 2005, and looked likely to drop further. The economy is close to satisfying the EU's criteria for joining the single currency, and Slovenia is therefore likely to succeed in its goal of adopting the euro as early as 2007. In contrast to many of its neighbours to the northeast, the country has not followed the 'flat tax' path, so both taxes and government spending remain high. It has also been slow in privatising former state enterprises.

Despite such promising economic fundamentals, Slovenia barely features on the fly-to-let radar; go to a property show in Britain these days and you will be hard pressed to find anything at all. This is probably because most Britons who have invested in Slovenia are classic second-home buyers, looking for traditional old houses, perhaps in need of restoration, probably in a rural or mountain setting – not, the kind of place, in short, where developers with big marketing budgets behind them will be putting up blocks of flats. Few opt for the coast (which is short and relatively expensive) or for Ljubljana. Another factor holding back interest in the country is the continued reluctance of the country's banks to provide mortgages to non-resident foreigners. This will certainly change, but until it does, lack of finance is a serious factor that will constrain the development of the market. While many of those investing £40,000 in a second home will be happy to pay for it out of savings or by remortgaging, larger-scale investors are unlikely to buy flats in Ljubljana with 100 per cent cash upfront when they could get 80 per cent loan-to-value in Warsaw or Prague.

Small Towns, The Countryside and The Coast

That being said, Slovenia has considerable tourism potential, and is of interest not just to downhill skiers, but also to those keen on outdoor pursuits such as hiking, riding, cycling, white-water rafting and golf. The tourist industry, although still relatively small, is developing fast, helped by the arrival of low-cost flights not just to Ljubljana, the country's only real airport to speak of, but also to Trieste and Graz, which lie a short drive away across its borders with Italy and Austria respectively. A number of pioneering Britons have moved to Slovenia, buying property and setting up in business there. During a visit to the country in summer 2005 I came across one intrepid man from Croydon, in south London, who is running a paragliding business from a house and adjoining barn that he had bought for a mere £22,000 in Poljubinj, a village in the southwest of the country near the Italian border. Another even more daring couple from Staines, Middlesex, had sold up at home and spent more than £270,000 on an enormous old mill and four other properties in the Prekmurje region in the far northeastern corner of the country. Besides offering family-friendly accommodation for visiting British tourists, they were hoping to make some money from renting out bouncy castles and other play equipment to the locals.

Such ventures are beyond the scope of this book, but there are certainly arguments to be made for buying a rural property, bringing it up to a reasonable standard and then letting it to British or other holiday-makers. Renovation could be a time-consuming business, especially if you are trying to arrange it all from a distance, while holiday lets take some organisation.

The mountainous parts of Slovenia are probably the most attractive from a touristic point of view. For downhill skiing, the largest and best known of the resorts is **Kranjska Gora**, in the north near the Austrian and Italian border. Although small by Alpine standards, with just 20km of slopes, it is suitable for different abilities and enjoys stunning scenery. New-build apartments in Kranjska Gora itself cost around £2,700 per square metre, which is not especially cheap by European standards, although prices are substantially lower in villages a few minutes' drive away. There are several other resorts such as **Maribor Pohorje** in the east, **Bovec** near the Italian border and **Bled** in the northwest, where prices are lower. You should not confine your search to the resorts themselves. Cross-country skiing and sledding are also popular winter activities, while growing numbers of people want to hike or mountain bike in summer. It is still possible to pick up houses in a reasonable condition a few miles away from the resorts for as little as £40–50,000, with both summer and winter rental potential. The area around Lake Bled is also especially beautiful, although prices will reflect this.

Very different is the northeastern part of the country near the Hungarian, Austrian and Croatian borders, which is rich in vineyards and thermal spas, but also boasts skiing around Slovenia's second city of **Maribor**. Prices for rural houses here can be extremely low (although not quite as low as on the Hungarian side of the border); it is still possible to pick up a smallish house with land for around £25,000, although making it habitable would cost at least another £15,000. The scenery, although beautiful, is not really spectacular. The coast, meanwhile, is short (just 46km long) and already expensive. The main resort, **Portoroz**, is popular with Italians (who know it as Portorose), for whom it is a short hop across the border. But the Slovenian coast risks being over-shadowed by the far longer and more spectacular Croatian coast to the south.

Ljubljana

With a population of just 270,000 people, Ljubljana may be the biggest city in Slovenia, but it is one of the smallest capitals in Europe. Prices are already relatively high there – new builds go for £2,000 and more per square metre – and the rental market is small, making it of limited interest to foreign investors. It is also extremely beautiful, though, so if you really fall in love with the place it might be worth buying an apartment there to let to tourists coming in on the daily easyJet flight from London Stansted.

Estate Agents

- **Domart, http://domart.nepremicnine.net,** t + 386 1 256 2888. Agency with properties across the country.

- **Gabra, www.gabra.si,** t + 386 1 300 2232. Agency with properties in Ljubljana and on the coast.

- **GBD Nepremicnine, www.gbd-nepremicnine.si,** t + 386 1 515 0000. Agency with a wide selection of properties in Ljubljana and elsewhere in the country.

- **Nepremianine, www.realestate-slovenia.info.** Property portal with offerings from various agents.

- **Slovenian Cottages, www.sloveniacottages.com,** t + 386 2 251 1865. Cottages for sale and rent in Prekmurje region of northeastern Slovenia.

- **Slovenian Properties, www.slovenianproperties.com.** Extensive list of properties and some useful information about buying in the country.

Western Europe

09

For those looking for a 'safe' investment, western Europe is often the first and most obvious choice. Physical proximity, stable societies and economies and the sheer familiarity of many of the countries in the area make for an irresistible combination. Much of the property bought in Spain, by far the most popular choice, and in France has traditionally been of second and retirement homes rather than of pure fly-to-lets. Yet increasing numbers of people have been acquiring property that they can both use themselves and let; others have gone for pure investments, often bought off-plan.

Developments in the Market

Safe certainly does not mean dull: starting in the mid-1990s, the Spanish property market has gone through one of the longest and most sustained booms ever seen, with year after year of double-digit growth. Ireland has performed even better over the past decade, although the rate of increase began to slow after the turn of the millennium; in France, by contrast, growth rates, still moderate in the mid- to late 1990s, have accelerated sharply in recent years. Several of the other western European markets such as Belgium and Denmark have put in impressive if less spectacular performances, providing solid returns to anyone who invested there.

At the other end of the scale, the German property market has been one of the worst-performing in the world, with stagnant or falling prices during the same period. Austria and Switzerland, whose economies have traditionally been closely intertwined with it, have also done badly. The Dutch market performed spectacularly well in the late 1990s, but has since fallen back.

A large part of the explanation for these developments lies in the introduction of the euro. The currencies of the participating member currencies were locked together (in January 1999, with the actual notes and coins introduced three years later). Imposing a single monetary policy on a group of countries with very different economies was a huge (and some would say foolish) undertaking. As part of the rules for adopting the single currency, the initial 11 members (joined two years later by Greece) were required to sign up to conditions that included cutting their budget deficits and national debts and bringing down inflation. The effect of this rigour, imposed by Germany on its partners to protect its beloved deutschmark from contamination by association with the Italian lira and other weak currencies, was dramatic. Those southern nations that traditionally had had high inflation and high interest rates suddenly found themselves in an unfamiliar virtuous circle of falling inflation and lower and lower interest rates. Much as in Britain (which stayed out of the single currency but has gone through a similar experience), the sharp drop in the cost of borrowing in the run-up to January 1999 gave a considerable boost to the real estate market. This encouraged many people across Europe to take out mortgages for the first time or to trade up to a more expensive property hitherto beyond their reach. Their willingness to take on such extra debt over 15 or 20 years was boosted by a clear signal from their respective governments and from the newly established European Central Bank in Frankfurt that this new low-interest-rate environment was not just a passing phenomenon but instead a genuine paradigm shift. The process was helped by rapid developments in Europe's financial services industries, which meant that mortgages, hitherto unattractive or difficult to obtain in some of the less sophisticated EU member states, became the norm. Investors got the message, too: with the interest paid on bank deposits dwindling towards zero, bricks and mortar became an increasingly attractive place to put their money, with a further sweetener from the capital gains likely to follow.

This cut in interest rates has also had an indirect effect on property prices through the boost it has given to the economy as a whole. The booms in Spain and Ireland, in particular, have coincided with years of strong economic growth, which have sharply boosted incomes and so stimulated the real estate market. Second or holiday homes, often in another country, still largely the preserve of the rich a generation ago, have also become increasingly common as Europeans have become more affluent and the cost of transport – especially air travel – has dropped in real terms. Many think nothing of flying most weekends to a holiday home several hundred miles away. Thanks to their attractive climate, Spain and, to a lesser extent, France and Italy have been the principal beneficiaries of this trend. But growing numbers of second homes have also been bought in Scandinavia, Ireland and other northern European countries with long coastlines. To a great extent, the whole process has become self-perpetuating: as the market value of their principal residence rises, so people have begun to feel more affluent and ready to splash out on a second one.

The picture has been very different in Germany, which had long enjoyed a low-interest-rate, low-inflation environment and so received little stimulus from the introduction of the euro. The country was anyway already in recession, as the boom which followed the fall of the Berlin Wall in 1989 was followed by a slump when the cost of reunification began to bite. The Austrian economy, highly dependent on that of its northern neighbour, slowed sharply between 2001 and 2003; the Swiss economy actually shrank in 2003.

For all the differences in the respective performances of the real estate markets in the various countries, those buying property in any of them will also notice similarities. In contrast to the emerging markets of eastern Europe and beyond, these are developed nation states, with well-functioning legal systems and few problems with title. Mortgages are also widely available for non-resident foreigners, with loan-to-value of 70 per cent or more and rates in early 2006 of around 3 per cent or less. Interest-only loans are largely unknown, but investors can sometimes stretch out repayments beyond 25 years.

With a few exceptions, these countries are also highly taxed. In France, Belgium, the Netherlands and some other countries, public spending is around

House price inflation in the EU 1994–2004

Year	France %	Germany %	Italy %	Spain %	Denmark %	Finland %	Greece %	Ireland %	Netherlands %	Sweden %	UK %
1994	0.0	10.6	-2.6	1.0	24.1	5.8	N/A	4.7	7.9	4.7	2.4
1995	-1.0	-2.2	1.4	3.5	7.4	-3.5	8.5	7.1	4.4	1.1	0.7
1996	1.0	0.0	-4.2	1.9	9.5	5.4	10.4	13.3	10.2	0.0	3.5
1997	2.0	0.0	-3.8	1.4	11.8	17.6	9.6	17.6	7.9	7.7	9.3
1998	2.9	3.0	2.0	4.7	9.2	10.2	14.4	28.8	11.0	9.2	11.0
1999	7.5	2.2	6.7	10.2	7.7	8.8	8.8	20.4	19.3	9.3	11.5
2000	7.9	2.1	8.6	14.3	7.8	5.9	10.5	15.3	14.4	11.1	14.3
2001	8.1	-2.1	7.9	17.5	7.8	-0.9	14.6	8.0	6.9	7.7	8.4
2002	9.0	0.0	10.0	18.1	4.1	7.4	13.0	3.6	4.9	6.4	18.0
2003	11.5	0.7	10.7	17.1	6.4	6.4	5.7	14.1	4.3	6.7	14.7
2004	15.6	-1.0	9.7	17.4	11.3	5.6	0.0	7.8	1.8	10.0	12.3
Average 1994–2004	5.9	1.2	4.2	9.7	9.7	6.2	9.6	12.8	8.5	6.7	9.6

Sources: ECB, National Central Banks, National Statistical Offices, Eurostat, European Mortgage Federation and Citigroup Investment Research (taken from *The View from the Rooftop*, Citigroup, September 2005).

45 per cent of GDP, substantially higher than in Britain (even though the margin has narrowed as spending in Britain has risen). This has an impact not only on the economy as a whole but also directly on property. The equivalent of stamp duty and other taxes and legal fees will add well over 10 per cent to the cost of buying in Italy and Belgium, for example. In France, property-owners are obliged to pay an annual wealth tax on the value of their assets in the country. Tax on rental income is also high in most (but not all) countries. So is inheritance tax.

There is nevertheless still money to be made on property in most of these countries. Average prices across the eurozone looked set to continue rising, albeit at a slower rate, in 2006 and 2007 after notching up average increases of 8.5 per cent and 7 per cent in 2004 and 2005. The countries' respective performances are also likely to become more similar, even though wide differences are expected to persist: as prices begin to grow more slowly in Spain, there are the first signs of a modest upturn in the German market.

The longer-term prospects are mixed. Overall economic growth in the 12 eurozone members has picked up slightly, but did not look likely to reach even 2 per cent in 2006 – around a third of levels in the 'new' EU members of central and eastern Europe and less than a quarter of that expected in China. The economic outlook in 2007 may be only slightly better. The scope for further house price rises in a number of countries may also be constrained by the extent to which they raced ahead of income in the last few years. In Spain, for example, average property prices are now more than five times income – a historic high for the country – while in the Netherlands they are close to six. As a result, the average age of first-time buyers has been increasing considerably. A further dampener may come from interest rates, which went up by a quarter of a percentage point to 2.25 per cent in December 2005, and by another quarter to 2.5 per cent in March 2006. Jean-Claude Trichet, the president of the European Central Bank, has warned that 'price dynamics in the housing market need to be monitored closely'.

The demographics, a key element in the demand for housing, present a more complicated picture: although much of the area suffers from low birth rates and an ageing population, social changes such as rising divorce rates and a continuing breakdown in the traditional extended family will boost the number of households.

Belgium

Let's face it: Brussels has a bad name with many Britons. It could be the thought of all those Eurocrats on fat salaries churning out directives stipulating the degree of curvature of our bananas. Or maybe it is because, unlike other European capitals, it is almost devoid of memorable tourist sights. After all, who can take seriously a city whose symbol, the Manneken Pis, is a small boy urinating? And don't even mention that most daunting of party games – naming five famous Belgians. Yet there is another side to Brussels. Much of the centre may have been ruined by tower blocks and multi-lane highways, but don't forget that the city is also the capital of Art Nouveau, the building style pioneered at the end of the 19th century by architects such as Victor Horta. Built in 1893 as a manifesto for the style, Horta's own splendid house still stands in the Rue Américaine in the St-Gilles district. The Horta House, now a museum, is not for sale, but the city boasts street after street of wide three- and four-storey terraced houses with high ceilings and imposing marble-clad entrances on sale for a fraction of the price of their equivalents in Paris and London. There is also a buoyant lettings market, thanks to the tens of thousands of EU officials, diplomats, lobbyists and assorted hangers-on looking to rent their own little corner of the self-styled capital of Europe. 'Brussels has become the little Washington DC of Europe. In fact, there are even more embassies here than in Washington,' declared Patrick Menache, head of Macnash Associates, a Brussels estate agent, as we sat over a fine lunch in his regular restaurant near his office in one of the smarter parts of Ixelles, just around the corner from Avenue Louise, the broad boulevard full of designer boutiques that radiates out from the centre towards the southeast.

Brussels is not as cheap as it was. Starting in the mid-1990s, as interest rates started to fall back in the run-up to the launch of the euro, prices in the city and elsewhere in Belgium began to rise, slowly at first, but then more rapidly; by the beginning of the current decade, annual rises were well into double digits. According to Stadim (**www.stadim.be**), an independent organisation that monitors the country's property market, a flat in Brussels that cost £100,000 in

1999 would have been worth just over £162,000 five years later; the cost of a similarly priced house would have risen to £140,000. Prices in Ghent, Ostend and other major towns elsewhere in the country generally moved in line with those in the capital, although the rises were slightly more modest.

This meant that, by Belgian standards, property was already looking rather expensive by the beginning of 2006. Although further annual double-digit rises are unlikely, so too is a crash, which means you should be able to get a good deal if you choose carefully. Thanks to the linguistic skills of the Bruxellois, there will be no problem with conducting negotiations in English.

The curious thing about Brussels, a city of just over 1 million people, is that the area near the Grand' Place, the splendid medieval market square in the heart of town, is not the place to be – with the exception of a few streets around the Place du Grand Sablon, another smaller square best known for its antiques market. There are splendid high-ceilinged apartments here, but the high prices and relatively low yields make them more suitable for owner-occupiers than fly-to-let investors. The euro-crowd who are likely to be your tenants prefer to be out further east instead. Most of the EU institutions, and the various other organisations that work with them, are in the so-called Quartier Européen around the Schuman metro station – site of the distinctive Berlaymont building where the European Commission has its headquarters. Nearby is the glorious Parc du Cinquantenaire, with its triumphal arch built to commemorate the 50th anniversary of Belgium's independence (it was meant to be ready in 1880, but was eventually completed only in 1905). The side streets here and in the nearby Etterbeek district are lined with terraces of period houses, mostly dating from the late 19th and early 20th centuries, with small back gardens. Some have had garages subsequently built in. It is all quite reminiscent of a British street scene, except that each building is normally different from its neighbour, rather than identical to it. Some remain as four-, five- and six-bedroom houses, while others have been converted into flats.

For around £130,000, it should be possible to pick up a generously sized 90-square-metre flat in one of these houses or in a purpose-built block, which could then be let to one of the many 20-somethings who come to Brussels from across Europe to work in the EU institutions. If you fancy playing the mini-property developer, you could buy an entire house for £300,000, divide it into two or three parts and sell it off for an immediate profit or else let it.

Potential tenants with more money to spend and families to accommodate will gravitate further out towards Woluwe-St-Lambert and Woluwe-St-Pierre, upmarket districts with newer houses and more greenery. Tervuren, which lies immediately to the east of the city, is popular with British families because of the British school there. Ixelles, in the southeast, is an also an attractive area, with some of the best streets in the city; Avenue Molière is especially beautiful, with prices to match. Uccle, to the south, is popular with French tenants because of its French school.

If you are looking for capital gains, then you should look beyond the established areas to something a little edgier. St-Josse, a relatively run-down district northwest of the EU buildings, or St-Gilles, another up-and-coming area near the Gare du Midi, the Eurostar terminus, are both possible. Schaerbeek, northeast of the EU buildings, is known jokingly as 'heaven and hell', because of the juxtaposition of large, lovingly restored *maisons de maître* and even grander *hôtels de maître* with more modest dwellings. The really intrepid might consider moving even further out towards the traditional working class areas of Jette and Anderlecht in the northwest, although you would probably then be letting to locals rather than Eurocrats.

Wherever you buy, the yields will not be spectacular. You may seem to be getting a lot of property for your money compared with other European capitals, but rents are correspondingly low, too. Bear in mind that Belgian salaries are appreciably lower than those in Britain, leaving people with far less

Case Study: *Buying a House in Brussels*

John Harrington, 35, who works for the EU, moved to Brussels for work in early 2000, initially renting in the southeastern district of Ixelles. After two years, he and his wife bought a small four-storey house a few streets away and sold it again after a year, making a small profit once all the tax had been paid (after getting back 60 per cent of the stamp duty because he had owned the property for less than two years). The couple used the proceeds to trade up to a larger, four-storey, four-bedroom house in a slightly dodgy but rapidly improving area near Place Jourdan. The house cost just £110,000, plus around £20,000 in stamp duty and notary fees. It had been lived in by students and was in a very poor state, and the couple spent another £30,000 on putting in central heating, a new boiler and lots of other work.

After living in the house for a year, the Harringtons moved out to Tervuren to be near the British school (and bought another property to live in), but kept the city house and now let it unfurnished to four French graduate students who pay £880 a month, just about enough to cover the mortgage. 'It's good because their parents guarantee their rent,' John said. He has another cause for good cheer: he had the house valued recently at just over £200,000 – which means he has made a healthy 25 per cent profit.

After spending a good part of the last few years in the close company of builders – some of whom, he believes, overcharged him because he was a foreigner – Harrington is wary about taking on another development project. He would nevertheless still advise others to buy in Brussels, provided they take their time to look around and choose the area carefully. 'It's a bit like London in 1997,' he said. 'Anyone buying now hasn't entirely missed the boat, but they would probably be climbing on the rear end of it. You can't just walk in and walk out again a year later with a bag of cash, but you will certainly see much higher returns than you would in the UK at the moment.'

disposable income. Given a chance, Belgians prefer to buy rather than rent, and owner-occupation rates are high. Count on earning around 4–5 per cent, just enough to cover borrowing costs. Rental contracts can run as long as nine years, and, although it can be difficult to get rid of tenants, much of the onus on maintaining the property lies with them; you are unlikely to get phone calls late at night complaining that a light bulb needs changing. Furnished flats, which are what many younger tenants want, will give a better yield (and require more intensive management), but also tend to suffer more voids.

The tax situation is favourable for landlords: rather than being liable for Belgian tax on your rental income, you instead pay a flat annual tax known as the *précompte immobilier*. In theory this is calculated on the property's rateable value, but in most cases this has not kept up with property price inflation. Check with an accountant too, though, on your liability to British tax.

Brussels is not the place to make a fast buck, not least because of the high transaction costs. Stamp duty is 12.5 per cent and the bill for the notary, who handles all the paperwork, will add several more percentage points. Although 60 per cent of the stamp duty (but not the notary's fees) is refunded if you sell (and complete) within two years, this can put a dampener on speculation. This has not prevented a number of the larger British and Irish investors from descending on the city in search of a killing. Few find what they are looking for. Agents warn there is too much money chasing too few good products, and admit that if they do come across bargains they are more likely to pass them on to regular clients rather than outsiders who approach them out of the blue.

The conclusion? If you are looking for adventure and risk, head for Bulgaria, Dubai or Croatia. But if you want a relatively secure medium- to long-term earner, then leave those preconceptions behind at the Eurostar terminal and take a look at the much-maligned capital of Europe.

Estate Agents

- **Agence Universal, www.agenceuniversal.be, t** + 32 2 646 55 55. Property for sale and rent in Brussels and its suburbs.

- **Atimmo, www.atimmo.be, t** + 32 2 331 55 11. Property for sale and rent in Brussels, including property with sitting tenants suitable for investors.

- **Capitol Invest, www.capitol-invest.be, t** + 32 2 663 65 80. Agency specialising in off-plan apartments in Brussels.

- **Crescendimmo, www.crescendimmo.be, t** + 32 2 660 50 50. Property for sale and rent in Brussels and in other parts of Belgium.

- **Eurimobel, www.eurimobel.be, t** + 32 3 829 00 80. Antwerp-based agency with property to buy and rent across Belgium.

- **Feeling Agence, www.agfeeling.be, t** + 322 289 10 00. Property for sale and rent in Brussels and its suburbs.

- **Housing Service, www.housing-service.be, t** + 322 732 99 20. A wide selection of flats and houses in Brussels for sale and rent.
- **Immoview, www.immoview.be, t** + 32 475 65 89 40. Portal with links to estate agents across Flanders.
- **Immoweb, www.immoweb.com.** Real estate portal with tens of thousands of flats and houses to buy and rent across the country.
- **Macnash Associates, www.macnash.com, t** + 32 2 347 11 47. Property for sale and rent in Brussels.

France

Thanks to its inimitable style, pleasant climate and wonderful food and wine, France has long been Europe's most popular tourist destination and a firm favourite with British second-home owners. The choice of properties is as diverse as the country itself: take your pick between a *gîte* in Normandy, a seafront villa on the Côte d'Azur, a *mas* in Provence and a *pied-à-terre* in a fashionable district of Paris. Many Britons who bought have done so with holidays or with retirement in mind. As elsewhere, though, this is changing. Increasing numbers of people now buy a holiday home with the hope of letting it at least for a few weeks a year to help cover costs; for a smaller number, income and capital gains are the principal motivation.

Certainly, from an investment point of view, anyone buying over the last few years will have done extremely well for themselves and be sitting on substantial capital gains. After making only modest gains through the early and mid-1990s (and, according to one measure, actually falling back during 1995), prices began rising sharply in 1999, with annual increases moving into double figures in 2003 and 2004. According to figures released in January 2006 by Notaires de France, the body grouping French notaries, the prices of apartments in the third quarter of 2005 rose by an annual 16.2 per cent, with houses up 13.4 per cent. This compared with 18.6 per cent and 14.1 per cent respectively in the previous year. The overall figure masked considerable regional differences. The market was especially strong in the Rhône-Alpes region, which includes Lyon and Grenoble as well as many of France's ski resorts (up 19 per cent in the period), and Provence-Alpes-Côte d'Azur, to the south (up 16.7 per cent). According to the same data, both areas also performed especially well over a five-year period – up 75 per cent and 86 per cent, respectively, compared with a national average of 65 per cent. Generally speaking, the cost of second-hand property rose more than that of new-builds.

Prices cannot keep on growing at that rate for ever, but the upturn looks likely to be more solid – and less 'bubble-like' – than in Spain. The principal reason is affordability: at just over three and a quarter times income (against five times or more in Britain, Ireland, Spain and Germany), average property prices in

France are around the lowest in Europe. Other factors also point to long-term gains: population growth is the fastest in Europe after Ireland, which results in more households being formed and so more demand for property. Owner-occupation rates, at 56 per cent in 2004, and outstanding mortgages, equivalent to just 27 per cent of GDP, are both low by European standards – leaving scope for growing demand for property.

While capital growth has been promising – with the prospect of more to come – the situation with rentals is more complex, especially when it comes to targeting the holiday market. The idea of buying a cheap rural property, renovating it lovingly and letting it to fellow Britons on holiday is an appealing one – so appealing, in fact, that rather too many people have done precisely that over the last few years, resulting in chronic oversupply. Put simply, there are just too many *gîtes* chasing too few punters. This is not to say that there is not money to be made. It just means you have to take more care in choosing your property. As far as rural properties are concerned, beauty counts for a lot; holiday tenants are buying, albeit only for a couple of weeks, into a French rural idyll – and the more idyllic, the better. But they will want their creature comforts, too – modern kitchens and luxurious bathrooms. For properties over a certain size, and especially those aimed at families, a pool is essential.

In areas such as the Dordogne, which are full of British barn conversions for rent, it may be worth going upmarket in order to make yours stand out from the pack. If your house is a large one, which would be suitable for two families sharing, then make sure it has almost as many bathrooms as it does bedrooms; no one wants to have to queue for their morning shower on holiday. To make it appealing, splash out on nice linen and crockery and maybe even offer optional services such as a cook as well. This is common with chalets in the mountains, so why not do the same with a property by the sea or in the countryside? Always remember that little things that may not actually cost you money can make a big difference to your tenants' stay. One useful guide to letting (**www. laymyhat.com**) also suggests quirkier things, like making picture postcards with a photograph of your house and leaving them for tenants, or welcoming them by name with those little magnetic letters you can attach to the fridge. Anything that can make people feel at home and want to come back next year can help; even better, it may encourage them to tell their friends too.

Location is extremely important. In general, the things that attracted you to the property in the first place should attract others as well, although accessibility remains a key. If you are looking at property in the north or northwest of France it is safe to assume that many people staying for a week or more will come by car, which means it is good to be close – but not *too* close – to France's excellent motorway network. Move further south, however, and you must think about your proximity to airports. This is also the case if you are targeting the long-weekend market; if people only have three days, they don't want to spend one of them on the road.

Travel to France has been transformed in recent years by the arrival of Ryanair and the other low-cost airlines. Not only have they drastically reduced the cost of flying relative to road or rail, they have also opened up the interior of the country to tourism by serving hitherto obscure regional airports such as Perpignan, Rodez and Bergerac. Property prices in these areas have undoubtedly benefited from a 'Ryanair effect' following the announcement and opening of such routes, even though the strength of this effect has varied from place to place. When making your choice, don't only think of flights from London, either. Nîmes, for example, receives direct flights from Liverpool and East Midlands as well as from Luton, while it is possible to fly straight to Marseille from Glasgow. Don't base your investment strategy entirely on an airline timetable, though; as some have found to their cost, carriers can go bust and routes be axed literally overnight.

It is not enough to have a beautiful, well-located property. You also have to market it well. For those looking only for a small amount of rental income to subsidise their holiday home, it may be enough to rely on friends and relations. If you see your property primarily as a business venture then you will need to advertise either in the print media or on the Internet and make sure you are coming up in the Internet search engines. The web plays an increasingly important role in people's holiday planning and there are large numbers of sites offering rental property either just in France or more widely. Your *gîte* or apartment will be up against dozens or many hundreds of rivals, though, and as discussed in Part One, Chapter 05, **Letting Your Property**, you should think hard about how best to differentiate it from them.

Be realistic about how much you can expect to earn in rent. One of the most important constraints is the length of the season. In Normandy or Brittany, for example, this is unlikely to exceed 10 weeks, with most money made during high summer. With the average *gîte* going for around £500 a week, this means a maximum of £5,000 a year – and that is before you have paid for cleaning, agents' fees and so on. In other words, if you have paid anything more than £100,000 to buy the property in the first place, your net yield will have dipped substantially below 5 per cent and, if you have bought with a mortgage, is unlikely to cover your monthly payments. Similar properties in the south, especially those near the Mediterranean coast, will command more, while the season will be several weeks longer, although the gains will be partially offset by the higher purchase prices. Property in cities could provide an attractive alternative; a flat in Paris, for example, can be rented out either short- or long-term. The advantage of the capital is that the season runs for the entire year; although it is not realistic to expect your flat to be rented continuously, even as little as 50 per cent occupancy should allow you to achieve more than 5 per cent. You will probably get slightly less letting out long-term.

If you think all this is too much hassle, then leaseback deals provide an attractive alternative. The concept behind these schemes – in which you buy a property and then lease it back to the developer – has already been discussed (*see* p.46). It is worth reiterating here that a variety of schemes is available all over the country, offering guaranteed yields of 3.5–5.5 per cent, depending largely on the amount of personal use allowed.

The buying procedure is well established and straightforward. As in Britain, it is a two-stage process; you first sign a *compromis de vente* (broadly equivalent to an exchange of contracts), usually accompanied by 10 per cent of the price, and then wrap up the process with the *acte de vente* (completion). The *notaire* (notary) plays a key role. Required by law to act impartially, he or she usually acts for both buyer and seller, but you can appoint your own if you wish. (This will not cost you more since the two *notaires* will split the fee between them.) As a foreigner, it may be advisable to hire a solicitor or English-speaking *notaire* of your own, who specialises in real estate; in case of a disagreement, you are far better off having someone who knows the law and can speak French.

Count on adding 8–10 per cent in taxes and fees to the purchase price. You will also be liable for an annual *taxe foncière*, calculated on the value of the property, while a *taxe d'habitation* is levied on whoever is living there on 1 January. Rental income is taxed, too. There is another nasty surprise in store in the form of the wealth tax, which in 2005, for example, kicked in if you owned assets in excess of €732,000 (£493,000). The tax starts at 0.55 per cent, but rises in bands, reaching a maximum of 1.8 per cent on anything more than €15,255,000 (£10,268,420). The tax is clearly an emotive subject, among French property-owners as much as among foreign ones, but it would be wrong to exaggerate its impact on those buying purely for investment, especially if they are doing so with a mortgage. If you own a £600,000 property with a £400,000 mortgage, for example, you only have £200,000 of wealth, which means you are well below the threshold. The problems really start if you become resident in France, in which case the tax is levied not only on your assets within the country but on those elsewhere in the world, too.

By contrast, the capital gains tax when you sell is not so onerous. Residents of other EU countries pay a basic rate of 16 per cent (those living outside the EU instead pay 33.3 per cent), but this drops by 10 per cent a year once you have owed the property for five years. You can also offset the cost of improvements, provided they are receipted. The precise amount due is calculated by the *notaire* handling the sale. (Although it is not in the legislation, the *notaires* have been told not to allow as a deduction any invoices that do not have a French VAT number on them. This is a problem for people who have informal arrangements with British builders.) Don't forget, though, that if you are a UK resident you will also have a liability to HM Revenue & Customs. French residents are subject to different and more complicated rules, but, as in Britain, should be exempt from paying any tax on profits made on their principal residence. Inheritance tax is reasonable, but be careful with rules on inheritance, which, unlike in Britain, oblige you to split your property between spouse and children.

Mortgages are generally available, with loan-to-value of 80 per cent or more and interest rates generally in line with those in other eurozone countries. French banks or the French subsidiaries of British ones are happy to lend to non-residents provided they can show evidence of regular income. Strictly speaking, however, under French law, the total of your mortgage payments worldwide should not exceed 30 per cent of your total income.

There is no room here for a complete guide to France; there are plenty of other books and websites that will do that for you. The following gives a quick tour of the regions and the kind of prices you will have to pay.

Paris

The Parisian property market requires a whole chapter, or perhaps even a book, for itself. Paris proper is relatively compact – at least, compared with London – with a population of 2.2 million, even though more than 11 million live in the Ile de France region of which it is the capital. It is divided into 20 *arrondissements* or districts (often referred to merely by their number); the 1st lies in the centre and the others radiate out in a clockwise manner around it.

At £6,000–7,000 per square metre, prices in some of the most expensive areas, such as the 3rd and 4th (the Marais), the 5th (which includes the fabled Latin Quarter), the 6th (St-Germain) and the 16th (which borders the Bois de Boulogne), are well up to London levels. They fall back to around £4,000 in edgier but still relatively central districts such as the 9th (Pigalle) and the 18th (Montmartre) and are lower still as you head out to the *banlieue* (suburbs).

By the middle of 2005 there were distinct signs that the Paris real estate market was cooling, at least in some of the more expensive areas. Agents reported that, rather than snapping up the first property that they saw, buyers were determined to shop around a little first. During the course of the year, average prices in the 5th and the other more expensive *arrondissements* actually fell back. The pattern across the city was not uniform, though, and prices in the trendy and more affordable 10th and 11th, around the Canal St-Martin, for example, shot up 18.8 per cent during the year.

There have been signs of oversupply in the short-term rental market, especially of smallish one-bedroom flats. It is not just Britons and other foreigners who are buying them. The French, too, have been purchasing small investment properties as an alternative to the stock market, spurred by tax breaks for landlords who rent out furnished apartments. You may do better with a larger, two-bedroom one instead.

The French Riviera and Provence

Generally regarded as one of the most luxurious, expensive and sophisticated areas on the planet, the French Riviera has been a fashionable resort since the late 19th century, when it first became popular as a wintering spot for wealthy

Britons. Starting on the Italian border in the east, it continues westwards through **Nice, Antibes** and **Cannes** along the Mediterranean coast of the Alpes-Maritimes department. Beyond lies the Var, which includes resorts such as **St-Tropez** and **Hyères**, on the outskirts of **Toulon**. The area still has its share of multi-million-pound villas, but there are also large numbers of more modest houses and rows of residential tower blocks.

It is difficult to generalise about prices, except to say that they have risen steeply. It is difficult to find a villa with good views for less than £350,000, although prices for more luxurious properties quickly rise to £1 million and beyond. A modern seven-bedroom villa in St-Tropez, with pool and 4,000 square metres of grounds, could cost more than £4 million. Prices of apartments along the coast go for £2,000–4,000 per square metre, depending on quality, proximity to the sea and view. The season begins earlier and ends later than in the rest of France, which helps yields. Nice, well served by the low-cost airlines, is a good choice and, on average, cheaper than Cannes; a small apartment there can make a good long-term let, yielding as much as 7–8 per cent.

Languedoc-Roussillon

Prices tend to fall back in Languedoc-Roussillon to the west, which stretches around and down southwards towards the Pyrenees and the Spanish border. Principal towns include **Montpellier**, **Béziers**, **Narbonne**, **Perpignan** and **Collioure**, a picturesque Catalan resort that was a meeting place during the early 1900s for artists of the Fauve school. Further inland is **Carcassonne**, a medieval city whose towers apparently served as the inspiration for the castle in Walt Disney's *The Sleeping Beauty*. It is possible to pick up easily lettable seafront apartments in one of the fairly nondescript resorts such as **Canet-Plage** and **St-Cyprien-Plage** near Perpignan for under £2,000 per square metre; prices could be almost double that in Collioure. The low-cost airlines have greatly opened up this area to tourists: Ryanair, for example, flies to Montpellier, Carcassonne and Perpignan.

Brittany, the Atlantic Coast and the Dordogne

Prices on the Atlantic coast are generally cheaper than on the Mediterranean, although the weather is far less reliable and the potential rental season shorter. Starting in **Brittany** in the north, the region stretches down through the **Pays de la Loire** and **Poitou-Charentes** to **Aquitaine**. Again, generalisations are difficult, although it should be possible to pick up a reasonable house with some land for £100,000–150,000. One of the most sought-after areas is the **Ile de Ré**, a delightful island off La Rochelle, appreciated by the French for its understated charm. Although the clientele is distinctly upmarket, it is the antithesis of the brash resorts of the Côte d'Azur – you will see many more bicycles than Ferraris and Porsches here. Not that many properties come on sale and, when they do, they are pricey. Count on paying at least £300,000 for a house; new-build apartments near the beach can cost upwards of £3,000 per square metre. Both the island and the mainland are extremely popular holiday destinations, which means an active rental market. For those with the time and energy there are also a large number of properties available in need of renovation.

Further south, **Biarritz**, near the Spanish border, is a grand old 19th-century resort, which became a favourite of European royalty after Empress Eugénie, the wife of Napoléon III, built a palace on the beach there in 1854. Queen Victoria became a frequent visitor. Flats there can range from £2,500 to £4,000 or so per square metre, depending on location.

The **Dordogne**, which lies inland from Bordeaux in the north of Aquitaine, has been nicknamed 'Little Britain' by the locals, even though it is just as likely to be the Dutch or Germans buying up land or property there. The appeal lies in its scenic countryside and picturesque towns and villages (it has 4,000 châteaux, 10 per cent of the total for the whole country). It is still possible to pick up serious renovation projects requiring considerable time and effort for as little as £30,000–40,000, although a large house with a pool, ready to move into, would cost several times that. Think carefully before buying purely as a rental investment; you will be competing with a lot of properties, many of them British-owned, that are already on the market.

Normandy and Pas-de-Calais

For sheer convenience, both for property-owners and those renting, it is difficult to beat the area south of Calais. Indeed, for those living in London, it can be a lot easier and quicker to access than Devon and Cornwall. Paris, Brussels and Lille are also within easy distance, enlarging your pool of potential rental tenants. The **Opal Coast** is dotted with a string of pleasant little seaside towns such as **Wissant** and **Hardelot-Plage**; there are also splendid larger resorts such as **Le Touquet-Paris-Plage** and **Deauville**, which lies much further down the coast, beyond the ports of **Dieppe** and **Le Havre**. The weather is not much better than in Britain, but property prices are far cheaper than in equivalent towns on the English south coast. Around £150,000 should get you a reasonable house.

The Mountains

Ski property can be an extremely attractive fly-to-let investment, with tenants generally prepared to pay substantially more for a week in a mountain resort than for the equivalent by the sea or in the countryside. Prices were growing at an annual 15 per cent in late 2005, slightly above the national average. A reasonable two-bedroom apartment in **Chamonix**, **Courchevel** or **Val d'Isère** will cost a minimum of £100,000 – or around £4,000 per square metre. Prices are lower in the lesser-known resorts. There are a number of leaseback schemes on offer, typically yielding 4–5 per cent and allowing some personal occupation.

Estate Agents

- **123immo, http://en.123immo.com**. Comprehensive French listing of property for sale and rent.
- **1st for French Property, www.1st-for-french-property.co.uk, t** 0870 720 2966. Portal site with a wide range of properties for sale and rent.
- **Azur Properties, www.azurproperties.com, t** (01527) 834 494. Flats and houses for sale in the south of France.
- **Coast & Country, www.coast-country.com**. British-run agency offering property in the south of France.
- **French Entrée, www.frenchentree.com, t** (01280) 817 766. Online magazine with property for sale and host of other features.
- **French Estate Agents, www.frenchestateagents.com, t** 08700 11 51 51. A wide selection of property in Dordogne and other popular areas, together with investment projects.
- *French Property News*, **www.french-property-news.com**. Magazine for those interested in French property, together with extensive listings.
- **Immostreet, www.immostreet.co.uk**. Tens of thousands of properties.
- **Internet French Property, www.french-property.com**. More than 3,000 properties for sale across France on the first French property website.
- **JB French Houses, www.jbfrenchhouses.co.uk**. A selection of houses for sale across the country.
- **Property Finder France, www.propertyfinderfrance.net, t** (01527) 834 494. Site full of detailed information on different regions and a wide choice of properties.
- **The French Property List, www.thefrenchpropertylist.com**. Internet forum for private buyers and sellers.
- **Un Mas en Provence, www.provence-properties.com, t** + 334 90 76 75 00. A choice of properties for sale and rent across Provence.
- **VEF, www.vefuk.com, t** (020) 7515 8660. Existing and new-build properties for sale across France.

French Leaseback Specialists

- **Assetz France, www.french-property-sales-france.co.uk, t** (0161) 456 5000. Property listings and information about how leaseback works.
- **EU Property Portfolio, www.eupp.co.uk, t** 0845 2265 093. Listings, information about how leaseback works and some market analysis.
- **Leaseback Investments, www.leaseback.co.uk, t** (0161) 976 2744. Listings and information about how leaseback works.

- **Le French Leaseback, www.frenchleaseback.net, t** (028) 9080 7952. Listings plus a forum for owners to discuss developments and pool their experiences.

- **Moving to France, www.movingtofrance.com**. Listings largely in France, but some in Spain, together with information about how leaseback works.

- **Pierre & Vacances, Property Investments, www.pierreetvacances-immobilier.com**. A wide choice of leaseback developments, largely in France, but also a few in Spain and Italy.

- **UK Overseas, www.ukoverseas.com, t** 08701 149807. Listings, mainly of Alpine ski properties, and general information about leaseback.

- **Your French Property, www.your-french-property.co.uk, t** 0870 787 3398. Listings and information about leaseback.

Germany

The words 'Germany', 'property' and 'buying opportunity' have not often been uttered in the same breath in recent years – and for understandable reasons. While real estate prices around the world have been surging, Germany, like Japan, has been a picture of unremitting gloom. The reasons are not difficult to find. Unemployment, at close to 5 million, has been at the highest level since the 1930s, and although well-known companies like Daimler-Chrysler, BMW and Siemens have ensured that the country remains one of the world's leading exporters, the German economy has been stuck in the doldrums since the post-reunification boom of 1990–92. Growth since has averaged just 1.3 per cent a year – the slowest in the EU. One of the principal problems is the continuing low level of consumer confidence. While their counterparts in Britain and America have been borrowing up to the hilt to fuel a consumer boom, the cautious Germans have been far warier of doing so, trapping their country's economy in a vicious circle. Many had expected the general election of September 2005 to provide a way out by giving victory to a Christian Democrat-led government that would reform the economy and usher in a new, more optimistic mood. The result instead was a hung parliament. Although the Christian Democrats were the narrow winners and their leader, Angela Merkel, became chancellor, she was obliged to form a so-called Grand Coalition with the Social Democrats, in power for the previous seven years under Gerhard Schröder. This has inevitably meant compromises, but, by the end of the year, the first green shoots of recovery were discernible. Growth, less than 1 per cent in 2005, was predicted to reach 1.5 per cent in 2006, adding to the sense that a corner has been turned. This, in turn, is expected ultimately to feed through to the real estate market.

Property prices in Germany have been out of sync with those in the rest of Europe for some time, booming from 1991 to 1994, when they were static in most of its neighbours, and putting in a miserable performance thereafter. In 1999, when prices climbed 20.4 per cent in Ireland, 10.2 per cent in Spain and 7.5 per cent in France, they rose just 2.2 per cent in Germany. They went on to fall 2.1 per cent in 2001 and, after remaining flat during the following two years, dropped another 1 per cent in 2004. Indeed, by the beginning of 2006 they were barely above the levels of the beginning of the previous decade. Germany is a highly decentralised country, however, and there have been big regional differences, especially between the west of the country and the former Communist east. Thus, while Berlin has been hit especially hard in recent years by the bust that followed the post-unification boom, the situation in Munich or Hamburg, for example, has been much rosier.

The underlying structure of the housing market is also quite different from, say, Britain or France. While Germans have traditionally been among the most enthusiastic buyers of second homes in Spain, Italy and Croatia, they have the lowest level of property-ownership in the EU at home. Only 43 per cent of Germans are owner-occupiers – compared with more than 80 per cent of people in Spain, 69 per cent in Britain and 53 per cent in France. The picture is far from homogenous: home-ownership in rural areas is far higher than in cities, for example, where many apartment blocks are owned by pension funds or other such bodies and tenants will rent all their life, protected by rules on tenure and rent controls that effectively allow them to treat their rented flat as their own.

Berlin is the most extreme example of this. A mere 11 per cent of the inhabitants of the capital are owner-occupiers, with the remainder living in property owned either by financial institutions or by the local government. This low level of owner-occupation is due in part to the eastern part of the city's Communist past. Most apartments in the former East Germany were owned by the state and, after the Wall fell in 1989, they were either returned to their pre-Communist owners or transferred to private companies rather than sold off cheaply to their tenants as was the case in much of the rest of the former Soviet bloc. West Berliners were also traditionally reluctant to buy. Part of the reason was the city's precarious location on the front line against Communism – who would want to put their life savings in an apartment in a city that could be overrun overnight by Russian tanks? It was also a strangely transient place: many people born there would move away to West Germany when the time came to start a family and buy a home, while students and other young people drawn to the city by its thriving 'alternative' scene in the 1970s and '80s would squat rather than do anything as 'bourgeois' as try to buy a home. There was an overriding economic logic, too: a series of special subsidies kept rents low, removing any real incentive to buy. One of the main effects of this predilection for renting rather than buying has been to keep purchase prices in Berlin, in particular, extremely low and running yields high, by western European standards. This has not gone unnoticed by foreign financial institutions, which began to buy heavily into the German real estate market in the first years of the new millennium, attracted by the fact that rents are now well above their cost of borrowing. In one of the largest such deals, Terra Firma, a British private equity firm, in May 2005 reportedly bought a job lot of 150,000 flats, many of them in Berlin. Fortress, a US private equity firm, meanwhile, announced plans to invest $10 billion in German real estate over a three-year period.

Individual investors have been far slower to follow, not least because of the dearth of estate agents who market real estate specifically to British or Irish buyers. There are nevertheless good reasons to buy in Berlin, in particular. The German capital is an increasingly popular long weekend destination, making a flat in a central location a good short-term holiday let. Letting a property long-term should also provide a good yield and considerable stability.

Given the low prices in Berlin, it does not require that much capital to go one step further and buy an entire block. Daunting? Not necessarily. You could pick up a small block with a dozen flats for as little as £400,000; with German banks prepared to offer around 70 per cent loan-to-value, the amount of capital required is not great. The gross yield on most buildings should be at least 8 per cent and, given that it is possible to borrow at 3–4 per cent, the return on capital invested will be in double figures.

When buying a flat elsewhere, you might shy away from somewhere with a sitting tenant. In Berlin, it is the opposite: the best deals involve buildings in which all the flats are already let. Before buying, you should consult the building's records and get an idea of how much each tenant is paying, together with details of their rental history. Given that the majority of Berliners rent for most of their lives, the law provides them with considerable security of tenure and imposes restrictions on rent increases. This means, in many cases, tenants will be paying quite different rents for what are effectively identical flats. Those who have lived there for some time may still be benefiting from the lower rents of the past, while landlords will typically take advantage of a change of tenant to push up the rent. If a number are paying below market price, there could be potential for a substantial improvement in the yield if and when they move.

Indeed, some agents will flag up this potential – rather than actual – yield when trying to sell a building. Such figures should be treated with caution. Any tenants who have an especially good deal will probably be extremely reluctant to leave, which means that, 10 years on, the potential yield will be just that – potential. It is not all negative, however. Such long tenancies mean far fewer voids than in a country such as Britain where, in the private sector at least, renting is seen as more for the short term. Management costs for an entire block are not prohibitive either; taken together with provisions for mainten-ance, they should come to around 15 per cent of rent.

When buying an untenanted property it is possible to get a good idea of how much it will fetch on the rental market by looking at a table called the Mietspiegel, which lists rents street by street. This can be consulted at the local town hall or online. (Just type 'Mietspiegel' and the name of the relevant city into an Internet search engine and you should find it relatively easily; it is likely to be only in German, though.) Although not legally binding, it will be consulted by owner and tenant in much the same way as someone selling a second-hand car might look at a car price guide.

The high yields that can be earned make German real estate an attractive option for those interested primarily in a steady, secure income. Whether it will also provide capital gains depends on whether the market is finally poised to rebound after years of stagnation or will simply remain flat. In a report published in July 2005, Merrill Lynch claimed, 'The greatest upside potential for house price lies in what is today one of the most depressed housing markets in the world – Germany.' This did not mean, however, that prices would automatically go up sharply, the bank warned. This would depend on three inter-related factors: a rise in home-ownership from its current low levels; a growth in consumption, which has been depressed by the economic gloom of recent years; and a greater willingness on the part of German banks to provide a variety of different mortgages of the type that have long since been provided by their British or other EU counterparts. There are plausible reasons why all three could be satisfied sooner or later, but don't hold your breath. Indeed, it is worth noting that, while foreign institutions have been piling in, their German counterparts have been decidedly less bullish.

According to some estimates, prices were still falling in early 2006; even the most optimistic scenarios called for a rise during the year of a mere 2 per cent – not even enough to cover buying costs – although some agents were more bullish, suggesting that sentiment and consumer confidence were finally improving, with the 2006 World Cup providing a further boost. Stamp duty and other taxes will add 5–6 per cent to the purchase prices. Those buying in Berlin will have to pay as much as another 6.9 per cent commission to the agent; in most of the rest of the country, it is the seller who pays.

This is clearly not the kind of frothy speculative market for those in search of quick capital gains. In Germany, as elsewhere, however, certain cities or districts will undoubtedly be moving up, either because of changing local economics or simply fashion. Choose well, and in addition to a running yield unmatched anywhere else in Europe you should see a considerable increase in the value of your investment. With prices flat for so long, the risks on the downside are fairly minimal.

Berlin

With a population of 3.5 million people, Berlin is easily Germany's largest city; the 12 districts that make up Greater Berlin cover 340 square miles, an area about nine times the size of Paris. The city has plenty of green space, including at its heart the massive Tiergarten, which originally served as hunting grounds for the Prussian princes until it was made into a park in the 18th century. From the end of the Second World War (and the subsequent building of the Berlin

Wall in 1961) until the Wall came down in 1989, Berlin was not one city but two, which developed in different ways. East and West have since been knitted together so completely that anyone visiting for the first time would find it impossible to see where the Wall once ran. The two parts of the city nevertheless still retain separate characteristics; many West Berliners are still reluctant to live in the east and vice versa. (Think of it as an extreme version of the aversion of some north Londoners to venturing south of the river.)

Berlin is unusual among European capitals in another way, too: although it has been the seat of political power in Germany since 1999, when the government and parliament moved there from Bonn, it has not regained its pre-war status as the centre of financial or industrial power. Many people had certainly expected it to become so: no sooner had the Wall come down than the bulldozers and builders moved in, triggering a construction boom that lasted for more than a decade – helped along by massive public investment and subsidies. But the boom was quickly followed by bust. Although the politicians, journalists, lobbyists and other associated hangers-on have dutifully flocked to the city, many big companies have preferred to stay in the west.

Case Study: Buying a Block in Berlin

Chris Lockley, 39, a pilot for DHL, the courier company, first became interested in buying in Germany when his company opened its headquarters in Leipzig, deep in the former Communist east. While visiting the city, he went on a trip to Berlin and decided the capital would be a better bet after all. Rather than a single flat, he decided to buy a whole block and, with Berlin prices, he could afford it. In spring 2005 Chris opted for a 1950s block of 12 flats in Wedding, a working-class district in former West Berlin, a few minutes' walk away from a U-Bahn (Underground) station. The building was not especially attractive architecturally, but the price was just £242,000, which was extremely cheap, considering the building was fully tenanted and generated £25,776 a year in rent. Chris made an offer of £218,880, of which he put down £61,560. He financed the rest with a repayment mortgage from Berliner Volksbank, fixed for three years at 3.3 per cent.

Chris was especially encouraged that the bank valued the block at £287,964 – such overvaluations are common in the slow-moving Berlin market. As is customary in Germany, the tenants, who have lived in the block for anything up to 20 years, remained in place regardless of the change of ownership. Chris wisely entrusted management and rent collection to a local specialist company. After mortgage payments, management fees, taxes and provisions for repairs, Chris reckons to be left with around £8,892 a year – giving him a healthy 14.4 per cent on his initial investment. And that is without factoring in any capital gain. 'It's as if someone is giving you money,' he said. In fact, he was so impressed that, at the time of writing, he was planning to buy a second, bigger, block with 16 flats and five shops on the ground floor.

Thus Frankfurt remains the heart of the financial and banking sector, while Hamburg, Munich, Dusseldorf and the cities of the Ruhr are regional power-houses. By German standards, Berlin also remains a relatively poor city: income per head is far lower than in most of the former west, while unemployment, at 17 per cent, is substantially above the national average. Despite some movement from the city out to the suburbs, the population of Greater Berlin has stayed more or less constant, which also means there is not the same demographic pressure on the city as on, say, Warsaw or London.

Prices in the city are well below those of other western European capitals and have even been overtaken by cities such as Prague, Tallinn and Budapest – a bizarre situation given that average incomes in Germany are still many times those in these former Communist capitals. This means it is still possible to pick up a studio flat for as little as £15,000, giving a price per square metre of as little as £500 or so. Inevitably, though, given the size of Berlin, there are huge variations, and a flat in one of the more sought-after areas could easily cost four or more times that.

Like London or Paris, Berlin is a collection of little communities rather than a single entity. Those looking for a little edge will head for the former Communist east, which includes the city's historic centre. Some of the main streets have been marred by ugly Communist-era blocks (don't knock them; they can make good investments), but there are other, more unspoilt areas, too. One of the most attractive areas is Prenzlauer Berg, a leafy area of late 19th-century Wilhelmine buildings north of Alexanderplatz. Berlin's answer to Islington or Wandsworth, it is increasingly popular with young, well-heeled couples with children. Walk the streets in this teutonic Nappy Valley and you will have to fight your way through waves of yummy mummies on their bicycles, all with the obligatory toddler on the child seat at the back. By Berlin standards, though, prices are already high, at around £1,300 or so per square metre, and although rents are also above average, the yields will not be as generous as elsewhere. Alternative punts are Pankow, to the north, a favourite with East Germany's former rulers, and Friedrichshain, slightly to the south, which is coming up fast in the gentrification stakes.

Parts of former West Berlin, such as Charlottenburg, are more solidly bourgeois, although those looking for more excitement might be lured by Moabit, a working-class area north of the Kurfürstendamm, Berlin's answer to Oxford Street, or else by Kreuzberg, a district with a high Turkish population where squatters and other members of the 'alternative' scene lived before the Wall came down. Some of that old spirit still lives on in parts of Kreuzberg today; other parts of it have moved distinctly upmarket.

More general considerations apply, such as proximity to shops and public transport, especially the excellent U-Bahn (Underground) network. The very bottom of the market is to be avoided; with rents so low in absolute terms, many tenants will be ready to pay a few euros a month more for something better, meaning your flat could remain empty for some time. It is well worth taking time to get to know the city. If you are lucky, you may also come across a bargain. The subdued nature of the market means many people are likely to have had their property on sale for weeks or even months and so will be more likely to accept an offer.

Estate Agents

- **Berlin Capital Investments, www.berlincapitalinvestments.com,** t (020) 7871 0695. British-based company with limited range of properties aimed at investors.
- **Berlin Residential, www.berlin-residential.net, t + 49 178 537 4234.** Agency offering entire apartment blocks for investors.
- **Immobilienscout, www.immobilienscout24.de.** Probably the most comprehensive site with private property for sale (only in German).
- **Nordstadt, www.nordstadt.com, t + 49 30 4053 9240.** Agency with wide range of flats and houses and whole apartment blocks for sale.
- **Norenva, www.norenva.com.** Berlin-based agency specialising in entire apartment blocks.

Greece

With its sandy beaches, whitewashed villages, olive groves and more than 2,500 islands, Greece should be one of the leading destinations for British foreign home-buyers in search of a place in the sun. Despite substantial British expat enclaves in certain areas, though, it still lags way behind Spain and France and risks being overtaken by Croatia, Bulgaria and the other new kids on the international property block. The Greek real estate market has also been going its own way: although average house prices in the country rose strongly from 1995 to 2002 (achieving double-digit growth in most years), the market, as a whole, slowed sharply the following year and ground to a halt in 2004. Things have picked up a little since, but there has been none of the spectacular rises of the sort seen in Spain or France – or even on the nearby island of Cyprus. Such figures, of course, are for the country as a whole and include big cities such as Athens and Thessaloniki. The markets on many of the islands seem to have been more resilient. Property remains relatively cheap, at least by western European standards, and can be attractive as an investment. Mortgage rates, at around 4 per cent in early 2006, were slightly above those in other countries in the eurozone, of which Greece is also a member, but still lower than in Britain. Greek banks have experience of lending to foreigners and are typically prepared to offer up to 75 per cent loan-to-value.

The buying process is relatively straightforward, although it pays to have a good English-speaking lawyer check all the documentation carefully to ensure there are no problems with title. Purchasing costs are relatively high. The buyer must pay purchase tax of 9–13 per cent, as well as legal and notary fees, each of 1–2 per cent. This is mitigated slightly by the fact that these percentages are calculated not on the sale price but on something called the 'officially assessed price', which can be as much as a third lower. Even so, with charges like this, Greece is clearly not the place for a quick speculative hit.

Most foreign buying interest is concentrated on the islands rather than the mainland, although Athens could be a good bet for long-term rentals. Choosing the right island is extremely important if you are planning to let your property. As an owner, you may be prepared to spend time and money trekking by air, land and water to your beloved stone-built house on an island at the back end of the Dodecanese, but, for those looking to rent a property for a week or two's holiday, ease of access assumes much more importance. Remember also that a place that is easily accessible in summer could be a nightmare to reach out of season. This may mean sticking to the larger, better known islands such as Crete, Corfu, Rhodes, Zakynthos, Kos, Skiathos or – for the sake of fans of *Captain Corelli's Mandolin* – Kefalonia. Other islands should not be excluded, of course, but before even thinking about buying on one of them you should sit down and spend some quality time with your air and ferry timetables.

Don't overlook the mainland, either. It may not sound as romantic as the islands, but access can be much easier, especially out of season. The Methana peninsula in the Saronic Gulf, for example, although close to Athens, is relatively untouched by mass tourism and has much of the same tranquillity as the islands and even similar scenery. Those in search of old properties to restore should look to the Peloponnese peninsula. Poros, although an island, is separated from the mainland by a channel only 200 metres wide and is a popular holiday destination for Athenians.

Crete

The fifth largest island in the Mediterranean, with a population of more than 530,000, Crete could almost be a country in its own right. The cradle of Europe's first civilisation, it was, according to legend, the birthplace of Zeus, king of the gods. Modern-day Crete offers something for everyone, from deserted beaches, traditional villages and sleepy tavernas to modern beach resorts and buzzing nightlife. Its southerly location means that it also benefits from the longest and usually sunniest tourist season in Greece, stretching from late March to mid-November, which can substantially boost potential rental yields. International airports at Hania (Chania) and Iraklio (Heraklion) make for easy accessibility.

Foreign buying interest has long been concentrated along the island's north coast, from Kastélli Bay to the Sitia area in the east, which has most of the best beaches. The western part of the northern coast is less developed and more fertile and green. The areas around the old, heavily Venetian-influenced towns of Hania and Rethymnon (Rethimno) are especially attractive. The eastern half of Crete is busier and more developed for tourism, but even here there are still many quiet villages. The rockier southern coast has been neglected largely because of its relative remoteness, but has considerable scope for future growth. The expansion of Sitia airport to take international flights will particularly help the eastern part of the south coast.

Despite Crete's countless charms, it is still possible to find small village properties in need of restoration for as little as £20,000, although a large, comfortable villa could easily cost £300,000 or more. You can still find properties with pools for £70,000, while apartments in new, upmarket developments start at around £80,000 for one-bedders. Crete is a well-established name with tourists and the rental potential should be good.

Estate Agents

- **Crete Homes, www.crete-homes.com, t** + 30 28410 28 804. Property and construction consultants with a good choice of stone-built houses and modern villas.

- **Crete Property, www.creteproperty.co.uk, t** (020) 7328 8209. Wide range of modernised and unmodernised properties on the island for sale.

- **Greek Island Property, www.greek-island-property.com, t** (0115) 932 2751. British- and Crete-based agency with a selection of property on the island.

- **Property on Crete, www.propertyoncrete.com, t** + 30 28430 28 005. Sitia-based agency specialising in property in eastern Crete.

- **WeAreHomesonCrete.com, www.wearehomesoncrete.com, t** + 30 69953 84 682. Sitia-based agency with a range of property.

Other Islands

Corfu and the Ionian Islands

Situated off Greece's western coast, only a few miles from the Albanian border, Corfu and the other five Ionian islands have a unique history that can still be felt today. Ruled for four centuries by the Venetians until 1797, they retain more of an Italianate than a Balkan character. Britain, which maintained a protectorate over them for half of the 19th century, has also left its mark: Corfu has always been a popular destination for British property-buyers, more than 6,000 of whom are thought to have homes there, making for a substantial expat scene which may (or may not) appeal to you and your potential tenants.

Corfu is generally considered to be one of the most beautiful Greek islands, although for some people the sheer number of olives, planted largely on the initiative of the Venetians when they ran the place, can make the colouring of its landscape monotonous. The island has acquired something of a reputation for mass market tourism, but there is nevertheless a wide variety of property on sale from old village houses and renovated historic buildings to modern apartments and villas in coastal resorts. The northeast coast between Nissaki and Ayios Stefanos Sinion is the most expensive part of the island; prices are substantially cheaper in and around mass market resorts like Benitses, Mesongi and Aharavi. A stylish alternative could be an apartment in a Venetian-era building in Kerkyra Town, the exquisite capital. Smallish new-build two-bed houses start at around £100,000, while double that should buy a substantial villa with good sea views.

What a difference a book makes. Louis de Bernières' best-selling novel *Captain Corelli's Mandolin*, and the subsequent film, transformed the fortunes of **Kefalonia**, a once obscure Ionian island, which has a permanent population of just 32,000. As many as 2,000 Britons now own homes there, while its celebrity visitors have included Madonna, Tom Cruise and Steven Spielberg. Prices have been rising by an average 10 per cent a year but are still not excessive. A new waterfront villa with enough land to dig a pool costs around £220,000, but it should be possible to buy an old unrenovated stone house for far less. Although there is some new building, the authorities are determined not to let it spiral out of control. On the downside, Kefalonia has a history of earthquakes – including a particularly devastating one in 1953, which wrecked the elegant capital of Argostoli and the island's southern villages. Although there are direct flights in summer, a stopover in Athens is required from November to May.

Rhodes and the Dodecanese Islands

Considered the sunniest place in Greece, **Rhodes**, one of the most southeasterly of the Greek islands near the Turkish coast, also has one of the most colourful histories. The Old Town is the oldest inhabited medieval town in Europe, a legacy of the Knights of St John. The Colossus of Rhodes, one of the seven wonders of the ancient world, was reputed to have stood astride the harbour entrance. Modern-day Rhodes is a popular and cosmopolitan tourist island, with many sandy beaches, particularly on its east coast. Kolymbia is an especially popular resort. Tsambika, Kalathos and Lindos, to the south, are also sought after. Property in Lindos itself tends to be expensive and is often handed down through families. Other places worth looking at include Pefkos, a popular resort in its own right, Aklipio, which is set back from the coast and boasts stunning views, and Genadi, an unspoilt village with tavernas on the beach.

Much of the property for sale in Rhodes is new-build, which, although generally of good quality, necessarily lacks charm. On the plus side, a number of houses are situated only a few metres from the beach. A typical new-build three-bedroom villa in Kolymbia with a swimming pool and sea view could cost around £160,000; for the same money you could have a luxury 120-metre apartment in Rhodes town. Many of the new builds come with rental guarantees, which can enhance their appeal for investors. As always with such guarantees, however, it pays to read the small print.

Despite the name, there are 163, rather than 12, islands in the Dodecanese, of which 26 are inhabited. **Kos** is the second most popular island for tourists after Rhodes. The other 10 most important ones are **Astipalea, Kalimnos, Karpathos, Kassos, Kastellorizo, Leros, Nisyros, Patmos, Simi** and **Tilos**. Many have a rich history, and even some of the smallest inhabited islands boast dozens of Byzantine churches and medieval castles.

Estate Agents

- **AGDev Kefalonian Developments, www.inkefalonia.com, t** + 30 26710 29312. Kefalonia-based developer offering a variety of properties on the island, together with useful information.

- **A Property in Greece, www.apropertyingreece.com, t** (020) 8467 5246. Properties for sale in Corfu, Rhodes and elsewhere.

- **Corfu Estate Agents, www.corfuestateagents.com, t** + 30 26630 64494. Agency specialising in selling and restoring old properties on Corfu.

- **Corfu Property, www.corfuproperty.com, t** + 30 26610 28126. Company that sells property and also offers design and construction services.

- **CPA Corfu Property Agency, www.cpacorfu.com, t** + 30 26610 28141. A wide range of old and new properties for sale on Corfu.

- **Hibiscus Real Estate Services, www.greekislandsproperty.com, t** + 30 22520 41885. Agency selling property on the island of Lesvos.

- **ProGC, www.progc.co.uk, t** 07726 736 747. British-based agency with property for sale across Greece.

- **Sawaides and Associates, www.rre.gr, t** + 30 22410 70017. Rhodes-based agency with large numbers of properties on the island.

- **Skopelos Property, www.skopelosproperty.com, t** + 30 24240 24617. Skopelos-based agency with land and property for sale on the island.

- **Vinieris, www.kefalonianproperty.com, t** + 30 26710 24202. Kefalonia-based agency with property for sale and rent on the island.

Italy

Despite its popularity as a holiday destination, Italy has long lagged behind Spain, France and even Florida as a target for second- and investment-home buyers. Although Britons have been purchasing property in 'Chiantishire' and other parts of Tuscany for decades, they have only relatively recently begun to look at other areas, such as Umbria, Liguria, Le Marche (The Marches) and Puglia. In contrast to Spain, off-plan developments have hitherto been only a small part of the market. Traditionally, most of the buying interest has been in old rural properties, often in need of loving – and expensive – renovation.

Things are changing, however. Sales of Italian properties to foreigners grew substantially in 2005, and although Germans and Americans have been the most active buyers – accounting for more than 40 per cent of the total – Britons followed with a 15 per cent share. The property market itself has been moving upwards, although more cautiously than its French and Spanish counterparts. After falling by more than a fifth during a long period of recession in the 1990s, prices began to pick up in 1998 and 1999 and have subsequently managed several years of annual double-digit growth. In early 2006 the market looked likely to continue its upward trend, albeit at a more modest rate. Future growth may be constrained by the anaemic performance of the Italian economy, which has been rivalling Germany for the title of the most sluggish in Europe; since 2002, annual growth has not once reached 1 per cent. With the average property already around four and a half times average earnings, prices are not especially cheap, either, while the demographics are distinctly unfavourable: both population growth and household formation rates during the rest of the decade are expected to be among the lowest on the continent.

An important factor worth watching is the size of the mortgage market: at just 15 per cent of GDP in 2004, the value of home loans in Italy was only a fraction of those in Spain (49 per cent), Germany (53 per cent) and Britain (76 per cent). The reasons lie both in the past lack of sophistication of Italy's financial markets and a traditional reluctance to run up debts: young people typically stay at home far longer than elsewhere in Europe and then buy a property outright, usually with their parents' help. With banks now far readier to lend, this is expected to change as people are encouraged to borrow more and trade up. Whether they will do so in large enough numbers to push up prices remains to be seen, not least because youth unemployment remains high.

The interest of foreign investors is likely to be concentrated on villas in the countryside or by the sea, or on apartments in historic cities such as Venice or Rome, which can be let short-term to visitors and retained for personal use during void periods. The prices of such properties, especially the high-end ones, can move differently from the market as a whole, reflecting the economic conditions back home in New York, Frankfurt or London as much as those elsewhere in Italy. Indeed, the slow-down in the UK housing market in recent years is believed to have had an adverse effect on those areas of 'Chiantishire' traditionally dominated by British buyers. Some agents have noticed a hesitation among those looking for properties in the £200,000–300,000 range, which have often been funded by remortgaging their own homes.

The rental yields achievable with such properties will also reflect the state of the tourist industry rather than the broader Italian economy. As elsewhere, the return you make will depend on the choice and location of the property. If you want to maximise rentals, then a decent swimming pool is essential, especially with a rural villa. So, too, is a reasonable piece of land; most people choosing to spend two weeks in rural Tuscany or Umbria do so because they want peace and quiet and privacy. If possible, though, they would also like a picturesque little village with shops selling wonderful local produce within easy walking distance. Proximity to airports is another important consideration: Italy is a long way to drive from Britain. Luckily, the country is well served by airports. In early 2006, Ryanair alone was flying to 14 destinations in mainland Italy (plus Palermo in Sicily and Alghero in Sardinia).

If you are buying in a city, then it is, of course, possible to let long-term, most probably to Italian tenants. But although the yields may be reasonable, it may be more trouble than it is worth: the whole system is weighted in favour of the tenant rather than the landlord, and rent controls persist.

Italy, it should be remembered, is a highly bureaucratic country. It is also a highly taxed one, despite concerted moves by Silvio Berlusconi, who was standing for re-election in April 2006, to reduce the fiscal burden after becoming prime minister in 2001. When buying, count on adding around 10 per cent to the purchase price to cover the local equivalent of stamp duty. (Many Italians reduce this simply by declaring an artificially low purchase price – but this has its drawbacks. Not only it is illegal, but if you are buying with a mortgage it will reduce the amount you can borrow.) Once you own and let the property you will become liable to a bewildering number of other taxes known by acronyms such as ICI and IRPEF. In another unpleasant surprise for the foreign buyer, properties deemed *seconde case* (second homes) have far larger taxes (and even utility bills and other charges) levied on them than primary residences. On the plus side, there is no wealth tax and no inheritance tax either, although your estate may have some liability in your home country. There is no substitute for a good local *commercialista* (accountant) able to guide you through all the paperwork. You may need to supplement this with a visit to an accountant back home as well.

Mortgages for foreign buyers are readily available. Banks are generally prepared to offer up to 80 per cent loan-to-value, with rates as low as 3 per cent. As an alternative to mortgages, some Italian banks have started offering leasing arrangements. Under this formula, the property is bought and owned by the bank and then leased back to the client for a set number of years, after which he (or she) is free to buy it at the original price. The payments will be broadly similar to a mortgage, although leasing can offer tax advantages. Discuss what is best with your *commercialista*.

Venice

The lagoon city is the ultimate dream place in which to live – no cars, beautiful architecture and palaces and churches at every turn. But space is at a premium, the historic centre is tiny, and bargains are few and far between. The city is divided into six *sestieri* or areas. The most expensive properties are around St Mark's Square and on the other side of the Grand Canal, in the Dorsoduro district. The ultimate Venice pad, an apartment on the *piano nobile* (first floor) of a *palazzo* looking out on the Grand Canal, could cost £4–6 million – and very few of them ever come onto the market. If you set your sights lower – and are prepared to forsake that canal view – prices are still reasonable, though; even in Dorsoduro, you can find property at around £4,500 per square metre – which means £150,000 for a reasonable-sized studio, with separate kitchenette, or £200,000–250,000 for a one-bedder. Property is slightly cheaper in Santa Croce, a lesser-known *sestiere* on the opposite side of the Grand Canal to the main railway station, or in Arsenale, site of the former shipyards, which lies in the eastern *sestiere* of Castello. But the price differential has narrowed over the years; Venice, after all, is a small place, and wherever you are in the city it is possible to walk to St Mark's within 30 minutes.

An interesting and cheaper alternative is the island of Giudecca a short boat ride from San Marco, the site of the Hotel Cipriani and also of Sir Elton John's waterfront home. The island offers spectacular views back towards San Marco but also allows you to get away from the crowds. Prices are considerably lower than in central Venice. There have been a number of stylish new developments, which are ready to move into. A 70-square metre, two-bedroom flat in a good building on Giudecca, for example, could cost £250,000. You could find a similar-sized property for under £200,000 on the island of Murano, famous for its artisanal glass-blowing industry. Although further from St Mark's and the centre, it has the advantage of being convenient for the airport.

The holiday rental market is good: people are increasingly attracted to the freedom that comes from renting an apartment rather than staying in a hotel. Venice also has a reputation as an expensive place, which means higher rates per night than in other Italian cities. Generally, the closer you are to St Mark's and the centre the better, although having some kind of terrace or garden can be important, too. Like property buyers, visitors are becoming more sophisticated, and although most first-timers want to be near the familiar landmarks, many of those returning prefer a base away from the crowds, especially during high season. It goes without saying that the more beautiful and unique your property is, the easier it will be to let.

Yields are helped by the fact that Venice is an all-year destination, with the only real low points from November to Christmas and from January until *Carnevale* (which normally falls in mid-February). Realistically, if you buy the right property, you should be able to let it 30 weeks a year. Remember, if you are buying into a *palazzo* in central Venice, you should factor in heavy maintenance costs, which are shared between residents. An alternative is to let to students long-term. Although this is not a suitable formula for those who want access to their property, there are two universities in the city and demand is high. The yields may also be better than with holiday lets.

Rome

As with Venice, anyone buying in Rome is likely to do so not purely for cold commercial reasons, but also out of sheer love for the place. The Vatican and St Peter's; the Colosseum and the Pantheon; the Spanish Steps and the Trevi Fountain – it is difficult to know where to start when describing the attractions of the Eternal City.

Until relatively recently, Rome was considered as undervalued compared with, say, London and Paris. The city was given a big boost, however, by preparations for the Jubilee year of 2000, declared a holy year of celebration by the Catholic Church, with buildings restored and grimy façades cleared.

As a result, the top end of the market is now extremely expensive: an apartment on or near one of the historic squares such as Piazza Navona, Piazza di Spagna or Piazza Farnese, with a large terrace and panoramic view, could easily cost £8,000–9,000 per square metre. Let to a diplomat or wealthy expat, such properties could generate a correspondingly high yield, but the amount of money that needs to be put down could deter all but the wealthiest investor. In any case, actually finding such a property will not be easy. Many of the best apartments are in the hands of the same Roman families who have owned them for decades or even centuries. And when they are sold, it is often in discreet private transactions through a *notaio* (notary) or other intermediary rather than in a public sale by an estate agent.

That being said, it is possible to buy more modest properties elsewhere in the *centro storico* (historic centre) for £2,000 to £4,000 per square metre. Trastevere, the Old Town just across the River Tiber and home to a very popular weekend market, with its lively *trattorie* and bars, is being rapidly gentrified. In the part closest to l'Isola Tiberina, historic 15th-century buildings are being restored, creating stunning apartments with very high beamed ceilings, thick walls and enormous charm. These apartments, within easy reach of the historic sites, are ideal for short-term lets to tourists. Move further out, and prices drop back substantially – but so probably, too, do your chances of making money by letting to tourists.

Tuscany, Umbria, Le Marche and Abruzzo

With its rolling countryside, medieval hill towns and unrivalled artistic heritage, **Tuscany** has long been one of the favourite parts of Italy for British home-buyers, especially the corner between **Florence** and **Siena** nicknamed Chiantishire. Prices there are correspondingly high; large, beautifully restored farmhouses with plenty of land can easily go for more than £700,000, although it is possible to find attractive properties for half that – but they will probably require work.

As prices have risen in Tuscany, attention has shifted over the years eastwards to landlocked **Umbria**, the so-called green heart of Italy, whose landscapes are just as beautiful as those of its more illustrious neighbour. Umbria also has its fair share of unspoilt towns with medieval centres, while local planning regulations are less strict, providing greater flexibility for those who want to restore a rustic property. **Assisi**, known for its Giotto paintings and monasteries, and **Perugia**, site of the famous university, are the main centres, but smaller towns like **San Sepolcro** can be more relaxed and just as attractive.

As an alternative, it may be better to keep heading eastwards towards **Le Marche**, on the Adriatic coast, which has 112 miles of coastline, wide sandy beaches and two lovely Renaissance art towns in **Urbino** and **Ascoli Piceno**. Its airports in **Ancona** and **Pescara** are served by direct flights from Britain. Prices, meanwhile, are around 40 per cent cheaper than Tuscany or Umbria, which means it should still be possible to find a three-bedroom town house in one of its many pretty medieval hilltop villages for as little as £50,000.

Keep going south down the Adriatic coast and you come to **Abruzzo**, a sparsely populated region that has hitherto been the stronghold of olive-farmers, shepherds and fishermen. Although the capital is not far away, it is only recently that more adventurous Romans have been heading to its mountain villages, many of which have long since been abandoned, in search of old stone houses that can be restored and turned into peaceful retreats. The winters can see heavy snowfalls, making the area popular with skiers.

Liguria

Situated in the northwest corner of the country, stretching up the Mediterranean coast from Tuscany to the French Riviera, Liguria remains a strangely undiscovered part of Italy. It is also a place of great contrasts. The hills of the Apennines and the Maritime Alps are full of isolated mountain hamlets with properties ripe for restoration. Like many parts of the country, these areas have suffered depopulation over the years, which means it should be possible to find abandoned houses ideal for transformation. Such wrecks can start from as little as £50,000 and, once renovated, have good rental potential.

Prices are considerably higher in the **Cinque Terre**, the string of five picturesque villages along the coast of La Spezia, which have become a major tourist destination. The resort town of **Lerici** in the Gulf of Poets (in whose waters Lord Byron met his end) is also pricey. Property is even more expensive – if you can find it at all – in **Portofino**, a highly exclusive Italian St-Tropez.

You may be pleasantly surprised, though, by prices further up the Ligurian Riviera, close to the French border. The Italian Riviera is known for its mild winter climate, while the faded grand hotels and neoclassical villas in resorts such as **San Remo**, **Albenga** and **Noli** are a reminder of the coast's traditional role as a place for wealthy northern Italians to spend the winter. The whole coast is currently undergoing something of a renaissance as the big developers move in with new-build projects and large-scale restorations, but prices are still considerably lower than in Monaco or Nice. A studio in San Remo, best known in

Italy as the home of the local equivalent of the Eurovision Song Contest, could cost as little as £30,000. At the other end of the scale, a large villa with spectacular sea views would leave little change from £800,000. Although the Italian coast has more varied landscapes than on the French side of the border, the beaches are small and can be overcrowded in summer. There is only a narrow gap between the sea and the mountains, and space is at a premium.

Puglia and the South

In the heel of Italy, **Puglia** is best known for its *trulli*, the little whitewashed cone-roofed houses found largely around **Alberobello** in the north of the region. Coming with a varying numbers of cones (and sometimes with a more conventional building, known as a *lamia*, attached), these make wonderful holiday homes and should be easily lettable. The region has been 'discovered' by British and other foreign property-buyers in the last few years and prices have been rising steeply. An unrestored *trullo* with one or two cones should start at around £40,000–50,000 – although making it habitable could turn out to be more expensive than you think. If you want a substantial one ready to move into (or let), with a decent amount of land and pool, you should count on spending at least £200,000. More conventional properties are also available, either in towns such as **Bari**, **Lecce**, **Taranto**, **Foggia** and **Brindisi**, or in the countryside.

Why confine your search to Puglia? The *mezzogiorno* (south) contains a rich mixture of beautiful coast, dramatic mountain scenery and vibrant cities, including, of course, **Naples**. The rental market is also developing well, thanks to the arrival of the low-cost airlines, which now fly direct from Britain to Pescara, Bari and Brindisi and also to the Sicilian capital, **Palermo**. Prices generally are substantially below those in Tuscany, although they vary widely depending on the quality and location of the property. Parts of the south and Sicily are blighted by poor infrastructure and high crime (this, after all, is the birthplace of the Mafia and the other various organised crime groups), so you should make enquiries before plumping for a particular area. Illegal building is also widespread, which means the title deeds should be checked, too, to make sure everything is in order.

The Alps and Dolomites

Italy has some of the sunniest slopes in the Alps, its food and wine are among the finest in Europe, and in February 2006 it hosted the Winter Olympics. So why do so few Britons buy ski property in Italy? It is a question to which there is no simple answer. It is certainly not through want of variety.

Situated in the middle of Italy, in the Brenta Dolomites, **Madonna di Campiglio** is an upmarket resort with an affluent, almost exclusively Italian, clientele and property prices to match. Flats and chalets go for around £4,000 per square metre, while some central newly built apartments can be double that. Prices fall back sharply in nearby **Folgarida** and **Vezza d'Oglio**.

Those looking for bargain basement prices and lively nightlife should head instead to nearby **Passo del Tonale**, a windswept purpose-built resort whose utilitarian architecture would not be out of place in a Russian provincial town. Desolate in summer, it is just about tolerable once it has a good dusting of snow, but the skiing, at 2,700 metres – or more than 3,000 on the glacier – is excellent. A series of newly built modern, well-equipped hotels with pools, bars and clubs is also attracting a young crowd. It should be possible to pick up a two-bedroom, 50-square-metre apartment for just £50,000, but don't expect to bump into any celebrities when you go for your *après-ski aperitivo*.

By contrast, you will find it difficult to avoid them in **Cortina d'Ampezzo**, a 150-mile drive through winding roads to the east. To Britons, at least of a certain age, the name will be forever linked with a utilitarian 1960s Ford, but for Italians Cortina has long been a byword for drop-dead chic. This is a place where the style with which you negotiate the designer boutiques on your evening *passeggiata* is just as important as your technique on the slopes. Don't even think of coming here without packing your fur coat and largest diamonds. If Cortina's atmosphere is very Gstaad or St-Moritz, then so are the property prices; you could be forgiven for thinking the estate agent has added an extra zero by mistake. A small two-bedroom flat in a good location could set you back more than £600,000.

While Cortina is a favourite with rich Romans, their Milanese counterparts prefer the **Val d'Aosta** in the western Alps, in the shadow of Mont Blanc where Italy, France and Switzerland meet. Val d'Aosta was once part of the French-speaking principality of Savoy, and the French influence is strong here, especially on the food. **Courmayeur**, a picturesque village just on the other side of the tunnel from Chamonix, is the classiest of the resorts; on winter weekends, Milanese society decamps here *en masse*, staying in apartments or houses they have rented for the season or which have been in the family for years. Prices in Courmayeur, although not quite at Cortina levels, are not bargain basement either. Expect to pay around £6,000 per square metre for anything in a good location, pushing the cost of a modest one-bedder over £300,000.

The **Piedmont** region of the Alps around Turin, which hosted the Olympics, offers some of best skiing in the country – helped by the more than £130 million pumped in by the government in the run up to the games. **Sestriere**, founded in the 1930s by Giovanni Agnelli, the Fiat boss, is one of the earliest and highest purpose-built ski stations in Alps. Although no one would call it picturesque, property there, at around £2,700 per square metre, is not expensive. The resort is also the gateway to the Via Lattea (Milky Way) circuit, which offers 250 miles of slopes – the second largest ski region in Europe after France's Trois Vallées. Other villages along it include the unpronounceable **Sauze d'Oulx** – whose centre is lined with bars offering wide-screen Sky Sports and cheap Guinness – and **Claviere**, Italy's oldest ski resort.

Estate Agents

- **Buy a House-Italy, www.buyahouse-italy.com, t** + 39 3280 930 519. Agency selling *trulli* and other more conventional houses in Puglia and elsewhere in the south.

- **Casa Travella, www.casatravella.com, t** (01322) 660 988. British-based company with property for sale across Italy.

- **Gabetti, www.gabettivenezia.it, t** + 39 041 522 2086. Venice-based agency offering properties for sale in the city.

- **Houses in Tuscany, www.housesintuscany.net, t** + 39 347 368 1090. Houses for sale and rent in Tuscany.

- **Italy Real Estates, www.italyrealestates.net, t** + 39 339 653 1677. Agency specialising in property largely in the Todi area of Umbria.

- **Key Italy, www.keyitaly.com.** Wide-ranging site with a large selection of properties and lots of useful information about various cities and regions.

- **Live in Italy, www.live-in-Italy.com, t** + 39 0763 629 073. Search service for those looking for property in Italy.

- **Properties around Italy, www.propertiesaroundItaly.com, t** 07710 464 695. Property for sale, especially in Abruzzo.

- **Sardinia Homes, www.sardiniahomes.com, t** (01394) 278 919. A wide selection of property for sale in southern Sardinia.

- **Toscana Houses, www.toscanahouses.com, t** + 39 0578 757 756. A wide range of properties for sale from a number of different agents in Tuscany and Umbria.

- **Venice Estates, www.venice-estates.com, t** (020) 8878 1130. A small choice of expensive, top-of-the-range properties in Venice for sale.

- **Wonderful Italia, www.wonderfulitalia.com, t** (01923) 893 764. Houses for sale in Tuscany, Sardinia and Puglia.

Portugal

If you really want to upset a Portuguese, mistake him or her for a Spaniard. Although they share the Iberian peninsula, the two neighbouring peoples have distinct languages, cultures and lifestyles. The same goes for their economies and their property markets, which have long been out of sync with each other, despite the fact that both countries joined the European Union and adopted the euro at the same time. Prices in Portugal grew strongly in the late 1990s into 2000, but then suffered a downturn in the following two years. Things have picked up since, with average prices rising by around 7 per cent in both 2004 and 2005. But the Portuguese economy is in a bit of a mess, and sentiment, especially among the locals, remains muted. Prices look set to continue moving ahead, albeit relatively slowly, but this is not a country for quick speculative gains, especially since buying costs are high and can add as much as 10–15 per cent to the purchase price.

The buying procedure in Portugal is straightforward. You are expected to pay the asking price and there is not much haggling, but before starting the whole process it is important to make sure the agents have checked ownership and title. You make an offer, wait for searches, and then put down a deposit and sign the *contrato de promessa de compra e vende*, which is binding on both parties. After around eight to 12 weeks, everything is wrapped up with the *escritura*, signed at the notary's office. The vendor pays marketing costs, while the buyer pays a property transfer tax on the 'declared value' of the property, which is usually a lot less than the actual price. In 2006 rental income is taxed in bands starting at 12 per cent for the first €4,266 (£2,928), while non-residents pay a flat 25 per cent on capital gains when they sell. There is no wealth tax. Mortgages are readily available, at around 3 per cent, with maximum loan-to-value of 70 per cent for non-residents (residents can get up to 90 per cent).

The Algarve

Mention Portugal and most Britons will immediately think of the Algarve, the region stretching almost 100 miles along the country's southern coast that has long been a popular holiday destination. Just over 400,000 people live there permanently, but in the summer the population swells to more than one million as tourists flood in, attracted by the superb beach resorts, traditional fishing villages, olive groves and vineyards, and, most of all, the multitude of golf courses. There are at least 30 of them, including San Lorenzo and The Old Course at Vilamoura, frequently quoted among the 100 best golf courses in the world; every year an average of one million rounds are played on the Algarve.

The most sought-after area has traditionally been the so-called 'golden triangle' of central Algarve between **Faro**, the administrative centre of the region, **Albufeira**, a former fishing village turned major resort along the coast to the west, and **Loule**, a charming inland town with a maze of narrow white streets and the remnants of a medieval castle. Popular with television presenters and sports celebrities, this is by no means pioneer country, but instead a mature, developed market, with facilities and prices to match.

A typical budget of £250,000 will no longer buy very much in the two most prestigious coastal destinations: **Vale do Lobo**, a luxury golf and beach resort three times the size of Monaco, and **Quinta do Lago**, a massive residential and recreational estate situated within 645 hectares of pine forest. In this part of the Algarve, villas costing £1 million and more are commonplace, especially near golf courses or on the heights overlooking the Formosa river, a protected area rich in bird life separated from the sea by a ridge of dunes. There are neverthe-less plenty of cheaper properties around: it should be possible to pick up a two-bedroom apartment in **Vilamoura**, a massive tourist complex covering 2,000 hectares some 15 miles west of Faro, for around £160,000.

The market has been volatile and, because of its dependence on British buyers, has often tended to move more in line with the UK economy than the Portuguese one. Thus the Algarve boomed in the late 1980s along with the British market and then collapsed with it too, so that prices in 1994 were only half what they had been in real terms in 1988. Although things took off again from 1999 to 2001, prices took another hit in 2003, when new laws were brought in penalising those who had bought property through companies in offshore tax havens, which had been a popular way for foreigners to avoid capital gains and inheritance tax.

More recently, the arrival of low-cost airlines in Faro has helped to boost prices and improve rental prospects – even though it all looks very flat compared with Spain. Rental yields are typically around 3.5–4.5 per cent, based on a 30-week rental season, although some developers offer guaranteed rental yields of 4–5 per cent. Flats and villas must be regularly inspected and have local tourism licences if they are let for 12 or more weeks a year; holiday-home owners and rental agencies who fail to comply can face hefty fines.

Those in search of substantial capital gains should probably look away from the 'golden triangle', perhaps northwards to the interior, with its flower-decked, whitewashed villages, many of which have still managed to maintain their traditional character, and countryside rich in eucalyptus, pine, lavender and rock-rose. Flats start at £60,000–70,000, with two-bedroom apartments on good-quality developments for £120,000 and detached villas with pools for around £250,000. An alternative is to stay on the coast but move east to **Tavira**, which lies on an estuary of the Ségua river, and the surrounding area where apartments in some new developments go for as little as £1,000 per square metre. The west of the Algarve, beyond Lagos towards **Martinhal** and **Sagres**, near the far southwestern tip of the country, has traditionally been less developed, but prices there are rising quickly, with buyers attracted by the lower-density housing and fishing villages. The market has been helped by construction of a coastal motorway, which has sharply cut times to Faro.

The Atlantic Coast

Moving round onto the Atlantic coast, there may still be bargains to be had in the Aljezur area, northwest of Sagres, a rugged and unspoilt region with many pretty bays and coves and fantastic – and often unsignposted – beaches famous for fishing and bird-watching. **Aljezur** itself, although little visited, is a quaint old town founded by the Arabs in the 10th century. A three-bedroom villa with a pool should still cost under £180,000. Golf courses, hitherto a little thinner on the ground, are also on their way: plans have been announced for a £286 million golf resort, **Amendoeira**, near **Silves** in the west, which will have courses designed by Nick Faldo and Christy O'Connor Jr.

The **Costa de Prata**, which lies further north between Lisbon and Oporto, has potential. It has long, sandy beaches and beautiful towns and villages inland. It is also somewhat exposed and windswept, although this does make it attractive to windsurfers. Property prices there are lower and golf facilities developing rapidly, making it a popular alternative to the Algarve. Daily Ryanair flights to Porto from Stansted and Liverpool have helped. The **Costa Verde**, to the north, is attracting more interest, too.

Those who want to turn their back on the Algarve's sea-and-sand culture should move inland to the **Beira Litoral**, an area of mountains, forests and subsistence agriculture, which has been described as 'Tuscany mixed with the Lake District and Wales'. **Coimbra**, Portugal's third largest city with an ancient university at its heart, is the gateway to the region. Other places of interest include **Arganil**, a market town, and **Oliveira do Hospital**, surrounded by vineyards, which is all cobbled streets and mountain views. Ruins start at around £25,000; habitable houses can go for double that, while a larger place with holiday cottage or annexe would cost upwards of £250,000.

Estate Agents

- **Algarve Estates, www.algarve-estates.co.uk**. Property for sale in the Algarve and in the Alentejo region.

- **Algarve Gold, www.algarve-gold.com, t + 351 282 770 640**. Algarve properties for sale, together with lots of useful information.

- **Casas do Barlavento, www.casasdobarlavento.com, t + 351 282 780 877**. Properties for sale and rent in the western Algarve.

- **Portugal Invest, www.portugalosinvest.com**. New-build properties in and around the Algarve.

- **Quadrant Overseas Property Services, www.quadrant-property.com, t (01276) 507 513**. A variety of properties for sale on the Algarve and elsewhere in Portugal.

- **Quinta Properties, www.quintaproperty.com, t + 351 289 396 073**. Property for sale in Quinta do Lago and other parts of the central Algarve.

- **Real Estate Algarve, www.realestate-algarve.com, t + 351 282 768 821**. Lagos-based agency offering property on the Algarve and beyond.

- **Superior Worldwide, www.portugal.superiorworldwide.com, t 0870 750 4477**. A selection of new-build properties in resort areas.

- **Venda Villa, www.vendavilla.com, t + 351 289 314 486**. Apartments and villas for sale in the central Algarve, from Albufeira to Faro.

- **Winkworth Portugal, www.winkworth-portugal.com, t + 351 282 769 341**. A variety of second-hand and new-build properties in the Algarve and beyond.

Spain

Since the beginnings of package tourism back in the 1960s, Spain has established itself as *the* destination for British holidaymakers in search of sun, sea and sand. Although the Costa del Sol and Costa Blanca still remain popular, the more adventurous visitors these days also explore the country's interior and historic cities such as Seville and Granada. Barcelona, surely one of the hippest places in Europe, has become one of the most popular city break destinations on the continent.

Over the last decade, Spain has also become a firm favourite for property-buyers from Britain and elsewhere in northern Europe. Of the 3.7 million holiday homes in Spain, 1.7 million are believed to belong to foreigners – at least 600,000 of them British. Despite recent challenges from Bulgaria and other emerging low-cost destinations, Spain consistently tops polls of places where people would like to buy. A survey carried out by Barclays Bank in late 2005 found that 30 per cent of Britons planning to invest in foreign real estate would opt for Spain; only half as many plumped for America, with France and Italy still further behind.

Spain is no longer the bargain basement destination it once was, however. Indeed, since the late 1990s the country has experienced a property boom of such length and intensity that even the British and Irish markets have looked flat in comparison. After barely keeping up with inflation in the middle of the decade, prices began to accelerate towards the start of the new millennium: according to figures from the Ministerio de Vivienda (the housing ministry) they rose by 12.4 per cent in 1999, followed by around 15 per cent in 2000 and again in 2001, and more than 17 per cent in each of the subsequent three years.

As elsewhere in Europe, one of the main catalysts has been the fall in interest rates, which are at historic lows for Spain. Because of the country's relatively high inflation rate relative to Germany and other eurozone members, rates have actually been negative – making borrowing to buy property even more attractive. A further boost has come from Spain's growing affluence since it joined the European Union along with Portugal in 1986.

Spain has become more European in other ways, too, which has affected its property market: a growth in divorces and in children leaving home earlier has meant greater demand for homes; the number of people per residential dwelling in Spain dropped by 20 per cent in the decade after 1990. Easier credit and longer repayment periods have led to an explosion in the mortgage market; the value of outstanding home loans, equivalent to 15.8 per cent of GDP in 1994, had leapt to 48.8 per cent a decade later. Home ownership, although at 83 per cent among the highest in Europe, has been growing further.

Foreign demand has also been an important factor. Britons are not the only ones to be attracted by the hot summers, mild winters and a proliferation of golf courses. The Germans, Dutch and Scandinavians have also been buying.

Foreigners seeking retirement or holiday homes have accounted for half of all the housing purchases on Spain's Mediterranean coast in recent years, and about a quarter of the homes bought in the country as a whole. A particular surge in buying came during the run-up to the introduction of the euro, which meant that deutschmarks, francs and so on had to be converted into the new single currency. Unwilling to declare money that had hitherto been hidden from the taxman, wealthy Germans, in particular, ploughed this so-called 'mattress money' into foreign property instead, particularly in Spain.

No boom can go on for ever, however, and by 2005 there were signs of a slowdown. Average prices are estimated to have ended the year about 12 per cent higher. Although a substantial rise by western European standards, this was markedly lower than in previous years (and, some experts believe, overstates the real picture, anyway). The global figure nevertheless masks considerable regional differences: prices in Valencia province, for example, rose by 27 per cent in 2005 – and 31 per cent in the city itself – largely because of the impact of preparations for the America's Cup, the world's richest yacht race, which Valencia will host in 2007. Other hotspots included Cadiz, in western Andalucía (26 per cent) and Tarragona in Catalonia (24 per cent). Growth was substantially lower elsewhere, while the price of new-build developments in parts of the Costa del Sol and Costa Blanca fell back because of serious oversupply. By late 2005, the average price of resale property in Spain stood at £1,200 per square metre – a figure which, according to a growing body of opinion, was simply too high: a study by *The Economist* found the house-price-to-income ratio in Spain (average house price divided by average income) at its highest level ever and 68 per cent above its long-term (30-year) average. This compared with prices that were 50 per cent above average in Britain, Ireland and the Netherlands and 23 per cent above average in the United States.

What happens next remains unclear. The hope is for a so-called soft landing in which the rate of increase will gradually slow to a more sustainable level; the Spanish housing ministry has predicted a rise of around 9 per cent in 2006. Of crucial importance is what happens to interest rates; a further increase, after the quarter-point hike in March 2006, would have a further dampening effect and hit hard many Spanish buyers who have taken out substantial mortgages.

The situation on the coast gives more cause for concern, due to the sheer and unrelenting scale of building there. The number of new properties started in Spain in 2004 was more than the combined total of France and Germany put together, and around a third of those begun in the United States – an economy seven times larger than Spain's. Another 484,000 of them were due to be started in 2006 (300,000 were expected to be principal residences, with many of the remainder for holiday purposes). The potential problem has been aggravated by the increasing marketing of off-plan developments not to end-users but, increasingly, to investors hoping to sell on at a profit on or before completion. In almost all cases this is no longer a viable option: oversupply in many parts of the coast means that, rather than making a healthy profit, you could end up stuck with a property you did not really want at an inflated price.

Not that the foreign villa- and apartment-buyers are about to give up completely on Spain. Despite competition from a variety of other destinations, the country continues to boast a unique package of climate, quality of life, ease of access and sheer familiarity. Live in Spain, an organisation backed by several leading developers, has forecast that the number of holiday homes purchased is expected to rise from approximately 117,000 in 2005 to 150,000 in 2010, with spending almost doubling from £17 billion in 2005 to £31 billion.

This is despite a series of scandals which by all rights should have dented foreign investors' confidence in the Spanish property market. One of the most bizarre issues has been in Valencia, where local authorities operate a controversial planning law, known as the Ley Reguladora de la Actividad Urbanística, which enables promoters to expropriate private property for development against an owner's will. Large numbers of British and other foreign buyers have fallen victim to it, prompting even EU authorities to become involved. The authorities in Valencia have been apparently unfazed by all the adverse publicity, despite a motion passed overwhelmingly by the European Parliament in December 2005 describing the law as a 'violation of the basic rights of many thousands of European Union citizens'. There have been other problems elsewhere in Spain. In spring 2005, the sales of more than 250 houses on the Costa del Sol were frozen pending an investigation into a £200 million building scam involving money allegedly stolen from a Russian oil company. Separately, the Andalucían government, based in Seville, said it planned to demolish up to 1,600 coastal homes – around 500 of which are believed to have been bought by Britons – after the regional high court ruled that they had been built illegally. In a third scandal, several thousand Britons found they had put down deposits on properties offered by a major developer which had been put on hold and may never be built because of problems with planning permission.

Such cases – although involving only a minority of purchases – highlight the potential perils of buying off-plan, in Spain perhaps more than anywhere else. Before putting down any money, you should take a few simple steps: the first is to do a quick Internet search on the developer; if they have had any problems with past projects, then these will come up very quickly. Past performance is never a perfect guide to what will happen in the future – but it can be an important indicator of trouble ahead. A good independent local lawyer will also have heard on the grapevine if a particular project is running into trouble.

If you are extremely unlucky, it might turn out that the planning permission might itself not be legal – as a number of Britons found after buying into a development in Marbella, which local officials had allowed to be built on green belt land in contravention of the rules. Before making the final payment and signing the public deeds of sale in front of a notary, you should also make your lawyer do further checks, such as ensuring that the developers are not passing on unexpected debts or charges and that they have received the all-important residential-use permit from the local authority.

Whether buying an off-plan or a used property, the buying procedure is fairly straightforward, with documents signed in front of the notary. Bear in mind, though, that Spain is a relatively high-tax country. The local equivalent of stamp duty and other fees will add 7–8 per cent to the purchase, with the notary taking another 1 per cent. Rental income is taxed and, as in France, there is a wealth tax, which starts at a modest 0.25 per cent but rises in bands – which means an annual £250 bill for the owner of a £100,000 flat. You will also be liable for capital gains tax on any profit you make; in early 2006, non-residents paid 35 per cent, against 15 per cent for residents, but this looked likely to be replaced by a unified rate after it was ruled discriminatory under EU law.

So much for buying property; how easy will it be to let once you have done so and what kind of return can you expect? According to Mark Stucklin, who runs Spanish Property Insight (**www.spanishpropertyinsight.com**), a highly informative real estate website, the lettings market on the two main holiday coasts, the Costa del Sol and Costa Blanca, is under threat from the sheer scale of the building programmes and the growing extent of speculative buying. As prices soften, then, rather than sell at a loss, many speculators will try to let their newly acquired property instead, adding to the supply on the market and depressing rents. Developers unable to shift their stock may do the same. This is not to say that there is no rental market as such on the Spanish coast; in fact, if there is a perception that purchase prices are going down, many would-be buyers will rent instead. It does mean, however, that you must do your research and choose your property carefully, rather than just buy into any development you come across on the Internet. Gross yields, therefore, are unlikely to exceed 5 per cent and could be lower than that.

Costa del Sol (Central Andalucía)

Mention the Spanish coast and most people think of the Costa del Sol, which has established itself as the number one destination for British buyers. It has had a chequered history. **Marbella** was a haven for the European aristocracy in the 1950s and '60s, but acquired a reputation as the centre of the Costa del Crime during the 1970s, when a number of British criminals fled there to escape justice at home. It has survived such influxes to remain popular with affluent people from northern Europe, as well as mega-rich Arabs and Russians.

The Costa del Sol is by far the most popular area for British property-buyers in Spain, accounting for more than 60 per cent of all purchases. The attractions are obvious: probably the best weather in mainland Europe, the large number of golf courses (40 of them in Malaga province alone), plenty of tourist attractions and the highly developed infrastructure. Many of the towns, like Torremolinos, Benalmadena and Fuengirola, are unashamedly mass market package tour resorts. The area further west around Marbella and the purpose-built pleasure resort of **Puerto Banus** is full of giant villas and gated estates. Tourists form the main rental market and the season is long, increasing the potential yield. Alternative targets are the young professionals and entrepreneurs from Northern Europe who come to work in the financial services and technology businesses that have been set up near Marbella and Puerto Banus. Not all of them will buy – at least not initially – creating a pool of potential tenants for year-round lets.

Don't believe anyone who tries to tell you that you are buying into a booming market. By early 2006, prices on the Costa del Sol were at least a third down on the peaks they reached in 2003, which means it should be possible to drive a hard bargain when you buy, especially from overstretched developers. This certainly does not make property cheap, though. Count on paying around £150,000 for a coastal apartment and at least £480,000 for a decent villa; prices in Puerto Banus and other upmarket areas are substantially higher.

Costa de la Luz (Western Andalucía)

To the west of the Costa del Sol, the windswept Atlantic coast known as the Costa de la Luz is increasingly popular with British buyers, although it is better suited to surfers than to those who want to lie and bake on the beach. The picturesque city of **Tarifa** (surely one of the windiest cities in Europe) is becoming a trendy destination. Moving inland, **Seville** is a delightful city, tipped by some as a second Barcelona. Well served by the budget airlines, it is developing into a popular city break destination, with good short-term rental prospects and investment potential.

Valencia and the Costa Blanca

The Costa Blanca is another firm and well-established favourite with British buyers, thanks to a good climate and plenty of cheap flights from all over Britain. More than 30,000 Britons, the largest concentration in Spain, live in Alicante province.

The southern part, including resorts such as **Benidorm** and **Torrevieja**, is what most people understand by the Costa Blanca, with its bargain-basement tourism and cheap properties. Despite recent rises, prices in the many high-rise blocks there are well below those on the Costa del Sol. A typical 60-square-metre two-bedroom flat in Torrevieja, a few minutes' walk from the sea, would cost around £70,000. The stretch of coast north of Benidorm around the towns of **Denia**, **Calpe** and **Altea** is far prettier, with rocky coves and rugged green mountains. It is also much more upmarket. A good-quality coastal apartment would probably cost around £130,000, with a villa going for double that. Prices have been falling here, too, so it is well worth haggling. As discussed above, **Valencia** itself has been booming thanks to the regeneration programme linked to the America's Cup. Completion of the new City Arts and Science Complex, a mix of iconic new buildings on reclaimed land, has added to the buzz. After several years of strong gains, however, property in the city is no longer cheap. Although it was still possible in early 2006 to pick up an apartment in a nondescript block for around £1,500 per square metre, properties in the historic centre can cost double that. Prices are expected to continue rising, however, and the city could be a good bet for long-term lets.

Barcelona and the Costa Brava (North Catalonia)

Think of what makes an ideal city and it is difficult to disagree that **Barcelona** has the lot: wonderful architecture, a great climate, vibrant night life – and both the sea and the mountains on its doorstep. A booming city of 1.75 million people, it is also a great fly-to-let location; the growing numbers of people coming to work in the city form an excellent potential pool of tenants. Around 15 per cent of the city housing is rented. Barcelona is also one of Europe's most popular city break and conference destinations, which means there is good money to be made letting to tourists, and a season that runs for most of the year.

Barcelona is well on its way to becoming one of the most expensive cities in Europe. Despite growing demand for housing, there has not been a corresponding building boom, owing in part to a shortage of land. The result has been several years of price increases above even the Spanish average; in the year to May 2003 the market surged by 25 per cent, followed by rises of 17 per cent and 10 per cent in the subsequent two years. The market had cooled a little by the beginning of 2006, but the overall trend still appeared upward.

One of the most sought-after areas among foreign buyers in recent years has been Barceloneta, one of the four districts that make up Barcelona's Ciutat Vella (Old Town). Situated directly on the waterfront, it was built 150 years ago to house local fishermen but is especially popular with young people who want to be near the beach, and has potential for short-term rentals to tourists. Although the housing stock is poor and the streets narrow, prices, at well over £3,000 per square metre, are already extremely high – a small studio would not leave you much change from £100,000. Prices are similar in other parts of the Ciutat Vella such as the fashionable Born district and the very touristy Barri Gòtic. Nearby Raval, traditionally home to successive waves of new immigrants, is cheaper and, according to some, ripe for gentrification. Petty crime is a serious problem throughout the Old Town, which could adversely affect rental prospects.

The atmosphere is very different in the rather grander Eixample district, to the north. Built in the 19th century during Barcelona's first expansion beyond its original city walls, it has wide streets laid out at right angles and grand buildings designed by Antoni Gaudí and other modernist architects. Prices are higher here, and a reasonably sized three-bedroom flat in a good building could cost upwards of £400,000. Your tenants will be much more comfortable and secure here.

Wherever you look in the city, yields will not be great; properties let out long-term will probably return around 4 per cent, barely sufficient to cover mortgage costs. Many foreign buyers have preferred instead to let out short-term (for anything from a few days to a month or so) to tourists or visiting business people; in the process, they have earned considerably more and also had the chance to use the property themselves when it is empty. For anyone buying now, though, the prospects are not as good as they were at the beginning of the decade. The supply of such properties has grown, increasing voids and pushing down rents, while purchase prices have continued rising. Another problem is competition from the hotel industry, which added an estimated 2,000 new beds in the city in the first five years of the new millennium and is keen to fill them. Determined to head off what they see as unfair competition, the hoteliers have successfully persuaded local authorities to introduce various rules regulating the short-term rental business.

The growing affluence of Barcelona has also spread to much of the rest of the **Costa Brava**, whose 'wild coast' was the inspiration for Salvador Dalí, the surrealist artist born in **Figueres**. Well-known tourist spots such as **Lloret de Mar** are best avoided, but prices elsewhere will not be cheap either: a small apartment in a mass market resort will cost at least £140,000, while a decent three-bedroom villa with a pool could set up you back £375,000. The highest prices are probably in **Begur** and **Aiguablava**, where villas will go for £700,000 or more.

Anyone buying to let should bear in mind that the rental season is appreciably shorter than on the Costa del Sol or Costa Blanca; this is not the place for winter golfers. Yields, consequently, are unlikely to be much above 4 per cent. There is a good resale market, however, among affluent Barcelona-dwellers in search of a second home.

Galicia and the Costa Verde

Known as the 'Green Coast', this northwestern region has a very different feel from the other *costas*, not least because of the rains that blow in off the Atlantic. Largely because of the climate, it also (so far) does not suffer the over-development that mars the south and east – although more buildings are on the way. Prices in Galicia have been rising, prompting people to look to nearby Asturias and Cantabria. An apartment in a popular coastal location such as Villaviciosa in Asturias could cost £95,000, while traditional stone country houses inland in need of refurbishment go from £55,000.

The Other *Costas*: Calida, Almeria and Dorada

Visit the area around Murcia and the **Costa Calida** and the first thing that will strike you is that the fields are covered in plastic sheets. Starting in the 1980s, this once poor backwater in the southeast of the country began to reinvent itself as Europe's market garden, producing winter fruit and vegetables for much of the continent. More recently, it has been discovered both by developers and by foreign buyers; according to Spanish government figures published in 2005, prices rose by 169 per cent in the preceding five years, more even than in Andalucía, where they were up a mere 132 per cent. As elsewhere on the coast, things have begun to slow quite sharply, particularly now the region has lost much of the price advantage it used to enjoy over the other *costas*. Unable to resist the large remaining stretches of virgin coast, the developers have been pressing on regardless, raising concerns of oversupply. The region suffers from a chronic water shortage, which looks likely to get worse once the current wave of properties and golf developments is completed.

The **Costa Almeria**, to its south, is largely unspoilt compared with other *costas* in Spain, with few villages and very few people. It is especially popular with nature-lovers and backpackers. Two very old towns of particular note are **Garrucha**, 'the city of prawns', and **Almeria**, which is crowned by the magnificent Arab fortress, Alcazaba.

Further up the coast, the **Costa Dorada** (or Golden Coast), with its main town, Tarragona, is another relatively undeveloped area, with great beaches and pretty seaside beaches such as **L'Ametlla de Mar**. Prices rose below the national average in 2005, boosting affordability. The former fishing village of **Sitges**, further up the coast towards Barcelona, has a reputation as a gay holiday hotspot. Temperatures are about 5°C warmer than on the Costa Brava, making the winter shorter and milder.

Estate Agents

- **Arriba Estates, www.arribaestates.com, t** (020) 7586 2456. Property for sale in Costa del Sol, Costa Almeria, Costa Blanca, Costa Calida and Murcia.

- **Barcelona Home Search, www.barcelonahomesearch.com.** Property to buy and rent in Barcelona.

- **Catalan Homes, www.jamescatalanhomes.com, t** + 34 97 740 1785. Property and land for sale in Tarragona and the Costa Dorada.

- **Direct Auctions, www.direct-auctions.com, t** 0871 990 3090. Auction site for property on the Costa del Sol.

- **Home Search Barcelona, www.homesearchbarcelona.com, t** + 34 93 409 3249. A wide selection of apartments in Barcelona and on the Costa Brava.

- **Ideal Spain Properties, www.idealspain-properties.com.** Thousands of properties across the country on sale from various agents, together with some useful information.

- **John Taylor Spain, www.johntaylorspain.com, t** + 34 93 241 3082. British-run company with property for sale in Barcelona and on the Costa Brava.

- **Masa International, www.masainternational.com, t** 0800 955 5266. New and resale properties on the Costa Blanca and Costa Calida.

- **Spain and Property, www.spainandproperty.com, t** + 34 64 778 7350. Property for sale in Valencia and the surrounding area.
- **Spanish Property Investment, www.spanish.property-investment.com.** Thousands of properties for sale and rent across the country, together with a detailed guide to different towns and regions.
- **Spanish Property World, www.spanishpropertyworld.com.** Site with property for sale on the main *costas*, together with useful information.
- **Valencia Property, www.valencia-property.com, t** + 34 90 274 7425. British-run agency with property for sale and rent in Valencia.
- **Viva Estates, www.vivaestates.com, t** 0800 298 9594. Thousands of second-hand and off-plan properties for sale mostly on the Costa del Sol and Costa Calida.

Switzerland

For most people, Switzerland is synonymous with skiing, and resorts such as Verbier, St-Moritz and Gstaad are renowned the world over. Although long popular as a holiday destination, the country has until recently been considered a virtual no-go zone for foreign property-buyers because of high prices and a raft of restrictions that seemed designed to ensure only the richest and most perseverant could buy there. Things are changing, however. Since 2002, as part of Switzerland's gradual *rapprochement* with the European Union, the rules have been relaxed to make it far easier for non-resident foreigners, especially those who are nationals of EU countries, to acquire property in the country.

Generally speaking, this means that you should be able to buy without problem in the mountains, by a lake or in any other place designated as a tourist area. This is not always the case, however. Under Switzerland's political system, it is up to the 26 individual cantons – and even individual towns and villages – to set the precise rules. The French-speaking canton of Vaud, in the west, is one of the most accommodating; neighbouring Valais (known as Wallis by the German-speakers), has slightly more restrictive rules. Zurich and the other German-speaking cantons of the east are far more reluctant to allow outsiders to buy. That is only the start of it. Some cantons forbid foreigners from selling within five or 10 years of purchase in order to prevent property speculation, and there are restrictions on the size and type of property that can be bought; foreign buyers are also generally limited to one each. Properties can be let, although leases must be shorter than a year. (Given the right lawyer, there are ways around all these obstacles, primarily through acquiring a so-called 'B' residence permit, but it can be an expensive and time-consuming process.)

Given such an array of problems, why would anyone even think of buying in Switzerland when things are so much more straightforward in France, Italy and

Austria, which also have their fair share of top-level ski resorts? For some buyers, perhaps, Switzerland has a cachet that its neighbours lack; a property there may be seen not only as an investment but also as an eventual retirement home, allowing the owner to benefit from the country's advantageous tax regime. Switzerland is also not as expensive as many people think. While property prices in France and Italy, in particular, have been rising strongly in recent years, they fell steadily across Switzerland in the 1990s, ending the decade lower than they began it. They have been rising moderately since the start of the new millennium, though, helped by cuts in interest rates and the general economic upturn, and look poised to notch up further gains. In a vote of confidence in the market, large foreign investors have also started buying.

One of the main attractions for individual buyers – as for the institutions – is the cheapness of borrowing. Swiss banks are ready to lend up to 80 per cent loan-to-value at 2.5 per cent or less. Transfer tax and notary and land registry fees, although varying from canton to canton, will add an average 5 per cent to the purchase price, but rental income is not taxed in Switzerland (although UK residents will have a liability at home). Capital gains tax and inheritance tax will also vary, depending on location. As you would expect, the legal procedures that govern buying are, like almost everything else in the country, simple, straight-forward and efficient.

Looking at the ski market, properties on offer are either flats in purpose-built blocks or one-off chalets, which can be bought 'off-the-peg' or built to order. A crisis in the hotel sector has meant some privately owned mid-market establishments are being converted into apartments, often with reasonable price tags and access to in-house spas and pools and other hotel-like services.

Yields will be modest. Some owners sign their properties over to tour companies for the entire season; such deals typically give a return of 4–5 per cent and allow some own use as well, but usually not during the peak season. Returns should be higher in developments and resorts with summer as well as winter potential. Although chalets appear more attractive than apartments, demand from the locals is greater, making it difficult to find bargains. Maintenance, permanent winter heating and the need for refurbishment every 10 years or so will also add substantially to costs, but they are more easily rentable in summer. Whether you buy an apartment or villa, capital gains are likely to be steady – typically a few percentage points a year – rather than spectacular, although much will depend on the choice of property and resort. Many of those buying in Switzerland do so primarily because they like the place rather than because of pure economics.

Valais

Situated in the Rhône Valley in the southwest of Switzerland, Valais is home to the famous Matterhorn, as well as some of the country's most popular resorts such as **Verbier**, **Leukerbad**, **Crans-Montana** and **Zermatt**. Rules on buying property vary from village to village; while foreigners can acquire property with relative ease in Verbier, a favourite with British skiers, they are effectively barred from doing so in Zermatt. Nearby **Saas-Fee**, a picturesque high-altitude traffic-free village surrounded by glaciers, is a good substitute. Anyone buying a property anywhere in the canton is obliged to hold on to it for at least five years before selling, but can then do so either to a Swiss national or to another foreigner. Purchase costs, at 2.5 per cent, are among the lowest in the country.

Prices in Verbier are more than £6,000 per square metre, making even an average one-bedroom flat well over £300,000. Property is substantially cheaper in nearby villages such as Les Collons, Mayens de Riddes and Nendaz, which are part of Verbier's Quatre Vallées ski area. A two-bedroom apartment in La Tzoumaz, part of Mayens-de-Riddes, should go for £90,000–100,000, including underground parking. You should be able to pick up a 35-square-metre studio for as little as £35,000, while a chalet could fetch more than £200,000.

With 28 lifts and 140 miles of slopes, Crans-Montana is a fully fledged resort in its own right, but substantially cheaper than Verbier. It is also a summer golfing destination, hosting the European Masters every September. It is possible to find property in a reasonable location for as little as £2,000–3,000 per square metre; a compact but high-quality studio could cost as little as £50,000, while a reasonable one-bedroom flat could come in at under £100,000. Prices in Saas-Fee are slightly higher at £3,000–4,000 per square metre, but still below Verbier levels. Leukerbad, another year-round resort with beautiful natural thermal baths and all possible sports facilities, is cheaper, with studios in new developments from as little as £60,000 and flats starting at double that.

Vaud

Situated around Lac Léman (Lake Geneva), in the far west of the country, the Canton de Vaud contains the mountain resorts of **Villars-sur-Ollon** and **Les Diablerets**, as well as the elegant 19th-century lake-side town of **Montreux**. Only 90 minutes from Geneva airport, Villars is one of the most attractive and easily accessible resorts. It also boasts a golf course, swimming pool and tennis courts, making it a true all-year resort. Properties on sale include second-hand chalets and apartments and new chalets built to order. Prices in Villars itself can be around £3,000–4,000 per square metre, but may be lower in nearby Gryon and Barboleusaz. Despite its grand style, Montreux is still affordable, with apartments available for as little as £2,000 per square metre. Purchase costs, at 4.8 per cent, are higher than in Valais, but rules on ownership are more liberal.

Ticino

The only canton situated south of the Alps, Italian-speaking Ticino offers a unique combination of Swiss efficiency and Italian flair in an idyllic setting of mountains, stunning lake views and palm trees. **Lugano**, an important financial centre, and nearby **Locarno**, known for its film festival, are both delightful lakeside towns with the sunniest weather in the country and lush subtropical vegetation.

Estate Agents

- **Gstaad Real Estate, www.gstaadrealestateservices.ch, t + 41 33 748 0404.** Property for sale and rent in Gstaad and the surrounding area, together with useful information on rules governing purchases by foreigners.

- **Immogalaxy, www.immogalaxy.ch, t + 41 91 941 0801.** Real estate portal with wide selection of property for sale in the canton of Ticino, together with useful information.

- **Investors in Property, www.investorsinproperty.com, t** (020) 8905 5511. A range of new-build apartments and chalets in various locations in Vaud and Valais.

- **Property for Sale Switzerland, www.homes.ch.** Property listings with more than 1,000 flats and houses for sale across the country.

- **Swiss Chalets, www.swiss-chalets.com, t + 41 24 498 2190.** Property for sale and rent in Villars and nearby Gryon and Barboleusaz.

- **Swiss Getaway, www.swissgetaway.com, t** (01202) 429 565. A wide range of properties in the mountains and elsewhere for sale, together with detailed information on buying and on Swiss life in general.

- **Swiss Property Sales, www.swissproperty.co.uk, t** (0114) 236 3655. A variety of new-build properties in Vaud and Valais.

- **Swiss Real Estates, www.swiss-real-estates.com, t + 41 79 599 4013.** Agency offering new chalets and apartments in Verbier, Crans-Montana and elsewhere in Valais.

- **Swiss Sun, www.swiss-sun.co.uk, t** (020) 8458 9379. London-based agency specialising in the sale of properties in Crans-Montana and Verbier.

The Middle East, Asia and Beyond

10

While the countries featured in the two previous chapters have shared a number of characteristics, those that follow in this chapter are a decidedly mixed bunch, with widely differing levels of income and economic systems. Some, but not all, were former colonies of Britain and other European powers; many, but not all, are Muslim. Indeed, the only thing almost all have in common is that until very recently foreigners would have been neither permitted to buy, nor even remotely interested in buying, property there.

Yet all these countries, like their European counterparts, have been exposed to the forces of globalisation and flows of capital across the planet. After first opening their financial markets to international investors, they have followed more recently by allowing foreigners to buy real estate as well. In some cases, such as in Egypt or Thailand, people from outside have effectively the same rights as the locals. In Dubai and the other Gulf states, foreigners are permitted to buy only in certain specially designated areas.

Turkey, hitherto the largest market for British buyers, shares a number of characteristics with Bulgaria, Romania and other countries covered in the **Emerging Europe** chapter, not least because interest in it has been enhanced by the prospect – albeit somewhat distant in Turkey's case – of membership of the European Union. Like those countries, it has undergone periods of economic turbulence and high inflation, but by the middle of the first decade of the new millennium it appeared on the right economic track. Coupled with growing demand from northern Europeans looking for a cheap holiday home in the sun, the result has been a booming property market, with rising prices.

Although they lie thousands of miles further east, Thailand and Bali have been experiencing similar property booms of their own. As with Turkey, much of the foreign interest has been not so much from investors chasing high returns but from people looking for holiday homes in locations that seem the closest thing to paradise on earth. Investors have also begun to realise that there is serious money to be made. The season in the tropics runs for virtually the whole year, producing far higher yields than in, say, Croatia or even Spain. Similar factors are at play in Egypt.

In the other countries covered in this chapter, investors have been very much to the fore from the start. The dramatic growth of the property market in Dubai, created out of nothing in 2002, has been largely attributable to investors, many of them from within the Gulf region, but also from Britain, elsewhere in Europe and North America. While some British buyers have undoubtedly been attracted by the idea of owning a holiday home in one of the most bizarre man-made environments on earth, many more have been attracted by the bottom line and by a boom which, until it began to falter in late 2005, looked as if it would go on for ever. This is even more the case with China – or rather with Shanghai and Beijing, the two cities where most foreign interest in that country has hitherto been concentrated. No matter that the government in Beijing still styles itself Communist; foreign investors have been attracted by the massive capital gains on offer, underpinned by the relentless growth of the Chinese economy. There have been warning signs there as well, though, with authorities stepping in during 2005 to try and deflate the property bubble, especially in Shanghai, before it got out of hand.

The size of the region and number of countries within it have meant there are omissions in this book. If you are really determined to find information on property in a country, though, it should be easy enough to do so on the Internet. The region has a wealth of English-language newspapers, accessible online or via stand-alone websites, with articles on the property market, while banks and other bodies produce research reports. The usual caveats apply: when viewing sites, always bear in mind that any predictions made about rental yields or future capital gains are best-case scenarios.

Bali and Beyond

Bali

Known variously as the 'Island of the Gods', 'Morning of the World' or 'Shangri-La', Bali is one of more than 17,000 islands in the Indonesian archipelago, which runs from Malaysia all the way to Australia. A chain of awesome volcanoes stretches across the island, helping to create an ideal environment for tropical rainforests, rice fields, mangrove swamps and beaches of both black (volcanic) and white sand, together with some world-class surf. The unique local culture is strongly rooted in ancient Hindu tradition rich in art, music and dance.

With 2.5 million people squeezed into just 2,150 square miles, Bali is also densely populated. The population is almost all Indonesian, with the usual small Chinese contingent in the big towns and a sprinkling of Indian merchants. Bali is also home to a large, dynamic community of professional and creative western expats, which gives the place a cosmopolitan feel. The island's infrastructure has been developing rapidly in recent years: dual carriageways now connect the international airport to the west and east coasts, while broadband satellite Internet connections and wi-fi hotspots can be found in all major tourist areas and in the residential enclaves of Seminyak and Canggu.

It is impossible to talk about Bali without mentioning the bomb attacks of 12 October 2002, which killed 202 people. The rental prices of villas dropped 10–50 per cent in the six to 12 months that followed, although they began to recover in late 2003 and 2004. Quality homes with pools in popular residential areas such as Sanur, Seminyak and Nusa Dua are now let for £600–2,500 a month. The attack also had an effect on sales: residential construction came to an almost complete standstill, leading to a severe shortage of high-quality homes. With demand for beachfront properties high, the result was that prices held up well. Land prices barely dipped and have since been rising sharply. The property market also largely shrugged off a second, smaller attack in October 2005, even though tourist numbers dropped briefly. Days after the second bomb, work began on the Canggu Club, Bali's first country club. Featuring an indoor sports hall, tennis courts and an associated school, it is aimed both at visitors and the foreign expats who live on the island.

Despite the ever-present fear of further atrocities, the market has been underpinned by Bali's unique charms and the ease of access from Singapore, Hong Kong and Australia. Indeed, around a third of those who buy on the island are expats based in southeast Asia, with the remainder mainly Australians and Canadians. It also helps that the cost of property is still about a third below that in comparable resorts in Thailand, its main competitor.

Prices vary widely, depending on size, quality and position. A typical three-bedroom villa with a large garden and a pool could cost around £200,000, and should be easy to let if it is well located. A great advantage of Bali for the fly-to-let investor is the year-round tourist trade. There are wet and dry seasons, but temperatures remain constant; visitors from Australia and New Zealand arrive in the middle of the year, while those from Europe, Japan and the United States come at the end. Domestic tourists fill the gaps between them. With average occupancy rates of 60–80 per cent, it should be possible to achieve yields of 10 per cent or more. Capital gains add to the attraction. Good property management is also important and has only recently become available.

The greater **Kuta/Seminyak** area in the centre of the island was the birthplace of tourism on Bali; its surfing beaches drew the first foreigners there in the 1960s. With its souvenir shops, cheap restaurants, bars and budget accommodation, it remains the most commercialised part of the island. This is also where the airport is. Legian, to the north of Kuta, has long been a favourite with expat buyers and visitors; adjacent **Seminyak**, which has a large number of high-end rental and residential properties as well as chic nightspots and restaurants, is increasingly popular. **Kerobokan**, just inland, has more rural surroundings and lovely scenery. **Jimbaran**, to the immediate south of Kuta and convenient for the airport, is also sought after. Those looking for somewhere quieter should try **The Bukit**, a large area to the south of that, with white sandy beaches. It is does not yet have much infrastructure and is far from nightlife and restaurants, which could make it more difficult to let property there.

Nusa Dua, located on the southeastern tip of the island, is renowned for its picturesque manicured beaches and five-star hotels and for the 18-hole Bali Golf and Country Club. It targets an upmarket crowd, and is free of much of the congestion of the Kuta area. Most villas built are for owner-occupiers.

Sanur, north of Kuta on the east coast, was one of the original holiday destinations, with some of the first hotels on the island dating back to the 1920s and '30s. These days it is more of a three- or four-star package destination, but it lacks a vibrant nightlife. Further north is **Ubud**, known as Bali's artistic centre. It has become increasingly popular as a rental area because it has not yet been commercialised as much as the southern parts of the island.

Ownership rules are relatively simple. Freehold tenure is not available for foreign investors; while buying in the name of a trusted Indonesian national provides a way around this, it is not an option for the risk-averse. The alternative is to lease land. This can be done at present for a maximum of 75 years; the lease can be rolled over for another 75 years, but this has to be done on a case-by-case basis. Purchase costs are relatively low: in addition to a notary's fee of 0.75–1 per cent (usually covered by the foreign buyer), both buyer and seller pay 5 per cent government transfer tax. This is based on the government-designated value of the property, which is usually far below the market price. Finance is more difficult: banks have been structuring special arrangements with foreigners, but this is not yet widespread. Investors would be better off funding a purchase on Bali by releasing equity from property in another location with which international banks are more comfortable.

Estate Agents

- **Bali Home & Property Sales, www.balipropertysales.com.** A variety of properties for sale, together with useful information about the market.

- **Bali Property Investment, www.balipropertyinvestment.com.** Properties for sale across the island, including investment opportunities.

- **Bali Real Estate Agents, www.balirealestateagents.com.** Portal with links to agents and developers.

- **Claire Brown Realty, www.clairebrownrealty.com, t** (07967) 258 121. Selection of property in Bali, the Philippines and Thailand.

- **Exotiq Real Estate, www.exotiqrealestate.com.** A wide range of property for sale in Bali, Phuket and Koh Samui.

- **Paradise Property Bali, www.paradisepropertybali.com, t** + 62 361 737 357. New-build properties for sale across the island.

The Philippines

The Philippines consists of 7,107 islands, only 2,000 of which are inhabited. They divide into three groups. First there is **Luzon**, the largest and northernmost island and the site of the capital, **Manila**, home to 8 million of the country's 67 million people. At the other end of the archipelago is **Mindanao**, the second largest island. In between them lies the tightly packed group known as the **Visayas**, which has seven major islands: Cebu, Panay, Negros, Bohol, Leyte, Samar and Masbate. **Cebu City** is a major tourist destination.

With GDP increasing at more than 6 per cent a year and booming regional tourism, the Philippines is one of the fastest-growing residential property markets in Asia, even though few developments have so far been marketed to foreigners outside the region. Cebu has been singled out because of its tourist potential; Macati, the Central Business District in Manila, is also of interest.

Since 2002, non-Filipinos have been able to own freehold property, but only provided it is a unit in a condominium. For zero worries on maintenance and rental operations, overseas investors should probably be looking only at condominium-style property or 'Condotel' projects, such as the Lancaster Cebu. There is also a strong market for resales: buyers in condo resorts are often Filipino nationals working overseas in America, Britain, China, Hong Kong or Taiwan, or western expats based in Manila or other southeast Asian cities. Such is the strength of the market that the prices of luxury off-plan condos in Macati have been rising as much as 80 per cent between release and completion.

Vietnam

Find all the above a little tame? Then why not try Vietnam, which some believe could be the 'next big thing'. Thanks to its hundreds of miles of white, sandy beaches, devotees see it eventually emerging as a rival to more mature resorts such as Phuket and Bali.

One of the first developments targeted specifically at foreign buyers is on the beautiful, unspoilt **China Beach**, a former playground of American GIs, near Danang in the centre of the country. The upmarket Nam Hai resort, which boasts more than half a mile of its own quiet beachfront, has a 60-room hotel and 45 privately owned villas, with prices starting from £500,000. It is possible to let them through the hotel when they are not in use. There may be more scope for development further south in places like **Phu Quoc**, **Nha Trang** and **Phan Tiet**. The weather there is generally warm most of the year, and there is not the same seasonal cold and rain found in central and north Vietnam.

Ownership is even more complicated than elsewhere in the region. Vietnam's Communist authorities prohibit foreigners from owning land. Setting up a Vietnam-registered company provides a way around that, but foreigners are not allowed to own more than 30 per cent of the company, which makes them heavily dependent on Vietnamese nominees, who retain overriding control. This is true even for buying apartments. There are imaginative ways around this: in the case of the Nam Hai development, for example, villa owners buy shares in an offshore company that has leased the land from a Vietnamese company which in turn has leased it from the government. With complications like this, Vietnam, at this stage, is probably only for the brave investor.

Estate Agents

- **Bahay.ph, http://bahay.ph, t + 632 914 1318. Property for sale across the Philippines.**

- **Claire Brown Realty, www.clairebrownrealty.com, t** (07967) 258 121. A selection of property in Bali, the Philippines and Thailand.
- **Garces Real Estate, www.garcesrealestate.com.** Houses and condos for sale across the Philippines.
- **Hanoi Property, www.hanoiproperty.com.** Property in Vietnam.
- **Invest PH, www.investph.com.** Cebu-based property portal with houses and condos for sale and rent across the Philippines.

China

Pick up almost anything these days, from a child's toy to a laptop, and the chances are that it was made in China. Pick up any newspaper and it is not hard to find predictions of how, a couple of decades from now, China, home to 1.3 billion people, will have overtaken America as the largest economy in the world. The figures speak for themselves: GDP has quadrupled since the country's rulers began to move towards a limited market economy in 1978, with growth averaging 9.5 per cent a year and exports surging more than 50 per cent from 1997 to 2002. Urban incomes have been rising at an average 8 per cent a year. China's admission to the World Trade Organisation in 2001 has obliged it to commit to the liberalisation of its economy according to a strict timetable. Foreign investment has also been rising at an annual 26 per cent, encouraged by a change in the law in the mid-1990s that allowed the establishment of wholly foreign-owned enterprises. This is still a nominally Communist country, but one that, in economic terms at least, is extraordinarily dynamic.

Such dynamism has fed through into a property boom. UBS Securities has estimated that urban land and property prices rose by 70 per cent between 2001 and 2004, as money, much of it from speculators, began to pour in. It has also become far easier for foreign investors to buy in China. Several British-based agencies have begun selling new properties, principally in Shanghai, but their numbers are growing and the list of cities is expanding to include Beijing and Guangzhou. (Under Chinese law, selling off-plan, as such, is not permitted; those properties offered are instead 70 per cent completed.)

The long march upwards began to falter in 2005, however. Worried about the development of a property bubble, Wen Jiabao, the Chinese premier, vowed in March to 'put the brakes on the rise in real estate prices'. The result, two months later, was the introduction of a series of measures to curb speculation, including a 5 per cent sales tax on anyone buying and selling within two years. The result was a sudden drop in prices, especially of properties in new developments. Shanghai, where 30–40 per cent of purchases are believed to have been made by speculators from Hong Kong, Taiwan and beyond, was particularly badly hit.

Opinions differ on what will happen next; for the optimists, the government's action was ultimately positive for the long-term health of the market. Letting steam out of the pressure cooker in this way, so it is argued, has reduced the possibility of a major crash in the future. International property consultants Jones Lang LaSalle warned that 2006 might see a further market correction, but like most commentators they see the long-term trend as upward, with annual rises of 10 per cent likely for some time. Indeed, the more bullish investors have seen any softening of prices in the short term as a clear buying opportunity.

Others have taken a negative view. In a report in January 2006, the Academy of Macroeconomic Research of the National Development and Reform Commission, China's top planning agency, claimed the long-running real estate boom in Shanghai and other cities had ended the previous summer and warned that it could be three to five years before things improved. There have also been fears of a knock-on effect on the rest of the Chinese economy, amid concern that falling property prices could hit banks who have been too free with their loans to developers. Although Shanghai's 20 million residents represent less than 2 per cent of the national population, the city accounts for an astounding 20 per cent of the country's property value. Around a million homes are under construction – about half the number of housing starts for the entire USA in 2004.

For the foreign investor, any falls in property prices may be mitigated by rises in the yuan. The yuan has become increasingly undervalued as the Chinese economy has grown. It is widely believed that the Beijing government will eventually have to bow to pressure from the USA and its other major trading partners and allow it to move upwards – in the process providing a windfall gain to anyone who has property or other assets there. A first move in this direction came in July 2005, when the yuan (also known as the renminbi or simply RMB) was decoupled from the dollar and went into a managed float (under the new system, it is allowed to move 0.3 per cent above or below the level set by the authorities). The immediate result was small: an effective revaluation of just 2.1 per cent against the dollar. But the currency remains seriously undervalued – by as much as 40 per cent, according to some estimates – and analysts expect the authorities to use the new system to allow a very gradual upward move. Theoretically, if Beijing allowed the yuan to rise by 0.3 per cent each day, it could gain more than 6 per cent in a month. Indeed, for many foreign investors, this currency effect is one of the main motivations for getting into the market at all.

Despite their continued adherence, in words at least, to Communist ideology, China's rulers are supportive of private ownership: in a landmark ruling, the parliament in 2004 changed the constitution to add a clause declaring that 'a citizen's lawful private property is inviolable'. The same rules on property ownership rights apply for foreigners and non-residents. In practice, though, such rights can be constrained by the arbitrary actions of local officials. Many older buildings are being demolished in faster-developing areas such as the northeast of Beijing, to be replaced with new residences, office buildings and department stores, but existing property-owners are usually paid less than the market value as compensation.

The careful foreign investor should be able to avoid being caught up in such an unfortunate situation. All cities have short- and long-term city development plans, and planning offices are usually willing to provide information. Often maps of the city can be found with huge chunks removed, where redevelopment will take place. Since Beijing was awarded the 2008 Olympics, several long-term city plans have been developed; studying these should make it clear which areas are likely to be safe from the bulldozer and for how long.

In Beijing, those traditional courtyard houses which have not already been demolished are now generally protected. This makes them a safe investment bet, although they can cost £600,000 or more and usually require considerable work. In Shanghai, colonial-style houses in the French Concession are also protected, but it is still worth confirming with authorities that the one you are buying is not in an area earmarked for demolition. Establishing 'friendly relations' with local officials is also a good idea. When doing any business in China, getting the right *guanxi* ('relationships') with officials is vital.

Buying a flat in a new building can be a lot more straightforward, even if the returns are not potentially as great. You should keep an eye on the quality of workmanship, which can sometimes be poor, with the first cracks and other defects appearing within months of completion. Building insurance is therefore essential; most properties offer between one and three years free, but check.

Whether buying older property or a flat in a newly completed building which someone has bought and is selling on, you should make sure the vendor is the real owner; fake legal documents are not unknown. A lawyer will be able to verify this, while the developers should also keep records of those to whom they sold. To make sure all the paperwork is in order, you should insist on seeing originals of the land use right certificate (*tudi shiyongquan zheng*), the building work certificate (*jianzhu gongcheng shigong zheng*), the project planning permit (*jianzhu gongcheng guihua xuke zheng*) and the commercial real estate presale permit (*shangpinfang yushou xuke zhengit*).

Generally, the Chinese property market still rates poorly on a broad range of issues, such as the availability of accurate financial and market information and the state of the regulatory and legal environment. Problem areas include the security of title and enforceability of property rights, financial disclosure and governance of listed real estate companies and zoning and building codes. In its 2004 Global Real Estate Transparency index, Jones Lang LaSalle ranked China 39th out of 51 countries. Some analysts maintain that the market is just too risky for small-scale investors. It is also worth noting that, for ideological reasons, foreign ownership of land is not permitted, which means that any residential property you buy will be on a 70-year lease. What happens when it runs out remains to be seen. The expectation is that you will be able to extend the lease, but even property agents admit that no one can guarantee this today.

For a Communist country, the tax regime is nevertheless surprisingly favourable: the local equivalent of stamp duty and other charges will add around 5 per cent to the purchase price, but thereafter a tax of just 5 per cent is levied on gross rental income. This may change, especially if the government feels it needs to do even more to cool prices. Mortgage rates are reasonable (around 5.75 per cent in early 2006), with loans offered by HSBC and other major international banks on most new development, and many, but not all, second-hand properties. Typically they are over 10–20 years and available only on a repayment rather than interest-only basis. Remember, too, that with property – as with many other things in China – it is important to haggle over the price, especially at a time when the market is slowing.

So where do you start in a country 40 times the size of Britain? Go to a grim, far-flung industrial town and you could pick up a flat for little more than the cost of a brace of Peking duck and a portion of fried rice. But let's be realistic. All things considered, the least-hassle choice for a UK-based investor must be Shanghai or Beijing. Also worth considering is Hong Kong, although, as we shall see below, its market has a completely different dynamic.

Shanghai

Located where the Yangtze River joins China's prosperous eastern coast, Shanghai has evolved from a small 19th-century fishing town into a modern metropolis with a population of more than 20 million people. It is the country's commercial and financial capital and has a port that is second only to Singapore in terms of the volume of freight handled every year. GDP, at around £3,000 per head, is almost five times the national average. Shanghai is continuing to grow rapidly in size, as multinationals relocate their regional headquarters from Hong Kong or Singapore, and locals move in from the surrounding countryside. Construction is under way of 11 new 'mini-cities' around the city (plus a further 22 satellite towns), each of which will accommodate around 1 million people. They are due for completion by 2020.

Arriving at the airport, you are whisked into town aboard the 170mph magnetic-levitation train, the first in commercial service in the world. In 2004, the first Formula One track was opened. In the next few years, Shanghai will be home to a series of events boosting its international profile; in 2007, Universal Studios will be completed, along with the world's new tallest building, the Shanghai World Financial Centre. The following year, the city will benefit from the spillover from the Beijing Olympics and then in 2010 will host World Expo.

Prices in Shanghai have risen strongly – up 25 per cent in 2003 and 20.4 per cent in 2004, according to data from the Shanghai Government Statistics Bureau – but, as discussed above, they were among the hardest hit by the government's attempts to cool the market in 2005. According to official figures, they had fallen some 15 per cent from their March peak by the end of the year. The strong economic fundamentals meant they are ultimately likely to resume their upward growth, although likely at a more modest rate. The question is, when?

The city of Shanghai is divided by the Huangpu river into the Puxi district, the traditional heart of Shanghai, on the west bank, and rapidly developing Pudong on the east side. Puxi is home to around 90 per cent of Shanghai's residents and remains Shanghai's cultural, residential and economic centre. The symbol of the city is the Bund, which winds less than a mile along the bank from its starting point at the Baidu Bridge. One of the world's most famous waterfronts, it began as a British settlement and became a major financial hub of East Asia at the end of the 19th and beginning of the 20th centuries. Its illustrious past is reflected in the grandeur of its architecture, a unique mixture of everything from Romanesque and Gothic to Beaux Arts and Art Deco. The Nanjing Road intersects the city, and property prices decrease as you move further away from it. Developments are still being built in the area, some of them at affordable prices, but most new apartment building on this side of the river is further afield, towards the universities and underground lines due to be completed in 2010.

Shanghai has some of the greatest surviving colonial architecture in Asia, predominantly in the stylish former French Concession. The district offers a mixture of houses, some with private gardens, and apartments dating from the 1880s to the 1900s. Property here, although already pricey, will undoubtedly continue to rise in value. Some foreign investors have done well by buying and renovating, but this requires considerable time, effort and local knowledge. Purchase prices can also be deceptive: many former colonial buildings need the same amount again spent on them to bring them up to modern-day standards. They are nevertheless extremely good rental prospects. Pudong, on the east bank, was until the early 1990s little more than a ramshackle suburb filled with villagers peddling vegetables. Today it symbolises China's economic growth with its rows of stylish skyscrapers; it is being given a further boost by the rapid development of Pudong International Airport, whose annual passenger capacity is set to triple from 20 million to 60 million by the end of 2007.

Although some investors have gone for the top end of the market, paying £750,000 or more, the rental market for such properties is limited. Many agents advise instead buying something in the £100,000–150,000 range or below, ideally near the city's rapidly expanding metro system. Such properties can be let out not just to foreigners, but also to the far larger numbers of Chinese graduates in well-paid jobs with large companies. Rental demand varies according to location, and yields are 4–8 per cent. Some new developments offer guaranteed yields, which in 2006 were typically around 7 per cent gross (or 6.5 per cent after rental fees and tax), although, as always, such deals should be approached with caution. Some agents have also begun offering hotel rooms for sale: one such scheme proposed rooms starting at £25,000, with a guaranteed rental return of 8.9 per cent over 25 years and a free annual eight days in any hotel operated by the same chain.

Ultimately, whether or not you buy in Shanghai depends on your interpretation of the events of 2005 and whether you see the fall in price merely as a correction or instead as the end of the boom. If the latter, then you may well want to stay away, at least until it looks as if the market has bottomed out.

Beijing

Home to just over 15 million people, Beijing has also been growing rapidly in recent years, with developers searching increasingly further afield in search of land to put up new apartment blocks. The 2008 Olympics will give the city a substantial further boost. Much of the interest has been concentrated in the northeast of the city, in and around the Chaoyang district, with developers encouraged by the opening of the airport expressway, which now runs all the way to the centre. Chaoyang district is home to the embassies and a large number of bars, restaurants and offices as well as being near several parks. While most properties here are modern apartments, the area around the Drum and Bell Towers north of the Forbidden City contains most of the renovated courtyard and *hutong* (lane or alley) homes. Property outside the third ring road is significantly cheaper than in the city centre, and larger homes are often half the price of those downtown. In 2005 studio and loft apartments became available for the first time in Beijing, focused on the art district of Dashanzi. Old factories are being snapped up by investors, gutted, redesigned and let out to arty types. Property there is currently cheap enough to buy on a 10-year lease, renovate and let out at a considerable profit as the area has become so popular. Other artistic areas such as the East End Village could be the places to look out for in coming years. Further out towards the airport, beyond the fifth ring road, are areas such as Shunyi, with villas popular with expat families. These generously sized four- and five-bedroom western-style houses have garages and gardens and are set in communities with shops and even Indian takeaways.

Prices in Beijing have been rising rapidly; the cost of new-build property rose around 20 per cent in 2005, to around £1,000–1,500 per square metre, depending on location and quality. Prices of existing flats and houses rose by a more modest 8 per cent. The rental market has not been quite so buoyant. Since the beginning of the new millennium, many expats and wealthier Chinese have left the centre for the greener, cleaner suburbs, leaving a glut of mid-range prop-erties in the £350–700-a-month range, many of which were being let at the end of 2005 for only two-thirds of the price they were achieving at the beginning. Spacious two-bedroom downtown flats that are let at around £800 a month are always in demand; anything much larger could be more difficult to let.

Hong Kong

Formally ceded to Britain in 1842 under the treaty of Nanking, during the 20th century Hong Kong developed into a major international centre of finance and trade, with one of the world's most liberal economies. At the stroke of midnight on 1 July 1997 it was handed back to China, and the last governor, Chris Patten, left with Prince Charles on the royal yacht. Under the terms of the Sino-British Joint Declaration of 1984 which governed the handover, the former colony was classified as a special administrative region, with its previous capitalist system due to remain untouched until 2047 under China's 'one country, two systems' policy. It also retains its own currency, the Hong Kong dollar, linked to the US dollar, and its own legal and judicial systems, administered by an independent judiciary, based on English Common Law.

Hong Kong's real estate market has consequently behaved very differently from those of Shanghai or Beijing. Prices, already high by international standards, rose sharply in the run-up to the handover. But they suffered badly during the Asian economic crisis of 1997–8, falling 44 per cent between their peak in October 1997 and October 1998, in what was one of the world's largest residential real estate busts. A modest recovery followed in 1999, but prices drifted back downwards thereafter, with the global economic downturn of 2001 striking a further blow. Then, just when developers thought they had hit rock bottom, along came the outbreak of the deadly Sars virus in 2003. This had a huge impact on Hong Kong, emptying restaurants, shops and hotels. Property prices came crashing down in its wake.

Continuing its rollercoaster ride, the market rose sharply in 2004, thanks to low interest rates and an erroneous expectation that the Hong Kong dollar might be revalued along with the Chinese currency; as a result, some apartments nearly tripled in value. Things slowed dramatically in May 2005, when the Hong Kong Monetary Authority changed the currency peg in a way that made it much more costly to bet on currency appreciation and ruled out any appreciation no matter what China did. Speculative money then flowed out of the territory's banking system and interest rates rose to US levels, further discouraging buyers. After all that, prices in early 2006 were still at least 20 per cent below their peaks, and anyone who invested in 1997 is likely to have suffered a substantial loss. Price rises were expected to remain in double digits in 2006 and 2007, underpinned by a shortage of supply; the number of new projects started during the slump years dropped sharply, with around 20,000 new units expected to come on stream per year, against an annual growth in demand of 40,000 in the previous 15 years. The long-term outlook is more difficult to predict. Although Hong Kong remains a vibrant place, prices, at £3,000 and more per square metre, are still high compared with other Chinese cities. The former colony may also suffer in coming years as the banking and legal sectors increasingly move to Shanghai once China is fully compliant with its commitments to the World Trade Organisation.

Estate Agents

- **Beijing Informer, www.beijinginformer.com, t + 86 135 5299 3800.**
Buying agents, providing information on the Beijing property market.

- **Beijing Real Estate, www.beijingrealestate.com, t** + 86 10 8231 8640. A wide range of apartments and villas in Beijing for sale and rent from different agents and private individuals.
- **City Trading Post, www.citytradingpost.co.uk, t** 0845 222 0085. London-based financial advisers offering a few off-plan developments in Shanghai.
- **Habitat Property, www.habitat-property.com, t** + 852 2869 9069. Hong-Kong-based agency with property for sale and rent.
- **Hidden Dragon Investments, www.hdilestates.com, t** (020) 7553 7103. A small selection of off-plan developments in Beijing, together with some useful information.
- **Landmark Asia Realty, www.landmarkasia.com.hk, t** + 852 2506 1008. A range of property for sale and rent in Hong Kong and Shanghai.
- **Landscope, www.hongkonghomes.com, t** + 852 2866 0130. A wide selection of properties for sale and rent in Hong Kong.
- **Lihong Property, www.lihong.biz, t** + 86 10 8580 2389. A large choice of Beijing properties for sale and rent, together with some useful information and analysis.
- **Shanghai Phoenix Property Agency, www.shanghaiagent.com, t** + 86 21 6240 4052. Property in Shanghai for sale and rent.
- **Shanghai Vision, www.shanghaivision.com, t** (020) 7072 8628. A variety of new developments in Shanghai, together with monthly market research reports and other useful information.
- **Shanghome, www.shanghome.com.** Comprehensive property portal with listings and lots of useful information about the city.

Dubai and the Gulf

Until recently, the Gulf was known for little other than its sand and its vast oil wealth. All this has changed since the start of the new millennium. Despite the Iraq war and its aftermath, several Gulf states, keen to diversify away from their dependence on oil, have begun to take advantage of their region's climate to turn themselves into holiday destinations – and also into a focus for foreign property investment.

Most of the attention has hitherto been concentrated on Dubai, one of the seven emirates that make up the United Arab Emirates (UAE). Although neither the largest nor the richest of the seven, it was the first to open up to foreign buyers in 2002, drawing in billions of pounds of investment as a result. Impressed by Dubai's success, other emirates such as Abu Dhabi and Ras al-Khaimah have begun to follow. Neighbouring Gulf states such as Qatar, Oman and Bahrain are also now getting in on the act.

Dubai

Anybody who thinks eastern European markets are hot should come to sweltering Dubai. This former fishing village turned wannabe desert megalopolis has been experiencing a property boom that takes the breath away. They don't just put up tower blocks in modest ones and twos here – they knock 'em up by the dozen, with armies of Third World labourers toiling around the clock under the blazing sun to finish 70- or 80-storey monsters of glass and concrete in record time. In early 2006, some 75,000 new units were under way or had been completed in Dubai, the most exclusive of them on three palm-shaped islands. Each adds some 38 miles to the shoreline of Dubai, increasing the UAE's beachfront by more than 160 per cent. Then there is the even more spectacular 'The World' – a cluster of 260 islands shaped like all the countries on the planet. Such is the pace of change that a part of the city known as the Old Town is still under construction. And then there are all the architectural superlatives that go with it – the Burj al-Arab, the world's first seven-star hotel; the Burj Dubai, which at a planned 160 storeys will be the world's tallest building when it is completed in 2009; Hydropolis, the world's first luxury underwater hotel, due to be finished in late 2006; and Ski Dubai, a massive snow dome featuring a chairlift, a 25-storey drop and five separate ski slopes up to 400 metres long (no mean feat with temperatures that can hit 48°C in summer), which opened in December 2005. The whole effect is rather 'Hong Kong meets Las Vegas'.

Things began to move in 2002 – aeons ago in Dubai time. Compared to Abu Dhabi to its south, Dubai has only small and dwindling oil reserves, which meant its far-sighted ruler, Sheikh Maktoum bin Rashid al-Maktoum, and the crown prince, his brother Sheikh Mohammed, were acutely aware of the need to find other sources of income. Inspired by Dubai's traditional role as a trading centre on the route between Arabia and the Indian subcontinent, they set out

Dubai Dreams

When looking for property in Dubai, there is one simple rule of thumb: if they have already started building it, then it's probably already sold. That, at least, was how it seemed to Daniel Simpson, a British property consultant at Landmark Properties, one of the emirate's numerous estate agents, whom I met during a visit to the emirate in early 2005, when the boom was at its peak. After a quick tour through a little cluster of pristine show homes, optimistically named the Street of Dreams, we went down to the marina (still under construction) into a large hall dominated by a huge architect's model. Although most of the buildings depicted were still little more than massive concrete skeletons, most of them, too, had been snapped up. 'About a year and a half ago, when one of the developments was released for sale, people queued all night, and they sold 900 houses in seven hours,' said Simpson. 'Things have calmed down a bit. But you still get developments that sell out in a day.'

to turn their emirate into a modern regional business centre. The first move was to create an attractive economic climate: there are no corporate taxes in most sectors, no personal taxes, and no exchange controls on the remittance of profits or repatriation of capital. Tariffs are low, and there are virtually no restrictions on foreign trade, either. Real estate quickly became an important part of the equation. Traditionally, only the locals, who make up fewer than one in five of the population of Dubai, had been able to buy property. But in 2002 the rules were changed to allow foreigners to do so as well. Certain areas, largely to the west of the creek that runs through the middle of the original city, were designated as suitable for foreigners to buy in, and parcels of land handed out to three master developers – Nakheel, Emaar and Dubai Properties. The big three, either on their own or in conjunction with smaller developers, then began to build tens of thousands of villas, apartments and townhouses.

The buyers were not just people from elsewhere in the Gulf, but increasingly from places further afield, such as Britain. In 2004 and into 2005, many projects were bought off-plan in record time; in September 2004, 7,000 villas at Jumeirah Village complex sold out within 24 hours, beating the previous record of 72 hours that it had taken to sell out 2,000 villas on the Palm Jumeirah, a palm-shaped island extending more than four miles into the Arabian Gulf, which developers styled the 'Eighth Wonder of the World'. Anybody who put down a deposit on a property in the early days found it had risen in value by as much as 60 per cent even before it was finished. The speculators had a field day, putting down an initial 10 per cent and selling on a few months later for a handsome profit. Some flats were 'flipped' half a dozen times even before the walls had been plastered. In an attempt to cool the market, some developers responded by levying a transfer fee of up to 7 per cent of the finished price on anybody selling on before completion. If you buy a flat on the 'secondary market', rather than from a developer, part of the price you pay will be the 'premium' – a mark-up of anything from 10–70 per cent of the launch price.

By late 2005, signs of a slow-down were becoming clear, with a growing body of opinion predicting that prices would level out – or perhaps even start to fall back. One of the most prominent doom-sayers has been Sultan Nasser al-Suweidi, the governor of the central bank of UAE, who warned in September that year that asset prices had been rising too rapidly and predicted a downturn for 2006. 'Next year we will have too many housing units, and if we don't take steps it will cause us certain problems,' he said. Several participants at the Cityscape property conference in Dubai the same month also expressed misgivings about possible oversupply. In contrast to other big cities such as New York or London, in Dubai there seems little to stop developers spreading out across the desert and building almost *ad infinitum*, they warned. Indeed, official figures released in early 2006 showed a sharp drop in the number of land deals in the second half of the previous year. Off-plan sales, meanwhile, were getting much harder, with sales incentives of various types becoming common. According to AME Info, a Dubai-based website that carries reports on the property sector, 'the year 2005 was a tale of two markets: re-sale of completed property continued strongly, with prices either holding steady at higher levels, or advancing 10 per cent or more in the case of villas; but off-plan sales slowed considerably, and the first negative premiums emerged on certain developments, such as the Golden Mile on the Palm Jumeirah.'

So how attractive is Dubai to somebody buying now? Although average prices in 2006, at around £2,000 per square metre, were already around three times 2002 levels, many analysts – especially those with a vested interest in the real estate market – see them continuing to rise, albeit not at the hectic levels seen in the past. Authorities have said they would like to achieve long-term stability at rates similar to those in Singapore, which are around twice as high.

The main reason for such optimism is that everyone, it seems, wants to come to Dubai, driving up the demand for housing. Some 100,000 extra people are expected to arrive every year from Europe, elsewhere in the Gulf and the Indian subcontinent, for the foreseeable immediate future. The emirate's population, which was 1 million in 2001, will soon reach 2 million and, at current growth rates, could be 3 million or more by 2010. Proof of this growing demand can be seen from the behaviour of rents, which have been rising in parallel with purchase prices in recent years, jumping an estimated 38 per cent in 2005. An apartment that cost £3,300 a year to rent in 2002 would have commanded £4,800 by early 2006. Yields, as a result, have stayed firm at 8–9 per cent. Another bonus is that rent is paid upfront, in some cases for a year in advance. The continuing high oil prices have also contributed to the buoyant mood. A further boost has come from interest rates, which at 8 per cent compared with general inflation running at 12 per cent are negative in real terms.

Those waiting for a property crash in Dubai could therefore be just as likely to be disappointed as those speculators who bought late into off-plan apartments and still hope to make a quick buck. With so many of the developments ultimately controlled by the Dubai government, there is also unlikely to be any panic dumping of property on the market. Yet there are undoubtedly causes for concern. In an attempt to rein in inflation, the authorities capped rent rises at 15 per cent in 2006, which is likely to feed through into capital values. There is also a large oversupply of property of certain types – mainly middle- to upmarket apartments – due to come on stream in 2007. This is almost certain to exert downward pressure on rents and, at the very least, prevent values from rising much above present levels. For this reason, prices for completed properties looked likely to hold steady during 2006, but with the possibility of some weakness towards the end of the year.

There are other clouds on the horizon. Some developers have found the transition from a 'sell, sell, sell' to a 'deliver, deliver, deliver' market difficult: several developments (including **The Waves** in Dubai Marina) looked set to be completed as much as a year or more behind schedule, while there have been complaints about poor quality at a number of other projects. British residents at Jumeirah Islands, a development of 800 villas and lagoons in the desert, were so angry at 'shoddy workmanship and poor management' that they wrote a letter of complaint to Crown Prince Mohammed, who heads Dubai's biggest property developer, Nakheel, which built the complex. Owners of properties in Dubai Marina, meanwhile, staged a service charge strike in late 2005.

There are other more general economic and political risks, too. The Dubai real estate boom has undoubtedly been helped to a great extent by the strength of oil prices. A sharp fall – although difficult to foresee – could severely cut buying power in the region, and reduce demand among Arab investors. Also important is potential political risk. Many of the world's current troublespots, from Iraq to the West Bank, are uncomfortably close. The atmosphere within Dubai remains surprisingly relaxed, but it would be an understatement to say that not everybody in this part of the world subscribes to western values.

An equally worrying issue, that of title, also continues to hang over the market. Properties in Dubai have always been advertised as freehold, but it was only in March 2006 that legislation was finally passed by the emiate's gvernment making it a reality for foreign buyers. Even so, it remians to be seen how the law is applied in practice

Given the importance of the real estate sector, Dubai authorities are unlikely to do anything to undermine foreigners' property rights. But this lack of a proper functioning land registry has not only had the effect of keeping away some investors; it has also adversely affected the availability of finance, since banks which lend are obliged to rely on bilateral agreements with major developers rather than having recourse to federal law. Despite initial misgivings, several mortgage providers, including Lloyds TSB and HSBC, have now joined local lenders, offering up to 70 per cent loan-to-value. Interest rates in early 2006 were around 6.5 per cent. In most cases, though, it is not possible to shop around for a loan: most projects each have only one bank that will lend on them. There can also be problems for those who buy an off-plan property at a 'premium', since banks have hitherto been prepared to lend only a proportion of the original price set by the developer rather than the actual price at which it changed hands. In an important development, Amlak Finance, a subsidiary of Emaar, one of the main developers, has begun offering loans based on the market value, with others likely to follow. As an alternative to a mortgage, one agency, Dubai Select, in January 2006 announced a new scheme under which it was possible to buy property in stage payments over 15 years.

Off-plan projects typically require an initial 10–15 per cent down-payment, followed by a series of further payments while the building is being constructed. A final payment, typically of 20 per cent, is due once the building has been completed. There are no taxes to pay in Dubai, either when you buy or sell or on rental income (although if you are a British resident, you will remain liable to UK taxes). But the Dubai Lands Department charges 1.5 per cent to register title, with a further 0.25 per cent of the value of the loan for those with a mortgage. Agents can charge commission, usually of around 1 per cent.

Whatever happens to the overall price level, conventional criteria such as location and quality of property will undoubtedly come into play as the market matures. What is on offer varies widely: those with £1 million to spend might want to join David Beckham on the Palm Jumeirah. Here you could buy a six-bed 'Signature Villa' for £1.3 million, although there are also more modest properties on offer: a one-bedroom 1,313-square-foot apartment (property in Dubai is quoted in square feet rather than metres) would cost around £200,000.

Like the **Palm Jumeirah**, the **Palm Jebel Ali**, just down the coast, is built in the shape of a date palm tree and consists of a trunk, a crown with 17 fronds and a surrounding crescent island, but is half as big again and will incorporate six marinas. Its exotic features include more than 1,000 four-bedroom 'Water Homes', positioned 30 feet above the sea between the palm fronds and the crescent, all with mooring for boats. The **Palm Deira** is also under construction. Even more spectacular is **The World**, due to be completed in 2008, offering 260 islands, ranging in size from 250,000 to 900,000 square feet, separated from each other by 300 feet of water.

At the other end of the market is **International City**, a 21,000-unit complex of 'country-themed architecture' featuring a reproduction of Beijing's Forbidden City together with other buildings in English, French, Russian and Moroccan styles. For £35,000, you could pick up a 473-square-foot studio. Set almost six miles back in the desert, it is not quite the stuff of dreams, but properties there certainly seem to be in demand. It is not due for completion until 2007, but prices have risen 50 per cent since launch. The units should also be easy to let, primarily to the less affluent expats coming in from Asia or elsewhere.

Those looking for already completed property should consider the **Springs** and **Meadows** developments, which comprise middle-market houses popular with expat families. Finished in 2005, they have generously sized rooms and excellent standards of finish, although, like many developments in Dubai, they are situated on plots that seem just a little bit too small. A three-bedroom, 2,400-square-foot Spring house would cost around £140,000. A four-bed, 5,800-square-foot mansion in the Meadows would be just over double that. Rental yields for both should be around 8 per cent.

There are many more complexes, details of which can be found by looking at the websites of any of the agents listed below. Your choice will be determined not just by budget and location but also by the completion date. The availability of finance will be important; so, too, will the precise structure of stage payments, which can have an important effect on the bottom line.

Estate Agents

• **Buy in Dubai, www.buyindubai.net**, t 0845 838 1490. A selection of off-plan properties for sale.

- **Dubai Luxury Homes, www.dubailuxuryhomes.com, t** + 971 4 303 9300. A range of properties for sale or rental, with some information.

- **Dubai Property Auctions, www.dubaipropertyauctions.com.** Online auction site allowing you to buy Dubai property.

- **Dubai Property Centre, www.dubaipropertycentre.com.** Portal with property search facility and links to a number of useful different sites.

- **Dubai Property Investment, www.dubai.property-investment.com, t** 0800 031 9018. Useful overview of the various projects on offer, together with market information.

- **Dubai Select, www.dubaiselect.co.uk, t** 0870 111 0000. Off-plan and resale properties for sale and rent, together with some property news.

- **Dubai Waterfront, www.dubaiwaterfront.com, t** + 971 4 321 3344. Off-plan and resale properties for sale, together with detailed guide to the various developments.

- **Edwards & Towers, www.dubaipremier.com, t** 0870 855 5722. Properties for sale and rent plus ancillary services.

- **Key2Dubai, www.key2dubai.co.uk, t** (020) 7749 3630. A selection of new-build properties to buy and rent.

- **Oryx Real Estate, www.oryxrealestate.com, t** + 971 4 351 5770. A selection of new-build properties and market information.

Ras al-Khaimah

Find Dubai a little too brash? Then try Ras al-Khaimah (RAK), the northernmost of the seven emirates, which lies just up the coast. An important maritime and trading centre for at least six centuries, RAK has been somewhat overshadowed by its wealthier neighbours since the discovery of oil in the UAE in the 1960s. Some oil and gas were found in RAK in the 1980s, but its reserves are modest: it has just 0.1 per cent of the UAE's oil and a mere 0.6 per cent of its natural gas. It has nevertheless shared fully in the growth and prosperity of the country; the population more than quadrupled from 44,000 in 1975 to 195,000 in 2003, while GDP rose tenfold from £102 million to £1.1 billion.

With such small energy reserves, RAK needs to diversify even more than Dubai and has seized on tourism, based on its miles of unspoilt coastline, mangrove forests, archaeological ruins, plains and mountains (real ones, that is, rather than the artificial peaks of the Dubai snowdome). The glitz-free Central Business District also bears little resemblance to those of the other emirates.

Its rulers don't just want foreigners to come on holiday; they want them to invest in property, too. In March 2005, the Ras al-Khaimah Real Estate Company was launched with the aim of constructing, selling and letting real estate. In early 2006, 5,000 units were either in the planning stage or under construction.

Sheikh Saud bin Saqr al-Qassimi, RAK's crown prince, has insisted his emirate is not trying merely to copy Dubai. 'The easy part is making land available to developers,' he said in an interview in the *Financial Times* in November 2005. 'The innovation is in bringing new and different products to the market – in our case, everything from luxury mountain lodges to eco-tourism resorts.' This means more upmarket developments and ones that also reflect the need to balance growth with environmental protection. There is also considerable investment in infrastructure: the extension of Emirates Highway 11 to RAK has brought it within an hour's drive of Dubai and two hours of Abu Dhabi. Dubai airport is just 40 minutes away. RAK Airlines, the emirate's own carrier, was due to start flights from Ras al-Khaimah airport in 2006.

Two developments were launched in 2005. The first, **Al-Hamra Village**, offered a total of 1,350 units, a mixture of flats, townhouses and villas with a view over the sea, marina or golf course. Prices started at £42,000 for a 517-square-foot studio and ranged up to £698,000 for a five-bedroom house fit for a (minor) sheikh. The second, **The Cove**, is a smaller and far more exclusive complex of 134 one-, two- and three-bedroom chalets on artificial islands and on the hillside, extending across 50 acres of prime beachfront with private access to the sea. There is also a five-star beach hotel. The resort offers a rental programme giving owners a guaranteed annual return of 7 per cent for three years together with one month of their own use. Other projects in the works include the **Port of Arabia** complex and **Khor Qurm**. There are also plans to build on **Marjan island**.

Despite its claims to modesty, RAK cannot resist the temptation to build some grandiose, Dubai-style projects. Plans were announced in July 2005 to build a massive indoor skiing project, **Desert Snow Village**, which will also be a self-sufficient town for 350,000 residents. The village, due to take around a decade to build, also includes an underwater hotel, monorail and 20-room ice hotel.

In a major plus, RAK does not suffer from the same uncertainties about freehold as Dubai: all ownership titles are registered with the government's Land Department. As in Dubai, though, mortgages are tied to specific projects and were not available on all of them in early 2006.

Estate Agents

Many of the agents which handle Dubai also sell property in RAK.

• **International Property Estates, www.rasalkhaimahproperty.com, t 0870 043 4292. British-based site with information about all the projects and some useful information about RAK.**

Abu Dhabi

The largest and richest of the emirates, Abu Dhabi accounts for 95 per cent of the UAE's oil and natural gas resources (which themselves represent about 9 per cent of the proven oil reserves and 5 per cent of natural gas reserves in the world). With that kind of wealth, its traditional and cautious rulers could be forgiven for sitting back and continuing to pump the stuff out of the ground. But they, too, have grasped the need to prepare for an eventual downturn in oil prices. Abu Dhabi has therefore set up its own airline, Ittihad, is developing its airport and has spent millions of pounds on developing the Emirates Palace, an extravagant seven-star hotel to rival Dubai's Burj al-Arab. It has also followed Dubai into real estate, kick-starting the market with a law announced in August 2005 allowing expatriates to own property on a 99-year lease. The law has paved the way for a number of developments.

Aldar, one of the leading developers, is planning more than 20 projects. The first, **Al-Raha Gardens**, contains a mix of three-bedroom townhouses and five-bedroom villas in a new, purpose-built community including two schools, a polo ground and equestrian facilities. The first phase, with a selection of town-houses ranging between £219,000 and £470,000, was on sale only to UAE nationals. They all went in a few hours. Foreigners were expected to be able to buy into later phases. Another project is **Al-Gurm Resort**, a waterfront resort and residential complex, which was announced in November 2005. The development consists of a 161-room international luxury hotel, together with 59 villas – nine of them on their own private islands. Each will have its own private pool and boat jetty, and some will also have a private beach. Prices range from £1.2 million for a three-bedroom villa to £5.5 million.

Other Gulf States

Oman

Dubai is acting as an inspiration not only for the other emirates; its example is also being followed by other Gulf rulers keen to attract tourists and open up their property sector to foreigners.

Like Dubai, the sultanate of Oman traditionally restricted property ownership to its own nationals. In 2004, a ministerial decree was passed allowing foreigners to buy freehold property there. They can only do so in specially designated areas classified as 'tourism zones', as part of a policy of preventing overdevelopment and maintaining the sultanate's character. A number of developments are being launched, providing golf and beach apartments, townhouses and Arab-style villas. One of the most spectacular is **The Wave**, a £450 million resort project stretching along five miles of virgin beachfront just west of the capital, Muscat. Work began in May 2005, with the first tranche of 200 villas going on sale in 2006. Another is the **Muscat Golf and Country Club**, near Seeb International Airport, offering a mixture of two-bedroom apartments, penthouses and three-, four- and five-bedroom villas. Prices in the project, due for completion in the second quarter of 2006, start at around £140,000.

Qatar

In 2004, Qatar, a gas-rich peninsula jutting out into the Gulf between Bahrain and the United Arab Emirates, also granted foreigners some rights to buy property. Under the decree, issued by the Emir, ownership was restricted to designated areas, namely the Pearl Qatar Island, West Bay Lagoon and Al-Khor developments. It is effectively leasehold rather than freehold, in that non-Qataris are only granted the right of usufruct for a renewable term of 99 years. The **Pearl Qatar**, the first of the developments, is a £1.4 billion man-made island, which is to cover 985 acres of reclaimed land, and will boast luxury hotels and marinas as well as housing for up to 30,000 people. As in Dubai, foreigners who buy property there will be granted permanent residency.

Bahrain

Bahrain, long home to a large western expatriate community, is also getting in on the act, as part of a policy by the ruling Al-Khalifa family of maintaining and building on the kingdom's status as the regional financial hub. In common with the other smaller Gulf states, Bahrain prefers to sell foreign investors land that is reclaimed rather than property on existing *terra firma*. There are five specified locations on the main island, however, where 100 per cent foreign-owned properties can be developed. One of the most ambitious projects is the $1.2 billion **Durrat al-Bahrain** resort city, with high-rise condominiums, two hotels, an exhibition centre, 18-hole golf course and village, shopping mall, marina, a string of other recreational facilities and several beaches. The residential rental property market is driven by demand from expatriates – who make up 40 per cent of the population – only some of whom will want to buy. Local landlords have also benefited from the presence in Bahrain of the US Sixth Fleet.

Estate Agents

- **Browns Properties Bahrain, www.brownspropertiesbahrain.com**, t + 973 177 10450. A selection of properties for sale and rent.
- **Hamptons International, www.hamptons-int.com**, t + 968 563 557. A small choice of property in Oman available for purchase by foreigners.
- **Oman Homes, www.omanhomes.com**, t + 68 244 88087. A large range of property for sale and rent.

Egypt

With a population of 78 million, Egypt is one of the most populous countries in the Middle East. It also has considerable tourist potential, from the majesty of the pyramids of Giza to the beauty of the Sinai Desert and the Red Sea resorts of Sharm el-Sheikh and Hurghada. Around 8 million people now visit the country every year (around 500,000 of them from Britain) and the numbers are increasing steadily. The country is also of interest to the foreign investor: prices are rising fast, rental yields are good and the tax environment is extremely favourable. By early 2006, mortgages were still difficult to obtain and the rates unattractive, but that is expected to change. In the meantime, a number of off-plan projects in resort areas aimed at foreigners offer payment by instalment: typically, you will pay for the property in a series of quarterly payments over three years; the building will be finished some time in the middle, meaning you advance the developer some money during the first few months, but they then effectively offer you an interest-free loan after completion.

Given the Egyptian government's appreciation of the importance of foreign investment and of the tourist industry, the future prospects for the property market look good. The only real question mark hanging over the country is political. Although one of the few countries in the region to hold elections, Egypt is not a democracy in the western sense of the word and, as in Morocco, there are clear indications of simmering dissent, increasingly of a militant Islamic nature, below the surface. The country has also had several terrorist outrages; the most recent, at the time of writing, was in July 2005, when 64 people, including several Britons, were killed in Sharm el-Sheikh by three bombs which exploded in a co-ordinated attack on hotels and shopping areas.

Sharm el-Sheikh and the Sinai

As recently as the early 1990s, Sharm el-Sheikh was little more than a small collection of hotels on the southernmost tip of the Sinai peninsula, of interest primarily to divers drawn by its crystal-clear water, rare coral and incredible variety of exotic fish. In recent years it has developed into a large resort, catering not just for tourists but also for the international conference trade. Although some people find Sharm soulless, the climate is attractive and the diving is still good, despite continuing fears of the effects of excessive development.

Sharm, together with Dahaba, Nuweiba and Taba, further up the coast, also provides a jumping off point for the Sinai desert, which has been fully under Egyptian control since 1982. The desert, rich in Biblical sites, is a delight to explore, either by 4x4 or, at a more leisurely pace, on camelback. Of specific interest are Mount Sinai and the nearby St Katherine's monastery, home to an order of Greek Orthodox monks founded in the 4th century AD. Sharm has its own airport, with a growing number of direct flights from European cities. London is around five hours away.

Sharm is not actually a single town, but rather a series of bays nestling between mountains. Most famous and developed is Na'ama, where hotel, resorts and diving centres first set up shop in the early 1980s. With its numerous beachside cafés and restaurants and vibrant nightlife, it is always bustling. About four miles north is Sharks Bay, which is quieter and (so far, at least) less developed.

Prices have been increasing by an average 15 per cent annually – albeit from a low base – with even sharper rises in some places. Rental yields are also good and may reach double figures, thanks to the long rental season; the resort really does boast year-round sunshine; even in December and January temperatures can still be up to 25°C, making it an attractive winter getaway. In early 2006, apartments were available for as little as £500 per square metre; a small studio could cost as little as £15,000. For £250,000 you could buy a luxury 230-square-metre, four-bedroom, three-bath villa with two reception rooms and pool.

Hurghada

Once a remote sleepy fishing village, Hurghada, on the Red Sea coast of Egypt proper, has been transformed in recent years into a vibrant, lively and busy beachside resort town. It offers an attractive mixture of the old and the new: **Sekala** and the tourist district south of it have exclusive upmarket hotels, while **El-Dahar** is rich in the sights, smells and sounds of everyday Egyptian life. Nearby is **El-Gouna**, the largest privately owned destination in Egypt. A perfect holiday resort, it is also an exclusive residential area, offering all the services and infrastructure needed for long-term stays. Many of its villas and apartments have lagoon and sea views; the lively **Abu Tig Marina**, harbouring yachts and sailing boats, offers elegant shops, restaurants and bars. An 18-hole golf course, a hospital and an international school are available.

Estate Agents

- **Coldwell Banker, www.coldwellbanker-eg.com, t** + 202 522 22 55.
Properties for sale and rent in Cairo, Alexandria, Giza and Sharm el-Sheikh.

- **Red Sea Property Services, www.redseapropertyservices.co.uk**. A variety of properties for sale in Sharm el-Sheikh and surrounding areas.

- **Sinai Real Estate Services, www.sinairealestate.com**. Agency offering a range of properties to buy and rent in Sharm el-Sheikh.

Jordan

If you want to be really ahead of the pack, then try Jordan. Property prices have been surging there since the American invasion of neighbouring Iraq in 2003, thanks to the billions of dollars being poured into the reconstruction of the country. Because of the continuing security problems in Baghdad and other Iraqi cities, contractors, businessmen and people working for multinational organisations have used Amman, the once sleepy Jordanian capital, as a base for their operations. Anything from 200,000 to half a million Iraqis have moved to Jordan while they wait for home to improve; some have bought property, while others are renting, providing a boost for the lettings market. Amman has also been helped by signs of political instability in Damascus and Beirut, its traditional rivals, which have boosted hopes among Jordanians that their city could take over as a regional centre. The process has been helped by the liberalisation and modernisation of Jordan's once state-controlled economy and by new laws on investment, which have made the kingdom an attractive place for Gulf investors flush with cash from the long run of high oil prices. It is now possible for non-Jordanians to buy real estate, although they still have to seek permission from the authorities. This can now come through in 10 days, though (it used to take a month). Foreign buyers are required to hold property for at least three years before they are allowed to sell it on. Mortgages are also increasingly available, with rates of 7.5–8.5 per cent and terms of 20 years. The banks' main target is Jordanians, but it may be possible for foreigners to borrow.

Both apartments and land in **Amman**, a sprawling city of 1.5 million spread over 19 hills, have notched up annual increases of well over 20 per cent since 2003, and a construction boom is under way as developers move to satisfy the demand. Prices in the city look set to rise further, not least because they are still well below levels in Damascus and Beirut. Perversely, the only real threat to the market would be the sudden outbreak of peace in Iraq, which would obviate the need for Amman as a stepping stone to the country. A new three-bedroom, two-bathroom apartment in a middle-class area of Amman now goes for about £70,000–80,000, while a four-bedroom apartment should cost £90,0000. Boosted by the influx of foreigners, rental yields in affluent parts of the city such as Abdoun, Deir Ghbar, Sweifi eh, Rabia and Jabal Amman were around 10–15 per cent in early 2006.

Investment, meanwhile, is also pouring into the Red Sea resort of **Aqaba**, which lies at the point where Israel, Jordan and Egypt meet. The Jordanian government is keen to turn the town into its own version of Sharm el-Sheikh and in 2000 designated it a special economic zone, with tax breaks and other incentives for potential investors. The zone process got off to a slow start, however: first came the Palestinian *intifada* (uprising), then the September 11 2001, attacks on America and finally the invasion of Iraq – none of which did tourism in the region any favours. Foreign visitors are returning, however, while more than £1 billion has been earmarked for five-star hotels, shopping malls and entertainment complexes in the resort. An important role is being played by two major residential complexes, **Tala Bay**, the first phase of which was completed in 2005, and **Ayla Oasis**, still at the planning stage, both of which are being marketed to European buyers alongside Jordanians and buyers from the Gulf. Prices are low by regional standards: apartments go from around £600 per square metre, making a basic 60-square-metre apartment just £36,000. Villas are around £1,500 per square metre. The Aqaba development corporation is making efforts to market the resort as a short break destination from Britain and other European countries.

Estate Agents

- **Abdoun Real Estate, www.abdoun.com.jo, t** + 962 6 592 0605. Property for sale and rent in Amman and elsewhere in the country.
- **Amra Real Estate, www.amrajordan.com, t** + 962 6 585 8563. Property for sale and rent in Amman.

Morocco

Think Britons in Morocco and the image that has traditionally come to mind is of Sebastian Flyte, from Evelyn Waugh's novel *Brideshead Revisited*, stumbling from one drinking den to another. Although still retaining many of the exotic charms that drew Flyte, Morocco has emerged in the last few years as a tempting destination for a very different kind of visitor: the property investor.

Despite its location on the northwestern tip of Africa, Morocco has a climate, geography and history linked as much to Mediterranean Europe as to the rest of Africa. In the north, the fine beaches, lush highland valleys and evocative old cities reinforce this Mediterranean impression. But leave the coast behind and you are plunged into a different culture and a landscape with spectacular mountains and the empty wilderness of the Sahara. The average summer temperature along the coast is 29°C; the period between October and April is slightly cooler, providing welcome winter sun.

High-profile figures such as Sir Richard Branson, the Rolling Stones and Malcolm Forbes have blazed the trail to Morocco, while other enterprising buyers started acquiring *riads*, traditional houses with interior gardens, in Marrakech (also written Marrakesh). The number of smart British estate agents that have set up shop in the city shows how foreign buying interest is growing. Casablanca, by contrast, has so far been considered too industrial, and Tangier too seedy, but they too may soon take off. The focus is also turning towards both the Atlantic and Mediterranean coasts. The country's property market is poised to enter a new phase, with growing numbers of apartment and villa projects targeted directly at foreign buyers. Morocco is being portrayed as 'the new Spain' – the climate is similar to that of the Costa del Sol, while prices are only a third to a half those on the north side of the Straits of Gibraltar.

The boom is underpinned by a realisation by Moroccan authorities of the benefits of tourism. Under a strategy named 'Vision 2010', the government is building new roads, developing regional airports and creating six new coastal resorts, with the aim of creating 600,000 new jobs in the tourist industry and boosting visitor numbers from 2 million to 10 million a year by the beginning of the next decade. The strategy appears to be working: tourist numbers in the first seven months of 2005 were up 19 per cent on the year before; the number of Britons rose 46 per cent. A further boost is expected from the 'open-skies' agreement which Morocco signed with the European Union in December 2005, liberalising air travel between Europe and Morocco. The country already has its own low-cost carrier, Atlas Blue, which began flying to Gatwick and several other European airports in 2004. EasyJet was due to join them in July 2006 with daily flights to Marrakech.

As part of its plans, the Moroccan government has come up with a series of tax concessions for foreign buyers: rent is tax-free for the first five years; no capital gains tax is levied on profits under £40,000 (and set at 20 per cent there-after, dropping to zero after 10 years); the proceeds of sale can be repatriated to the UK; and there is no inheritance tax to pay if the property is passed on to another family member. Mortgages are also becoming available for foreigners – although not normally for more than 60 per cent loan-to-value, with interest rates in early 2006 about 8 per cent. The payment structures for off-plan developments are fairly advantageous and dovetail neatly with the mortgages; normally a maximum of 40 per cent must be paid as an initial deposit and during the course of the construction, with the remainder due on completion.

In theory, buying procedures are simple and straightforward and similar to those in France, with all transactions overseen by *notaires* (notaries). Expect to pay about 2 per cent of the purchase price to the *notaire* and a further 3–4 per cent on land registration fees, stamp duties and other small expenses. You should not run into title problems when buying in new developments, but matters may become more complicated with second-hand property. Some old properties may simply not have been registered at all; inheritance rules, under which property is automatically shared between children, could complicate the process of securing the agreement of all the existing owners.

Morocco is a Muslim country and, despite the keenness of authorities to attract foreign investment, the threat of militant Islam is never far away. Morocco has also been a target for violence; in this case, a series of suicide bombing in Casablanca in May 2003 that killed 45 people. Although the country has appeared calm since, poverty and high unemployment providing a breeding ground for discontent among the young.

Marrakech

Marrakech, with its historic *médina* (Old Town), in the southwest of the country in the foothills of the Atlas mountains, is a magical place. Jema el-Fna, the main square, comes alive at night with its musicians, dancers and fire-eaters, and in the nearby *souks* (or markets) you can buy anything from spices and shoes to teapots and tagines. On the property front, Marrakech is best known for its *riads*. Over the last decade, more than 650 *riads* and palaces in the *médina* have been bought up by foreigners, initially mostly French, although with the Italians and British following hot on their heels. Prices have soared, both for properties in their original state and modernised ones. Although it should still be possible to buy a basic renovated *riad* for £200,000, you could pay more than double that; they are popular with tourists looking for the authentic Marrakech experience, and the rental market is good. More conventional apartments can be a lot cheaper, at around £300–400 per square metre. The Marrakech suburbs may also be an attractive alternative for those keen to escape both the tourists and the touts who cling, limpet-like, to their forearms, although the market for short-term rentals may not be so good.

The Coast

Developments so far targeted at foreign buyers have been on Morocco's long Atlantic coast stretching from Tangier in the north, down through Essaouira, to Agadir, and on the shorter Mediterranean coast, extending eastwards past the Spanish enclaves of Ceuta and Melilla towards the Algerian border.

One of the biggest complexes being developed is at Saidia on the eastern edge of the Mediterranean coast. Known as **Mediterrania Saidia**, it is composed largely of low-density, low-rise buildings and boasts a 750-berth marina, three 18-hole golf courses and various other facilities, including an aquapark, cinema complex and commercial centre. Sold off-plan, air-conditioned two-bedroom, two-bathroom apartments start at around £100,000; large three-bedroom villas with sea views are priced from £180,000. An alternative is the Playa Vista resort in the Tétouan area, 45 miles southeast of Tangiers and near the Cabo Negro golf course, where two-bedroom apartments start at around £45,000. The developers claim they can be let for £60 a night during high season, with high occupancy rates, which should give a double-digit yield.

Second-hand apartments can be substantially cheaper: in **Essaouira**, an ancient fishing port, it is possible to buy two-bedroom flats closer to the beach for as little as £17,000, or a large villa with sea view for £150,000. The Atlantic coast can be windy, though, and many of the *riads* and apartments on sale need major renovation. Don't underestimate the amount of time and money needed to organise this at a distance.

Estate Agents

- **Bab Menara, www.bamenara.com**, t + 212 44 42 25 70. Property for sale and rent in Marrakech and Essaouira.

- **Karimo, www.karimo.net/en/index.html**, t + 212 44 42 01 13. A wide selection of flats, villas and *riads* in Marrakech and the coastal resort of Essaouira for sale and rent.

- **Marrak Villas, www.marrakvillas.com**, t (01666) 861 049. A small selection of luxury properties in Marrakech for sale and rent.

- **Mauresque Immobilier, www.mauresque-immobilier.com/en**, t + 212 6000 6666. Several hundred *riads*, together with villas and land.

- **Morocco Property, www.morocco-property.com, t + 34 695 059 468.** A range of new developments, largely on the Mediterranean coast.

- **Ryad Plus, www.riad-plus.com, t + 212 44 42 73 82.** *Riads*, apartments and villas for sale in Marrakech, Essaouira, Tangier, Agadir and Fez.

- **Superior Worldwide, www.morocco.superiorworldwide.com, t 0870 750 4488.** Off-plan apartments and villas for sale.

Thailand

The only southeast Asian country never colonised by a European power, Thailand is a fascinating blend of the ancient and the hyper-modern, where saffron-robed monks walk barefoot past glistening skyscrapers and ornate temples are tucked away beside eight-lane highways. With its amazing coastline, exciting cuisine and friendly people, it has long been the region's most popular destination for western tourists; the population of 80 million is joined every year by millions more visitors from abroad. Once seen as a destination for backpackers, it has also moved upmarket; the cafés selling banana pancakes and all-day breakfasts have been joined by luxurious hotels and beach resorts.

Some of those who have been to Thailand on holiday over the years have since returned in search of a place of their own. The first foreign buyers were predominantly expatriates based either in Bangkok or in other regional hubs such as Hong Kong, Kuala Lumpur or Singapore, looking for holiday homes. Recently, they have been joined by people from Britain and other places further afield who have acquired condominiums and villas that they can use them-selves but which are also good investments.

Like other countries in the region, Thailand was hit hard by the Asian economic crisis of 1997 and 1998, although property prices stalled rather than collapsed. By 2003 the economy had bounced back with a vengeance and people started buying and selling again. Property prices in the most popular locations have been growing at an average 30 per cent a year since, despite a temporary blow to tourism from the 2004 Boxing Day tsunami. In a sign of growing confidence, international fund managers have begun moving in.

For the fly-to-let investor, Thailand is attractive not only because of the expectation of further rises in prices but also because of the high running yields available; it should be possible to earn at least 12 per cent a year on your investment, thanks to a rental season in the tropics that lasts for almost 52 weeks a year. The resort rental market in Thailand is extremely robust: potential customers come from Britain and Europe and from expat hotspots in China, Japan and across southeastern Asia. Many people travelling to and from Australia also stop off en route in Thailand for a beach break.

Buying costs are relatively low, and should add the equivalent of up to no more than 5 per cent of the purchase price. There is also a 12.5 per cent tax on rental income. Foreign individuals can only buy leaseholds; to acquire the freehold you must set up a Thai limited company. This is straightforward; in fact, most good real estate lawyers will set up a company for you as part of the conveyancing process. Choosing this path also means you can avoid inheritance tax and capital gains tax, which starts at 25 per cent for private buyers. When the time comes to sell your property, it is simply the company that is sold. The annual running costs of a company will be £300–500, but the tax advantages will be far greater. More sophisticated investors seeking an extra layer of security will set up an offshore company (typically in the British Virgin Islands) which will in turn own the Thai company. It is this offshore company that then changes hands. Temporary visitor visas of one month are granted to most nationalities on arrival in Thailand, although it is also possible for foreigners to apply for one-year multi-entry non-immigrant visas. Rules are relaxed for the over-50s as a way of persuading foreigners to choose Thailand to retire in.

Finance has traditionally been difficult to obtain, but at least one bank, the Bangkok Bank, is ready to lend to non-resident foreigners, offering up to 70 per cent loan-to-value in US or Singapore dollars and an interest rate that in early 2006 stood at 6.25 per cent. It also offers mortgages for off-plan property purchases, but will release the funds only once construction has reached the point when the roof is put on the building. Savvy developers are structuring their stage payments accordingly, so only 30 per cent has to be paid before the 'roof on' point is reached. The repayment period is so far limited to 10 years, but given the high yields available it should still be possible to earn enough in rent to cover the mortgage repayments.

Thailand covers about 197,000 square miles, roughly double the size of the United Kingdom. It is divided into four distinct areas: the mountainous north, which includes the city of Chiang Mai; the fertile central plains, with the capital, Bangkok, a bustling city of 6 million people, and the vibrant resort of Pattaya; the semi-arid plateau of the northeast; and the peninsular south, with its many beautiful tropical beaches and the resort islands of Phuket and Koh Samui.

Phuket

Phuket, set in the blue waters of the Andaman Sea an hour by air from Bangkok, is Thailand's largest island, boasting swaying palm trees and beautiful beaches. For almost four decades it has also been one of the most popular tourist destinations in southeast Asia, attracting an average of 3 million visitors each year. The tsunami took its toll, and in its immediate aftermath tourism dropped sharply, with some hotels reporting occupancy rates as low as 10 per cent. Despite the tragic loss of life, the damage to property and infrastructure was not that great, however, and property prices did not ultimately suffer much. The tourists began to return in the second half of 2005, and there was a further boost towards the end of the year, with the resumption of and even an increase in the number of flights from Asian-Pacific and European cities. Beachfronts and businesses have since been rebuilt, land prices continue increasing at pre-tsunami levels, developers have continued their projects, and people are still buying property. In a report in 2005 on the Phuket property market, post-tsunami, CB Richard Ellis (Thailand) Co. Ltd. found it had been remarkably resilient, with projects already under way closing sales without discounting. 'We believe the reason customers are actively proceeding with acquisition is that they believe that Phuket's residential property market is in the early stages of a long-term growth curve,' said chairman David Simister.

The island offers a wide variety of properties, from luxurious condominiums to basic beachfront dwellings. Land is in short supply; the west and south coasts of the island are relatively well developed, especially the beachfronts, which bodes well for future capital growth of existing property. New developers have therefore had increasingly to go inland in search of hillside sites with sea views.

The challenge for authorities is to prevent Phuket from being swamped by low-cost, low-quality developers. The first warning signs have already appeared: in August 2004, around 12 per cent of the homes on sale were flats; by early 2006, the figure had risen to 26 per cent. The government is nevertheless taking action: since the tsunami, all new construction has been banned within 200 metres of Phuket's high-water mark, even though plenty of existing homes are much closer. Schemes of 90 homes or more must undertake rigorous 'environ-mental impact studies' before getting planning consent to deter Spanish-style overdevelopment. Height restrictions, meanwhile, prevent developers from building above three storeys, which means that, as land prices increase, only the more professional, well-funded ones can remain in business.

Around half the mid- to upper-end second homes – that is, those priced at £250,000 or more – are bought by Hong Kong, Chinese and British buyers, with Europeans, Australians and Americans accounting for the rest. Although Thailand has traditionally appealed to the young, it is also becoming popular as a retirement location. One development at Kamala beach launched in 2005 was aimed specifically at the over-50s, who, as discussed above, benefit from a more flexible visa regime. One- and two-bedroom bungalows and apartments start at around £80,000, while a three-bedroom, two-bathroom, two-storey house could cost £175,000. Apartments in luxurious new condominium developments go for around £160,000, while a high-end villa with three or four bedrooms and a private pool and sea view will fetch from £500,000 right up to £1 million. Some super-luxury villas on the market are even selling at over £2 million.

Further enhancing Phuket's growing status as a destination for the well-heeled, there is now a Marriott Resort; Grand Hyatt Resorts have just purchased land; and there are already three professional golf courses and a marina. Two more marinas and a casino are also planned.

Koh Samui

Unknown just a decade ago, Koh Samui now rivals Phuket as Thailand's most popular island resort. Situated off the east coast on the other side of the Gulf, it is accessible by air, car and passenger ferry from Surat Thani on the mainland. With its quiet beaches of powdery white sand and sparkling blue waters and its lush green hinterland of coconut plantations and rice paddies, it is an ideal place to relax in the sun. There are several smaller islands dotted offshore, where you can find some of the best dive sites in the world.

Chaweng Beach, the main resort on the island, on the east coast, offers shopping, a wide selection of restaurants and lively nightlife, while the villages of **Bophut**, on the north tip, and **Lamai**, on the east side, are becoming increasingly popular with tourists and expats. There is a marina under construction on the north of the island near to Bophut, and plans for a new airport in the southwest have been approved so that the island can receive large passenger jets from Europe (the current airport is almost at capacity). Samui is now home to numerous, stunning five-star resorts and some of the world's finest boutique hotels. The region's first six-star hotel, the Evason Samui Hideaway, opened in 2004. Indeed, for its fans, Samui is well on the way to becoming the Monte-Carlo of the east.

In the early years of the new millennium, prices were surging ahead at 30–40 per cent a year, buoyed by interest from Hong Kong and from Australian and European investors based in Singapore. Growth has since slowed to an annual 20 per cent or 25 per cent for exceptionally well-located or especially well-designed properties. The northeast tip of the island is still the most popular area with buyers, because of its natural beauty, established infrastructure and proximity to the island's main amenities. But interest in the south is growing, thanks to its unspoilt feel away from the traffic and mass of tourists. South of Lamai there is much coastal land yet to be developed, which is of potential interest to the shrewd investor looking for capital gains.

A variety of properties is on offer, ranging from homes directly on the beach, with the waves lapping the sand a few feet from the verandah, to those located up on the hills with spectacular views of turquoise seas through coconut palms. It is possible to pick up a two-bedroom, 100-square-metre apartment with a sea view for under £100,000 or a two- or three-bedroom house near the beach for £180,000. At the other end of the scale, a luxurious 600-square-metre, new-build, four-bedroom, three-bathroom villa with pool, sea view and 800 square metres of land could cost more than £1 million.

Pattaya

The most established of all the Thai beach resorts and only two hours' drive from Bangkok, Pattaya was always known as a big, brash tourist mecca, attracting up to 5 million visitors a year in search of sun, sand and fun. Little more than a remote fishing village during the 1960s, it has grown spectacularly since: the long, sandy beaches of its half-moon bay are littered with restaurants, bars and discotheques and the sea is churned by speedboats and jet skis. It also boasts an extraordinarily sleazy red light district, which grew up in the 1960s and '70s to cater for American soldiers and airmen fighting the Vietnam War and which has been going from strength to strength since.

Pattaya has done much to shake off this negative image, with a raft of higher-end resorts and more sophisticated restaurants. There is also some very cool and contemporary real estate on offer. The resort's location a mere £25 cab ride from Bangkok has encouraged expats working in the capital to purchase property in the area and spend holidays and weekends relaxing on its many tropical beaches. The transition to a family holiday destination has been good news for both property and land prices, which have been rising at an annual 20 per cent. From a place that many would keep at arm's length, Pattaya is rapidly turning into the country's hottest property market.

Property in Pattaya has long been much cheaper than in Phuket and Koh Samui, but the eastern coast is undergoing a massive regeneration, with new shopping centres, a cinema complex and several golf courses within easy reach. Pattaya has received a further boost from the construction of the new Suvarnabhumi international airport, due to open in 2006, from which it is just an hour away. Plans to extend the Sky Train service to the resort could cut the journey time between the two to just 20 minutes.

There was relatively little new building in the second half of the 1990s and early years of the new millennium, leading to a limited supply of upmarket new properties. A number of new projects began to come on stream in late 2004, with more to follow. The most promising area for city residential projects is the stretch of coast between Pattaya Beach and Jomtien Beach. Resort-style developments are concentrated between the Ambassador Jomtien Hotel and Bang Sarey, where the quiet beachfront location ensures privacy for residents. One of the largest of the new schemes is **The Sails**, a 43-floor condominium tower with 151 apartments, which will share its site on outer Jomtien near Ocean Marina with a luxury hotel. It also boasts its own 100-square-metre stretch of beach. It is due to be completed towards the end of 2007.

Although apartments in The Sails and other upmarket developments start at more than £1,000 per square metre, it is still possible to pick up a second-hand 30–40-square-metre studio near Jomtien Beach with a sea view and use of a communal pool for as little as £15,000–20,000. A top of the range 470-square-metre, four-bedroom, four-bathroom villa with separate maid's quarters and pool in one of the more exclusive districts could set you back closer to £300,000.

Krabi

Two hours' drive from Phuket, Krabi offers a mixture of mountains, river valleys and tropical beaches, which provide stunning panoramas and plenty of activities for tourists and residents. The province of Krabi also includes more than 130 islands in the Andaman Sea, including **Koh Lanta** and **Koh Phi Phi** (the backdrop for the film version of Alex Garland's *The Beach*, starring Leonardo di Caprio). Far less developed than Phuket, Krabi has so far attracted tourists and home-buyers looking for relaxation rather than wild nightlife. Planners are trying to keep it that way, with carefully crafted plans for sustainable development, although the opening of a new international airport with flights to Hong Kong in October 2006 will substantially boost tourist numbers and property and land prices.

The largest resort project so far seen in the province is **The Cove** at Krabi on the mainland beach of Haad Yao. The first of many such large-scale schemes, it is being managed by the Marriott hotel group. Land prices increased more than twofold during 2005, with a likely knock-on effect on property prices. The largest group of investors is once again European and Australian expats living in the financial centres of southeast Asia, many of whom made considerable money buying and 'flipping' property in Phuket and then Samui. They are clearly confident Krabi will do the same thing for them. There is already a Sheraton resort, and other high-end hotel chains are also looking for a share of the action.

Hua Hin

The oldest Thai beach resort, Hua Hin was the original destination for royalty and jet-setters, who would escape from Bangkok's heat every summer on a procession of elephants. Its status was further enhanced in the 1920s with the arrival of the railway and the building of Thailand's first hotel. The country's first golf course was laid out here in 1926; two years later, King Rama VII built his Klai Kangwon Palace, which is still an official royal residence. Located a three-hour drive from Bangkok, it has remained a place for wealthy Thais to have their holiday homes, and the nightlife and general atmosphere are far less rowdy than some other resorts.

Hua Hin is very much on the regional investor's radar at the moment, as the present King of Thailand has chosen to live there permanently. The government is also building a new highway which will cut the travelling time to Bangkok to just over one and a half hours. The speculators are moving in. The beachfront is more built up than some of the islands in the south, but the hotels and resorts are truly world-class – Hua Hin is home to numerous five-star resorts including Hilton, Dusit Thani, Grand Hyatt and the famous Chiva Som Spa. This is a place that is all about fine dining and pampering.

Bangkok

Prices in Bangkok have been rising steeply since 2003. Probably of most interest to foreign investors are Sukhumvit, Silom, Sathorn and other parts of the Central Business District where most expats live and work.

With its high-rise apartments and air-conditioned shopping centres, stylish boutiques and restaurants, Sukumvit epitomises modern Bangkok. Many embassies and the headquarters of financial institutions lie along the Sathorn Road. The Silom Road has the head offices of local banks, law firms and multi-nationals. Count on spending at least £100,000 for a reasonable property. Yields should more than cover borrowing costs, and substantial capital gains are likely.

The Bangkok market is extremely buoyant at the moment, as many Thai nationals who could not previously afford to buy are now climbing on the property ladder, fuelling movement right the way up the scale. The rapid rise in oil prices in 2005 made many developers nervous about the knock-on effect on building costs, which it is feared may increase by 20–30 per cent. Any large scale projects already under way, such as the prestigious Watermark development, are on a fixed-price construction contract, however, and so will provide the investor with 20–30 per cent of additional equity on completion.

Estate Agents

- **Bangkok Property, www.bangkokproperty.com, t** + 66 19 86 31 38. Property for sale and rent in Bangkok.

- **Claire Brown Realty, www.clairebrownrealty.com, t** (07967) 258 121. A selection of property in Phuket, Koh Samui and Krabi, together with useful market information.

- **East Coast Real Estate, www.thaiproperty.com, t** + 66 38 72 36 15. A selection of property in Pattaya and the surrounding area.

- **Exclusive Homes, www.exclusivehomes-phuket.com, t** + 66 76 26 44 91. A wide choice of properties for sale in Phuket and the surrounding area.

- **Holt Realty, www.holt-realty.com, t** + 66 26 93 41 46. A wide range of properties across the country, coupled with useful information on the market and buying procedures.

- **Ko Samui Properties, www.kosamuiproperties.com, t** + 66 77 41 36 24. A range of new-build and existing properties on the island.

- **Pattaya Properties, www.pattayaproperties.com, t** + 66 38 30 35 15. A selection largely of off-plan properties, together with some useful information.

- **Pattaya Property Finder, www.pattayapropertyfinder.com, t** + 66 38 30 10 90. A wide choice of flats and houses for sale and rent.

- **Phukethouse, www.phukethouse.biz, t** + 66 10 81 29 26. A variety of new-build and second-hand properties for sale in Phuket.

- **Town & Country Property, www.townandcountryproperty.com, t** + 66 38 37 41 36. A range of property in Pattaya and along the eastern seaboard.

Turkey

Of the many countries vying to become the 'new Spain', Turkey, with its 5,000 miles of coast and 300 sunny days a year, has one of the strongest claims to the title. Situated at the crossroads between Europe, Asia and the Middle East, it has been a popular tourist destination for several decades, drawing as many as 14 million visitors a year. Its array of beaches puts the Spanish *costas* to shame; the Aegean offers some of the best sailing in Europe, while the interior boasts skiing and some highly exotic landscapes. The country also has more ancient sites than Italy or Greece.

Since 2002, when a ban was lifted on purchases by foreigners, Turkey has also become an attractive destination for people looking both for holiday homes and somewhere to retire; hitherto sleepy fishing towns are being transformed into bustling resorts as developers move in to satisfy the demand from British and other international buyers. According to research published in 2005 by Pega, an Istanbul-based property services company, 12,000 properties were sold to foreigners over the preceding two years. International home-buyers now account for nearly half of all foreign investment in the country.

One of the main reasons is affordability: although prices in some resorts doubled between 2002 and 2005, they still have a long way to go before they reach Spanish levels. Expectations of further capital gains makes the country doubly attractive to people buying property not only for their own use, but also as an investment. Much of the Aegean and Mediterranean coast is of interest to the fly-to-let investor. Istanbul, the country's commercial (but not political) capital, also has potential; an apartment or house could be a long-term let or be let to tourists by the night or by the week.

A further boost has been given by the European Union's decision in October 2005 to open membership talks with Turkey. It could be as late as 2015 before the country actually joins, but in the meantime the economic and legal reforms required to prepare for membership should make Turkey a more attractive place in which to invest. The fall in inflation, running at an annual 90 per cent at the beginning of the millennium, to reasonable levels, coupled with the stabilisation of the Turkish lira, have also helped. (A currency reform at the beginning of 2005 which turned 1 million liras into one lira gave a psychological boost, too.) Indeed, the real estate market appears to have become caught up in a virtuous circle: reform of Turkey's banking sector has attracted foreign financial institutions, which has in turn encouraged global developers to move in.

Despite the hype, bear in mind that the tourist season is relatively short – you can count on around 14–16 weeks in a coastal resort, compared with 20–25 weeks in Spain. Although temperatures across the country will be in the 30s from June to October, they fall back quite sharply in the winter. In Bodrum and Marmaris, on the Aegean coast, it can average 10°C in January and February (only three degrees warmer than in London). The Mediterranean coast in the south is warmer, but even in Antalya, for example, it is an average 15°C in winter.

This does not necessarily make Turkey a worse bet: although the rent you will be able to charge per week will slightly lower than the Spanish equivalent, the purchase price will be considerably less. Given the speed with which prices are rising, there is also far more scope for capital gain. To be conservative, count on letting a flat or villa by the coast for around 12 weeks a year, which could realistically give a yield of around 5 per cent. A flat in Istanbul will not be so dependent on the weather, and, if you are letting it short-term to tourists, you should be able to keep it filled for as much as 35 weeks a year.

The usual rules apply for choosing a property that you are planning to let out to foreigners: it should ideally be pretty, near shops, restaurants and ideally a golf course and, if possible, within an hour's drive of an airport. If you are buying an apartment, make sure you do so in a complex with a pool. A decent-sized pool will also make a villa much more lettable, especially if you are targeting the family market. Officially, owners are required to register their property with tourist authorities if they want to let it, but many ignore this.

Most people buy as individuals, although to do this one must obtain permission from the military. This should only be a formality, unless you are buying in an area deemed to be of military significance. (The definition of this can be wide; it may be in a strategically sensitive position overlooking Greece or the Greek islands or simply too close to an admiral's back garden.) The alternative is to set up a Turkish company and buy the property through that, which should be fairly cheap and easy to do.

In a curious development, foreigners were barred from completing purchases in 2005 when the country's title deeds legislation was suspended after being challenged in the constitutional court. This did not prevent people from continuing to shop for property and start payments on off-plan projects, but they were unable to register their ownership. In January 2006, President Ahmet Necdet Sezer approved a new law allowing them to buy again.

Such hiccups confirm the impression that the Turkish property market is not for the faint-hearted. Jones Lang LaSalle's global real-estate transparency index rates it as 'opaque', with poor supply-and-demand data, weak title and corrupt practices – so having access to good impartial advice before jumping in is all the more important. Projects are often begun without proper planning permission by developers who expect that, when it comes to the crunch, the authorities will cave in. This is often but not always the case, which can prove a problem if you have been dutifully making your stage payments all the way along. You should check the paperwork – or, better, have it checked by a Turkish lawyer or one familiar with the country – to ensure you are not caught in this way.

Many Turkish vendors also deliberately under-declare the value of the sale and demand a substantial proportion in cash. This is not just the case with private sales. Large-scale developers often do the same – prompting suspicions that the Turkish property market, like that of Spain before it, is being used by organised crime as a means of laundering money. Many agents selling to British buyers appear all too happy to go along with the irregularities. As a buyer, this can put you in a difficult position. However much you may be told that 'everybody does it', the practice is illegal. Also, although it may save the seller a lot of money, there is very little in it for you: as a buyer you are liable for only half the 3 per cent property transfer tax – in other words, declaring a £200,000 home as worth just £100,000 will save you a mere £1,500. Any such saving will be easily outweighed by the extra capital gains tax that you will have to pay on the artificial gain when you come to sell (provided you don't under-declare then as well). Although you are currently not liable for Turkish capital gains tax if you hold the property for more than five years, this may change – and you will also still have some liability in Britain. Furthermore, if you are buying with a mortgage, under-declaration will reduce the amount you can borrow. You should also not underestimate the physical danger in which you could put yourself by travelling around with large amounts of cash. You could face a dilemma, though, if the owner makes under-declaration a condition for selling.

The Aegean Coast

The area south of Izmir, Turkey's third largest coast, is one of the most popular with British buyers. Despite the plethora of modern, Spanish-style resorts, the Aegean coast still boasts long stretches of pine forests and rugged coastal scenery. One of the most popular resorts is **Kuşadasi**. Just 40 miles from Izmir airport, it has a yacht marina and bustling town centre, with shops, beach clubs, restaurants and non-stop nightlife. Ephesus, one of the wonders of the ancient world, and Adaland, the largest aquapark in Europe, are within easy reach. Although high-rise developments are not permitted on the shoreline, there are large numbers of them elsewhere in town. Despite claimed annual rises of as much as 25 per cent a year, prices are relatively low because of the slack application of planning law, which allows the supply of property to more than keep pace with demand.

Further south is the **Bodrum peninsula**, with its unspoilt forest-clad mountains sweeping down to the sea and deserted coves, beaches and marina. The town of Bodrum, with its low-rise whitewashed, bougainvillaea-covered villas, is one of the most beautiful and sophisticated resorts on the Turkish riviera. Home to one of the Seven Wonders of the World, the Mausoleum of Halicarnassus, the town's large double harbour is guarded by the picturesque Castle of St John, which now houses a fascinating museum. The long waterfront promenade is lined with restaurants, bars and cafés; Bodrum is said to boast more bars per square mile than any other Turkish resort and the nightlife is even louder and goes on longer into the morning than in Kuşadasi. Although the peninsula still retains much of its unspoilt character, it is rapidly being developed into another Costa del Sol. Indeed, some agents who have made the journey east from Malaga and Marbella claim gleefully that it is 'like Spain a decade ago'. Most of the new homes around Bodrum, which range from two-bedroom apartments priced at £60,000 to detached villas with a pool at £180,000, are built in gated communities.

Marmaris, to the east, where the Aegean and the Mediterranean meet, is a once quiet fishing village situated on the marvellous natural harbour where Nelson organised his fleet for the attack on the French at Abukir in 1798. The picturesque old part of town around the harbour and castle has now been all but lost in the concrete sprawl. The town is Turkey's premier yachting centre, with the 700-berth Netsel Marina and an annual regatta organised by the internationally renowned Marmaris Yacht Club.

The Mediterranean Coast

Stretching from Dalyan and Fethiye in the west, through Antalya and Adana and on to Hatay on the Syrian border in the southeast, Turkey's Mediterranean coast offers warmer weather (especially in winter) and some of the country's finest and sandiest beaches. The most popular area for tourism and foreign property investment is the westernmost part between Fethiye and Antalya known as the Turquoise Coast. It is easily accessible from two international airports, Dalaman and Antalya.

Dalyan, which lies less than 30 minutes from Dalaman airport, is a charming traditional Turkish fishing town in an idyllic position, situated amid the orange groves on a lazy river meandering near the sea, within a wildlife sanctuary and surrounded by lush green fields backed by spectacular mountain ranges. The main street is pedestrianised and lined with shops, cafés and restaurants. The stunning white sand beach at Iztuzu, protected against development because it is a nesting ground for giant loggerhead sea turtles, is 30 minutes away. Dalyan has its fair share of new developments, but planning restrictions prevent anything higher than two storeys from being built.

Almost entirely rebuilt after the 1957 earthquake, **Fethiye** is a bustling market town of around 50,000 people overlooked by pine-forested mountains. Yachts and *gulets* (traditional wooden sailing boats) moor along the waterfront promenade, which is dotted with waterside cafés and several excellent seafood restaurants. To the west of the town centre, Karagoz is a quiet, leafy suburb of villas and apartments overlooking the new marina; in the opposite direction the resort area of Calis has beachfront apartments with wonderful views across the Gulf of Fethiye. Within easy reach of Dalaman international airport, Fethiye also has excellent public transport, with minibus and boat services from the centre of town to the various suburbs. There are also regular bus services to local beaches, such as Oludeniz (Dead Sea), a picture-perfect lagoon with crystal-clear water and a long, sandy beach. Many properties in the nearby villages of

Hisaronu and Ovacik have views over the surrounding forests and meadows. To the northwest of Fethiye is **Göcek**, a sophisticated town with shops, restaurants and cafés, which lies on an attractive bay almost enclosed by mountains dotted with pines. It does not have a beach, but is good for watersports and is popular with rich Turks and yachting types who pop down from Istanbul at weekends. Prices are relatively high by Turkish standards, but, with Dalaman airport just 15 minutes away, properties here have good rental potential.

Continuing eastwards round the coast, **Kalkan**, a small, peaceful fishing town and resort, was for a long time untouched by mass tourism. Narrow streets twist down to the harbour through the historic town and are lined with listed whitewashed villas with shuttered windows situated alongside small local speciality shops and restaurants. The developers are moving in and so, too, are British buyers; by some counts as many as one in five of the local population are from the UK. It was not until 2002 that the town got its first estate agent; now it has more than 70. Prices have risen correspondingly and will receive a further boost from the opening of a mountain tunnel, which will cut the time from Dalaman airport from two hours to one and a half. New-build apartments with a sea view cost £1,000–1,200 per square metre. Villas work out at similar prices; a 175-square-metre property on a modest 350-square-metre plot with pool and terrace could cost around £200,000. Four- to five-bedroom villas are let for anything from £500 to £1,000 a week.

With more than 500,000 inhabitants, **Antalya** is the largest city on the south coast and its airport is by far the busiest, making it an important hub for tourism. The symbol of Antalya is the Yivli Minaret, which was built in the 2nd century BC when King Attalos II established the city. Since then, the Romans, Byzantines, Seljuks and Ottomans have all conquered it. In the picturesque old city centre called the Kaleiçi, traditional wooden houses line the narrow maze-like streets and old people sit outside their houses drinking Turkish tea.

Much of the property-buying interest has been concentrated in **Side**, which lies within an hour's drive along the coast. Founded around 600 BC, it is a virtual open-air museum that boasts a wealth of Roman temples, statues, amphi-theatres and ruins, which thread throughout the town and on into the sand dunes behind the beach. Prices are higher here than in Antalya, with decent two-bedroom apartments already costing well over £50,000.

Alanya, which lies another 85 miles east, is a thriving port city, nestling on a rocky cape between two glorious sandy beaches: the eight-mile-long eastern beach and the two-mile western beach, known as 'Cleopatra' beach, because this is where the Egyptian queen is said to have bathed. On top of the cape is a fortress built by the Seljuks in the 1200s. Alanya remains open for 12 months of the year, with direct charter flights from Britain even during the winter months. It is often warm enough in January and February to eat out during the day.

Cappadocia

Fancy a fly-to-let cave? It is not as far-fetched as it sounds. Situated in the centre of Turkey, southeast of Ankara, Cappadocia (or Kapadokya in the Turkish spelling) is a unique geological wonderland of strangely shaped pinnacles, crags and canyons carved by nature from the soft volcanic rock. This breathtaking landscape has been inhabited since the earliest times; people have added to it over the centuries by excavating homes, villages and even whole cities under the ground. Cappadocia was a centre of early Christianity and is dotted with subterranean churches and monasteries, some decorated with stunning frescoes. A UNESCO World Heritage site, the area forms a national park. It is centred on the village of **Göreme**, but also encompasses the towns and villages of **Urgup**, **Nevsehir**, **Uçhisar**, **Ortahisar** and **Cavusin**.

Cool in the summer and warm in the winter, many of the area's cave houses are still inhabited and are increasingly being bought by foreigners. You could get a basic and rather bare starter cave house for as little as £20,000. Prices for refurbished ones, some of which even have swimming pools, can reach more than £150,000. Cappadocia is a popular tourist area and such a property could be let by the night or week, providing a good return.

Istanbul

With a population of 12 million people stretching out on both the European and Asian shores of the Bosphorus, Istanbul is by far Turkey's largest and most vibrant city. It is also growing fast, with as many as 700,000 new people arriving every year. While the market on the coast is dominated by foreign buyers, prices in Istanbul are determined largely by domestic demand. For this reason, prices were relatively stable during the recession that followed the financial crisis of 2001 and lasted until 2003. They rose the following year, however, and look likely to continue upwards.

A major factor will be the growth of the domestic mortgage market. A series of restrictions, especially on the maximum length of loans, has meant that traditionally even affluent Turks have rented rather than bought. According to a study by Colliers International, published in 2005, mortgage-lending amounted to just 0.3 per cent of GDP, compared with an average of 40 per cent in EU countries and 50 per cent in the United States. The Turkish government is in the process of changing the law to allow the development of a western-style market. With some 60 per cent of the population under 20 years of age, the availability of loans over 20, 30 or even 40 years will bring home-ownership within the reach of many.

As with any large city, prices in Istanbul are determined largely by transport links and the proximity of shops, offices and factories. The 1999 earthquake centred on Izmit, east of Istanbul, which killed 18,000 people, also had an important effect: it immediately boosted demand for new low-rise housing in the northern suburbs of Istanbul, which escaped the tremor largely unscathed. There has since been a gradual move back towards the city, especially by affluent young Turkish 'creatives' who want to be near their jobs in advertising agencies or production companies. Wherever you buy, it is worth employing a surveyor to assess whether your new investment is likely to survive the next 'big one'. Anything built since 1998 should comply with higher new standards, although many buildings erected earlier have been reinforced.

For tourists, the most familiar part of Istanbul is the Sultanahmet district of old Istanbul, where the bustling narrow streets link tourist sights such as the Blue Mosque and Santa Sophia. This would be the ideal spot if you are looking for a holiday let, but, with its crowds, plethora of carpet shops and appalling traffic jams, it may not appeal to the expat banker or Turkish middle-manager who wants to rent long-term. If you want to target that market, a better bet would be the Beyoğlu district on the other side of the Golden Horn, from the Galata Bridge to Taksim Square. This is the heart of modern Istanbul, with its wider streets and late 19th- and 20th-century Art Nouveau architecture. Upmarket districts include Tesvikiye and Nisantasi, and other areas to the north within easy commuting distance of the Levent, where many banks and multinationals have their offices. Especially popular are flats and houses with views of the Bosphorus, such as in Bebek, which lies further north on the European side. Although a view of the water can add up to 30 per cent to the purchase price, homes there command far higher rents and are easier to let out than property elsewhere. Prices are lower on the more residential Asian side. It may also be worth looking at new-build projects in the suburbs.

The rental market has remained fairly buoyant, with rents in early 2006 higher than two or three years earlier. This is expected to change as mortgages become more widely available, although the process could take many years to work its way through the system.

Prices vary widely from area to area: an average property in a good area in the centre could go for £1,000–2,000 per square metre, dropping to half that in the suburbs. Surprisingly for what is still a relatively poor country, apartments are often large by British standards: flats of 200 square metres or more – well over the floor area of a typical Victorian semi – are common, while studios are few and far between.

Estate Agents

See also the Turkish embassy's guide for foreign property buyers at **www.turkisheconomy.org.uk/buying_property.html**.

- **1-e-1 Emlak, www.1-e-1.com, t** + 212 327 4901. **Istanbul-based agency with a selection of property in the city.**

- **Aquavista, www.villas-apartments-turkey.com, t** (01580) 850 170. **Agency with a wide range of properties in dozens of locations.**

- **Avatar, www.avatar-turkey, t** 08707 282 827. British-based agency with a variety of coastal properties and useful information about the resorts.

- **Best Bodrum Villas, www.bestbodrumvillas.com, t** + 90 252 382 2294. A choice of largely new-build property on the Bodrum peninsula.

- **Canterburys Overseas, www.canterburys.com.** A selection of largely new build properties on the Aegean and Mediterranean coast, together with some useful information about the resorts.

- **Cappadocia Houses, www.cappadociahouses.com, t** + 90 535 618 2865. Agency with a selection of cave houses in Cappadocia.

- **Home in Turkey, www.homeinturkey.com, t** + 90 242 753 3910. Antalya-based agency with new-build projects largely in the Side area.

- **Home Made Real Estate, www.homemaderealestate.com, t** + 90 242 512 6890. A variety of new-build properties in the Alanya area.

- **Ibak Homes, www.bestbodrumvillas.com, t** + 90 252 382 2294. For new-build villas on the Bodrum peninsula.

- **Let's Go Turkey, www.letsgototurkey.co.uk, t** + 90 242 513 62 56. A selection of new-build property in the Alanya area.

- **Second Home Turkey, www.secondhometurkey.com, t** + 90 (0) 242 814 4342. Antalya-based agency with a wide choice of coastal property.

- **Turkish Property People, www.turkishpropertypeople.co.uk, t** (01622) 764 200. British-based agency with a wide range of property on the coast and in Istanbul.

The Americas

11

The United States

The US housing market began to hot up later than those in, say, Britain or Australia, but it has been rapidly making up for lost time since, with prices up an average 50 per cent across America – and even doubling in some of the hottest cities – during the first half of the current decade. Despite considerable regional variations, the main driving force has been the extraordinary strength of the US economy, which has expanded steadily in recent years, and was expected to grow by more than 4 per cent in the first quarter of 2006.

Also important has been the expansive monetary policy pursued by the Federal Reserve, the American central bank, in the aftermath of the 9/11 terrorist attacks on New York and Washington in 2001. This not only kept the economy out of recession, it also sharply cut the cost of borrowing, encouraging property-owners to trade up and new buyers to enter the market. This in turn has fed back into the broader economic picture; as in Britain, as the values of their homes have risen, property-owners have felt richer and more inclined to spend money on other items, fuelling the consumer boom on which the economy has been so dependent.

The ever inventive financial services industry has also been playing a part by offering new, riskier forms of mortgage finance that allow buyers to borrow more and more of the cost of their new home. Those offering conventional loans are increasingly ready to offer up to 105 per cent loan-to-value, which effectively covers the buyer's purchasing costs as well as the property itself. Potentially even riskier are so-called 'negative amortisation loans', in which the buyer initially pays less than the interest due – effectively a gamble that prices will continue to rise, allowing the borrower to sell for a profit or re-finance before any principal has to be paid. Around a third of all loans in America in 2005 were of this type.

Like their British counterparts, increasing numbers of Americans have seen the real estate market as a place to invest. According to a study by the influential National Association of Realtors (NAR), 23 per cent of all houses bought in America in 2004 were for investment rather than owner-occupation, and a further 23 per cent as second homes. The expectation of further price rises has encouraged people further; with purchase prices rising far faster than rents, many investors have been ready to buy property that they could only let at a loss, convinced this would be more than compensated by a rise in capital values – the classic definition of a financial bubble. The process has been exacerbated by short-term speculators, who have been 'flipping' condos, often two or three times before completion, in a process reminiscent of the late 1990s, when investors were busy buying and selling dotcom stocks. In Miami – the 'flipping' capital of America – as many as half of the original buyers have resold new apartments in this way. The practice has been widespread in Las Vegas, too. In certain areas, especially Florida, interest from foreign buyers has helped push the market from one record high to another. Even after the huge price increases seen in the self-styled Sunshine State in recent years, British buyers sitting down with a glossy catalogue of homes in Orlando or the Gulf Coast, complete with pool and generous back yard, are still pleasantly surprised by how far their money will go – at least compared with prices back home.

All the best parties are followed by a hangover, though, and by late 2005 there were clear signs that this was on its way. According to reports in the American press, a combination of rising mortgage rates, growing supply and media talk of a 'bubble' were making many potential buyers wary of taking the plunge – cutting the number of sales and prompting fears that prices would level out and perhaps even fall back. 'The air is coming out of the balloons,' declared David Lereah, a leading American property economist.

The signs of a looming slowdown have continued to multiply. By early 2006, a number of developers were reporting falls in orders, while stocks of unsold properties rose a staggering 38 per cent in the course of eight months – the largest such increase on record. In February 2006, the NAR reported that there was a 5.1-month supply of unsold homes on the market – against a record low of 3.8 months' worth a year earlier. Condos appear to have been especially badly hit. As the most obvious target for speculators, they tend to benefit most when prices are rising and suffer most when the market turns, as already happened during the real-estate slowdown of the early 1990s. Repossessions, meanwhile, have been growing. RealtyTrac, an organisation that monitors them, said numbers rose 24.5 per cent from the first quarter of 2005 to the fourth quarter, in a reflection of the effects of higher property prices and mortgage rates.

What was once a sellers' market has been swiftly transformed into a buyers' one. According to a detailed study by the *Wall Street Journal* in February 2006, the changing climate has been especially noticeable in once-hot markets such as Miami, Phoenix, Arizona and Washington, DC, and also in places such as Detroit, where price increases have been modest but the job market is weak and heavily dependent on the fortunes of the automobile industry.

Developers, faced with mounting inventories of unsold property, have begun offering all sorts of perks and incentives. A survey conducted by the National Association of Home Builders found that 19 per cent of builders were cutting prices to shift stock, while 64 per cent were using other incentives, such as contributions towards buying costs and free upgrades. Anecdotal evidence suggested that others are offering more unusual sweeteners, from golf and country club memberships in Florida to free plasma screen TVs and opera tickets.

While the number of sales was falling quite sharply by late 2005, prices were initially more resilient, except in particularly overheated markets such as Boston and California's Silicon Valley, which were beginning to show small falls. According to the NAR, the median house price in the United States rose 13.6 per cent in 2005, with much of that rise occurring during the first three-quarters of the year.

The overall figure masked considerable regional differences: Phoenix, Arizona was the hottest metropolitan market in the USA, up 48.9 per cent, narrowly ahead of Cape Coral and Fort Myers, Florida, where prices soared 48 per cent. The worst performing was South Bend, Mishawaka, Indiana, down 5.3 per cent. Notably, there were signs of cooling in what had been the best performing markets in 2004, such as San José, in California, which at US$747,000 (£430,000) has the highest median property prices in the country (making the median home there more than eight times the cost of its equivalent in Youngstown, Ohio). Prices there ended the year only 3.7 per cent higher; Denver and San Diego, which also did well in 2004, rose only slightly more.

Opinions have been sharply divided on what will happen next. As always, the optimists are hoping for a soft landing, despite clear indications in early 2006 from Ben Bernanke, the new Federal Reserve chairman, that more interest-rate rises were on the way. The NAR said it expected prices across the country to keep going up in 2006, but at a far slower national average rate of 5 per cent – which, given the different influences at work from state to state, appeared to leave the door open for absolute falls in some areas. Others have posited more gloomy scenarios. As discussed in the first part of this book, *The Economist* published a detailed survey in June 2005 claiming that property in America was seriously overvalued and predicting that the housing market would collapse, taking down much of the rest of the country's economy with it. In early 2006, it was not clear who would turn out right. 'No one really understands how these things behave,' admits Robert Shiller, the Yale economist and author of *Irrational Exuberance*, who presaged the dotcom crash and has since moved to study the American real estate market. 'Looking for indicators is a little bit futile because we've never seen this kind of growth in housing before.'

Florida

With its balmy climate, wonderful ocean front and plethora of theme parks, Florida has long been a popular destination for British property-buyers, even if the well-publicised trail of destruction left by Hurricane Katrina in August 2005 may have provided pause for thought to some would-be investors in the Sunshine State. Florida has also had one of America's fastest-moving property markets, delivering double-digit annual capital gains for anyone who has bought in the last few years. Cape Coral, with Fort Myers, was one of six Florida cities in the list of the top ten best-performing property markets during 2005. Prices in Orlando, Ocala, Tampa, Sarasota and Daytona also grew by at least 28.5 per cent. As elsewhere in America, there are concerns that boom will turn to bust. The broader market nevertheless remains underpinned by a number of factors, not least immigration from elsewhere in the USA. Despite Katrina, Florida's population grew by 400,000 in 2005, with many people from other states drawn in by the booming economy; Florida led the USA in job creation in

2005. The state's reputation as the ideal place for retirement has also helped. As the baby-boomers get older, many are cashing in equity in their principal homes, and either buying holiday property in Florida or selling up and moving there permanently.

Even if many Florida-dwellers are beginning to take hurricanes as a fact of life (just as Californians are ready to put up with earthquakes and Midwesterners with tornadoes), the recent spate of them has undoubtedly had an impact on home-buyers. With insurance costs for some properties going through the roof, location is becoming increasingly important. Buyers are also paying greater attention to their property's structure and how resistant it is to high winds.

Hurricanes or no hurricanes, for many British buyers the first choice must be **Orlando**, jumping-off point for the Walt Disney World Resort. Other attractions in the area include SeaWorld, Universal Orlando Resort and Gatorland. It also has the world's largest McDonald's. There has also recently been considerable development in downtown Orlando itself, even though it is relatively far from the main tourist attractions. Prices vary widely, but you should generally count on spending £140,000 to £220,000 for a three- to four-bedroom detached property, with some land and a heated pool. With an estimated 52 million tourists a year visiting Orlando, there is also a large potential supply of rental tenants.

Miami, with its subtropical climate, has been a favourite vacation destination since the 1920s, when the first of its wonderful Art Deco resort hotels was built. Although other parts of Florida have been dubbed – somewhat unkindly – Heaven's Waiting Room, this city of around 600,000 people (half of them Latinos) is a young, vibrant and fast-moving place. (Go into the wrong street, though, and it can also be a quite scary one.) Condo fever has transformed the cityscape in recent years, with more and more new residential blocks going up. It is still possible to pick up a reasonable two-bedder for £130,000 or so, but prices can easily be double that if you want something close to the ocean, especially in South Beach. Don't worry overly if you cannot afford a property in Miami itself. A string of other cities such as **Coral Cables**, **Hollywood** and **Fort Lauderdale** stretches along the coast, offering cheaper and less hectic alternatives which are still within easy driving distance.

Over on the west side, the **Gulf Coast** is less developed and is known for its relaxed pace. The south is taken up largely with the swamps of the Everglades, although the southern town of **Naples** is famous for its tennis and golf and is popular with British buyers. Nearby **Marco Island** has been a centre of frenetic condo-building. Moving northwards up the coast, **Fort Myers**, **Sarasota** and **Brandenton** are heavily dependent on tourism – and especially popular with the 'snowbirds', the retirees who descend every year from Canada and northern parts of the United States. **Tampa**, slightly further north, is the largest city on the Gulf Coast and an important business centre. Prices generally are more reasonable than on the east coast. It should be possible to find a large three- or four-bedroom house in Fort Myers or Tampa for less than £150,000.

The **Florida Panhandle**, situated on the north of the Gulf Coast, has a different feel from the rest of the state. The **Emerald Coast** (or Redneck Riviera to its detractors!) has glorious white sandy beaches and a quieter, more family-orientated feel. Resorts include **Pensacola Beach**, **Gulf Breeze**, **Destin**, and **Seaside**, a development community whose iconic pastel-paint and tin-roof construction was made famous in the Jim Carrey film *The Truman Show*. Parts of the coast were hit especially badly by Hurricane Katrina.

Wherever you buy in Florida, there are some important considerations to bear in mind if rental income is your main concern. Many potential buyers have gone on holiday in the state, fallen in love with it and are all too happy to be sold a property which, by British standards at least, seems a bargain. The prospect of rental income subsidising the mortgage payments makes the dream complete. Agents will tell you that if you buy a property with a 60 per cent mortgage you will typically need to let it for around 30 weeks a year to cover your costs. This seems a manageable target, given the mild climate, but there are some dangerous potential pitfalls to watch out for. The first is that, surprising though it may seem in a country that epitomises private enterprise, there may be restrictions on how long you can let out your property for. Until 1990, no such curbs existed. But, as growing numbers of Britons and other foreign buyers started buying-to-let, a couple of counties began imposing land-zoning ordinances that restricted the number of weeks a year they could do so for. Other places within Florida have since followed. The rules vary widely: some communities and counties allow two-week rentals, while others prescribe a minimum of four weeks or even six months, which could seriously reduce your property's ability to generate income. For this reason, it is vital to check before buying whether the property concerned is in an area zoned for short- or long-term letting. A reputable realtor should be able to provide this information, although it never hurts to double-check with the county or city governments. Don't listen to anyone who says such rules do not matter; they are strictly enforceable.

As elsewhere, there are other, more general questions, such as the suitability of the property for renting and the competition it will face from other such properties, many of them also owned by Britons. Rental guarantees given by travel companies, although often ostensibly good deals, should be examined closely. You should also not forget strict immigration rules that will limit the amount of time a year that you can spend in your own home.

Estate Agents

- **David Beroset and Company, www.smartfloridaproperties.com, t** (020) 7993 8487. Agency offering properties in central Florida and the Gulf Coast.
- **Florida Homes 1st, www.florida-homes-1st.com, t** (020) 8460 9903. British-based agency specialising in new-build and second-hand property in Orlando, Kissimmee and on the Gulf Coast.

- **Florida Properties, www.floridaproperties.co.uk, t** (01256) 799 855. British-based agency offering holiday homes with investment income.

- **Florida Realty UK, www.floridarealtyuk.com, t** 0870 162 0772. British-based agency offering a variety of Florida property.

- **Floridian Homes, www.floridian-homes.com, t** + 1 (407) 932 1426. Property in the Orlando area for sale and short-term let.

- **Househunt, www.househunt.com**. Gateway to extensive real estate listings in Florida and across the USA.

- **Miami Real Estate Buyer, www.miamirealestatebuyer.com, t** + 1 (305) 610 6698. A selection of property for sale in Miami.

- **Sun Sentinal, www.sun-sentinel.com/classified/realestate**. Newspaper website with extensive listings of real estate in southern Florida.

California

The eighth largest economy in the world in its own right, with a population of almost 34 million people, California is America's powerhouse, and the location not just of much of its entertainment industry but also the heart of the 'new economy'. After suffering a serious property slump during the early 1990s, prices have been booming in recent years – so much so that many buyers have been priced out of the most expensive coastal areas such as Los Angeles and San Francisco and been forced to look to the cheaper central valley, or else to neighbouring Nevada and Arizona.

After increases of 18–21 per cent in the previous three years, average prices in California rose 16 per cent in 2005, taking the median cost of a one-family house above US$500,000 (£288,000) for the first time. In Silicon Valley, the median house price in December 2005 was US$734,975 (£423,499).

Prices look likely to continue rising in 2006, albeit at a slower rate, but the warning signs are there. The number of default notices – the first stage towards repossession – rose more than 15 per cent in 2005, and almost 20 per cent in overheated southern California. Sensing trouble ahead, many lenders have been scrutinising mortgage applications and adopting a more conservative lending policy. If the market does turn, things could quickly get out of hand, locking prices into a downward spiral. Californians have been even more enthusiastic than other Americans in borrowing with 'negative amortisation loans' and other riskier forms of finance (60 per cent of all loans were of this type in the state, three times the national average). Such loans are fine as long as the market is rising, but potentially disastrous if it is falling.

One of the hottest areas has been in **Orange County** in the south of the state, an area of 3 million people, which is home to Disneyland, the Knott's Berry Farm theme park and miles of sandy beaches (and which is of course the setting for the TV show *The O.C.*). After tumbling along with those elsewhere in California in the early 1990s, prices began to pick up towards the end of the decade, and by early 2006 were up a staggering 195 per cent on 1997 levels.

The market looks set to continue registering double-digit gains for the time being, thanks to the strong economic fundamentals. Unemployment, at 3.2 per cent, is the lowest in California, and the area was ranked fifth in job growth nationally in 2005. The market has also been underpinned by expectations of continued price growth; surveys have shown that people in Orange County predict prices continuing to rise at an unsustainable 23 per cent a year and have been happily mortaging themselves up to the hilt.

Estate Agents

- **California Moves, www.californiamoves.com**. Site with more than 170,000 properties for sale across California.

- **California Real Estate, www.californiarealestate.com**. Property listings throughout the state.

- **Househunt, www.househunt.com**. Gateway to extensive real estate listings in California and across the USA.

- **Prudential California Realty, www.prudentialcal.com**. Listings with a large amount of property for sale in Los Angeles, San Diego, Orange County and the rest of Southern California.

- **Real Estate for Sale in California, http://realestateforsaleincalifornia.net**. Site with agents listing property, and links to sites with real estate news.

Las Vegas

Las Vegas, the self-styled 'Entertainment Capital of the World', is an oasis of gambling and other hedonistic delights rising out of the Nevada desert. The property market there has been one of the hottest in America in recent years, fuelled by a building boom and by investors keen to place what has increasingly looked like a one-way bet. Between the second quarters of 2003 and 2004, single family home prices in Las Vegas shot up 52.4 per cent, according to the NAR – the greatest year-on-year increase ever for any US metropolitan area. At the height of the boom it wasn't unusual for sellers to get a dozen offers on a house and sell it in a single day. Builders had waiting lists for new developments and agents reported that buyers – many of them 'investors' from out of state – were so eager to get their foot in the door they made offers on property that could be easily flipped or let without even bothering to see it.

This has been particularly the case with condos. Researchers at Marcus & Millichap, a California-based real estate research firm, have estimated that as many as 70 per cent of buyers in Las Vegas have been speculators or people looking for second homes. The upper end of the market was especially buoyant in 2005: about 4,500 condos and townhouses priced at US$500,000 (£288,000) or more were sold – a fourfold increase over the previous year. Buyers have been encouraged by schemes that have allowed them to secure non-binding purchase contracts by putting down just 10 per cent of the purchase price.

Yet, as any Las Vegas gambler knows, it is also only a matter of time before your luck changes and the money that flowed in so fast has begun to flow out again. As the market slows, speculators have been getting cold feet and demanding back their 'non-binding deposits'. As the slowdown sets in, several prestigious projects have been scrapped before construction had even begun. Falls of as much as 15 per cent have been predicted in the price of luxury condos.

The crisis appears, initially at least, to have affected the top end of the market. 'This is not New York. This is not Miami. We are still in the desert,' says Irwin Molasky, whose company built one of the first high-rise luxury condo developments in the city. 'There isn't enough wealth [in Las Vegas] for these prices. To pay $1 million for a place in New York is not a big deal. Here it is a big deal.' Any softening at the top, however, looks almost certain to trickle downwards, casting a shadow over the rest of the market.

Estate Agents

- **Dana Anderson-Whittaker, www.danaanderson.com, t** + 1 (702) 300 7653. Property for sale in Las Vegas and Clark County.

- **Househunt, www.househunt.com.** Gateway to extensive real estate listings in Las Vegas and across the USA.

- **Jacqulyn Richey, www.lvrealty.net, t** + 1 (702) 493 8033. A wide selection of property in the Las Vegas area.

- **Las Vegas Real Estate, www.greatlasvegashomes.com, t** + 1 (702) 596 7821. Agency with a range of more than 8,000 homes for sale and information about the city.

- **Vegas.com, www.vegas.com/realestate.** Comprehensive guide to buying in Las Vegas, with links to agents' sites.

New York City

The New York property market has been one of the fastest-growing in the United States over the last few years, with prices more than doubling on average between 1997 and 2006, fuelled by the continued strength of Wall Street and the financial services industry, and the tight supply of property on Manhattan Island. Even the usually irrepressible New Yorkers were beginning to show signs of fatigue by late 2005, however, with annual growth slowing from double digits to more sustainable single-digit rises. By early 2006, the newspapers were full of stories suggesting that in New York, as elsewhere in the country, it was now a buyers' rather than a sellers' market. Realtors were quoting as expressing relief that reality of sorts was returning to the market.

Property in **Manhattan** is still expensive. A survey by Prudential Douglas Elliman, one of New York's leading realtors, put the average sales price of a Manhattan apartment in the fourth quarter of 2005 at US$1,877,404 (£682,841), up 3 per cent on the previous quarter and 20.3 per cent on the same quarter of the previous year. This worked out at US$780 a square foot (£4,820 per square metre), up 1.8 per cent on the previous quarter and 28.5 per cent on the year earlier. At the same time, prices in the **Nasau/Suffolk** region were beginning to stabilise, while those in **Queens** continued upwards. **The Hamptons**, the traditional seaside playground of affluent New Yorkers, continued to surge ahead, however, with the average price of a residence reaching a record US$1,380,198 (£793,405) in the third quarter of 2005, up 5.2 per cent from the previous quarter and 33.5 per cent from the year before. Much of the demand appears to have been investment-driven; with some of the top houses commanding rents of as much as £100,000–150,000 for the summer season, some people buy them specifically to let and then use themselves in the winter.

With prices at such levels, and signs of a slowdown multiplying, it would be a brave – and a wealthy – outside investor who would enter the top end of the New York property market just as it looks as if the great party is coming to an end. There could be money to be made lower down, however. A survey by *The New York Times* published in November 2005 concluded that it was after all (just) possible to buy a property in the city for US$220,000 (£126,000), the nation's median price, although it was a struggle to find anything bigger than a studio. Indeed, another study showed that the market for studios and one-bedroom apartments had performed the best, rising 11 per cent between June and September, while the price of larger apartments dropped an average 16 per cent. The explanation lies partly in the dramatic price rises of the last few years, which have meant that the latest crop of first-time buyers have been obliged to make do with a smaller property than before.

Estate Agents

- **HH Realty Group, www.hhrealtrygroup.com, t +** (212) 734 1800. Agency specialising in New York apartments for sale and rent.

- **Househunt, www.househunt.com.**

- *New York Times***, www.realestate.nytimes.com.** Extensive real estate listings from New York's most prestigious newspaper. Also try the real estate sections of the city's other main newspapers such as the *New York Post***, www.nypost.com,** the *New York Daily News***, www.nydailynews.com,** and *Newsday***, www.newsday.com.**

- **Prudential Douglas Elliman, www.elliman.com.** Large agency with property for sale and rent in New York, Long Island and The Hamptons.

Latin America

Stretching from Mexico in the north to Chile in the south, Latin America is one of the last frontiers for the international property investor. Until recently, military dictatorships rather than democracy were the norm on much of the continent, and outsiders were viewed with suspicion. Some countries, such as Chile and Nicaragua, were the scene of serious bloodshed in the latter years of the 20th century, while large areas of Colombia were turned into no-go areas by the drugs mafia. Matters were not much better on the economic front: although Brazil and Argentina, for example, have considerable natural resources, much of their wealth has traditionally been concentrated in the hands of a small ruling élite, with the majority left in abject poverty; economic mismanagement has led to periodic bouts of hyperinflation and the need for bail-outs by the International Monetary Fund (IMF).

Since the turn of the millennium, however, there have been growing signs that some of the countries, at least, have been beginning to get things right. The last of the generals has gone, replaced with democratic systems of varying degrees of durability; after years of boom and bust, the continent also looks set again on a path of growth. According to IMF figures, GDP in the Latin American and Caribbean region increased by an estimated 4.1 per cent in 2005 and was due to expand by 3.8 per cent in 2006. Such figures mask enormous contrasts: while the Argentinian economy, for example, has been growing strongly since the financial crisis of 2001–2002 and both Brazil and Chile are economically and politically stable, several countries are in the grip of a left-leaning populism that draws its inspiration from Cuba's Fidel Castro. Venezuela, for example, may boast a long Caribbean coastline and some dramatic scenery – not to mention huge oil reserves – but it also has a fiercely anti-American and anti-globalist president in Hugo Chavez, who has ruled the country since 1998. The election of Evo Morales, a former coca farmer with equally anti-American views, as president of Bolivia in December 2005, demonstrates that the populist model still holds appeal for a people impoverished by long years of economic mismanagement and corruption.

The message for the property investor is clear: although the political and economic risks in some countries are probably still too great for all but the bravest, several Latin American countries are attractive targets for investment. It is on these that this section concentrates.

Brazil

Long known for its music, beaches and the Rio Carnival, Brazil is becoming an increasingly popular place for foreigners to buy property either for holidays, retirement or investment. With a population of 184 million spread over an area larger than Europe, it is by far the largest country in Latin America and, given its huge resource base, it should also be one of the richest nations in the world. Like the rest of the continent, however, Brazil has had a mixed history: its economy grew an average 7.4 per cent a year from the end of the Second World War until 1980, but the country subsequently turned crazy, with 80 per cent inflation and horrific trade barriers. Since the 1990s, Brazil has been on the path to recovery. Inflation is back down to acceptable levels and the economy is expanding, even though growth, at 3.3 per cent in 2005, was modest by the standards of other developing countries. The political situation, nevertheless, remains stable, thanks largely to President Luiz Inácio Lula da Silva. The former trade unionist, known to his people simply as Lula, was elected in October 2002 on a populist left-wing ticket, but has shifted markedly to the centre since coming to power and has proven himself an effective and pragmatic leader.

Brazil offers a relatively benign environment for foreign property-investors. Purchase costs are low, with a mere 2 per cent transfer tax on property. The payment structure for off-plan developments is also advantageous, which in a rising market means there could be money to be made by buying early and 'flipping on' before completion.

Rio de Janeiro

For most foreigners, Brazil means Rio de Janeiro, a bustling city of more than 6 million people dominated by the statue of Christ with open arms above Guanabara Bay. One of the most attractive parts of the *cidade maravilhosa* (wonderful city), as the Brazilians call it, is the Zona Sul (southern zone). Taking in Ipanema, Leblon, Gavea and Copacabana beaches, this is the most exclusive part of Rio and the place where the upper middle classes, luxury shops and a good part of the nightlife converge. Space is limited and the area is almost entirely built over, so prices are relatively high by Brazilian (if not European) standards and are continuing to rise. A one-bedroom 70-square-metre apartment in an average block around 50 metres' walk from Copacabana beach, for example, would cost around £70,000, and could be let to tourists for £60 or so a night for most of the year (and considerably more at New Year or Carnival). Prices in Ipanema and the nearby district of Leblon are 30 per cent or so higher, but so, too, are rents, and the prospects for capital gain may be greater.

Other parts of Rio may be well known for their tourist attractions, but are less interesting for investors. An exception is Santa Teresa, one of the oldest neighbourhoods in the city, which lies high on a hill over the centre, with a number of impressive colonial-style houses and great views to the sea and the bay. Once one of the most élite areas in Rio, it became run-down in the 1960s and '70s, but has remained a favourite with the intellectual and artistic élite and is now being rediscovered by a new generation. A large 350-square-metre house with five bedrooms and small pool could cost less than £200,000. Prices there look likely to rise, thanks to Santa Teresa's proximity to the downtown/business district, which lies five minutes' ride away on the old wooden tramway.

The district's hilltop location also means it enjoys cooler, fresher air than most of the rest of Rio.

Also of interest are Barra and Recreio, which lie in a modern Miami-like area on the beach south of the city. Made up largely of high-rise beachfront condos, set in gated developments with gardens, pools and leisure areas, they have little of the charm of old Rio. The comfortable lifestyle afforded by such projects appeals to many middle-class Brazilians, however, and investing in off-plan projects here could yield good long-term capital gains.

Bahia and the Northeast

While much of Brazil's economic power remains concentrated in Rio, Sao Paulo and the other cities of the south, foreign property-investors are looking increasingly at Bahia and the other smaller states on the northeastern coast, which offer a winning combination of stunning beaches and a tropical climate. The authorities in Bahia, in particular, have seized on tourism as a way of providing much-needed income for the state, and have put considerable resources into building both a new airport and the Linha Verde, a 100-mile stretch of toll road along the coast. Air connections are improving.

Property prices have risen rapidly since the beginning of the decade, but remain below those in the south of Brazil and are still only a third or so of those in comparable locations in Europe. The northeastern coast is extremely beautiful, not only because of the exotic vegetation and fauna, but also because of the combination of beaches and rivers that create beautiful lakes and estuaries separated from the sea by spectacular white dunes. For this reason, not only the frontline beach, but also the area behind it, offers great develop-ment potential.

Bahia's capital, **Salvador**, a city of 3 million people which was also the national capital until 1763, still retains the colonial atmosphere of the early Portuguese settlers; property in the city is relatively cheap and it is possible to buy luxury villas nearby for around £120,000. **Itacaré**, and the **Marau peninsula** to the south, are two emerging hotspots. A number of new developments have sprung up, among them the mega-resort of **Costa do Sauipe**, an hour north of Salvador. **Praia do Forte**, a former fishing village, was created in the 1990s by Peter Klaus, a visionary investor who turned it one of the world's first truly ecological resorts. The smaller states which lie north of Bahia also have considerable potential. **Fortaleza**, the capital of Ceará, is a lively city of 2 million people, with a string of attractive beach resorts such as **Prainha, Iguape** and **Porto das Dunas** nearby. The area around **Natal**, capital of the state of Rio Grande do Norte, is also developing. One of the fastest-growing areas is **Ponta Negra**, a former fishing village which has turned into a major tourist area since the 1990s. A typical 50-square-metre, two-bed, two-bath apartment in a new block could go for around £55,000. Developers talk of yields of 10–12 per cent.

Estate Agents

- **Beachfront Brazil, www.beachfrontbrazil.net, t** (020) 7193 1472. Agency offering a selection of beachfront properties on the northeastern coast.
- **Apartments Rio, www.apartmentsrio.com, t** + 55 21 9474 8148. Rio-based agency with a choice of property in the city for sale and rent.
- **Brazil Estates, www.brazilestates.com.** A wide range of properties for sale across the country, together with detailed information on the property market in different areas.
- **Homes in Rio, www.homesinrio.com, t** + 55 21 8633 0846. Properties for sale and rent in Rio.
- **Property Bond, www.propertybond.co.uk, t** (020) 7538 0102. British-based company offering off-plan and ready-built new property on the north-east coast.
- **Property Brazil, www.property-brazil.com.** Agency offering a wide selection of apartments and houses on the northeastern coast.

Argentina

While the Brazilian economy has experienced some swings over the years, Argentina has been on a veritable rollercoaster since the crisis of December 2001, when its finances went into freefall, the banks closed their doors and the country seemed to be getting through a president a week. The recovery since then has been remarkable. Argentina's creditors were persuaded to accept a formula that effectively forgave the country a large chunk of its debt, the peso was devalued and, after shrinking by 11 per cent in 2002, the economy grew by 9 per cent in 2003, 8 per cent in 2004 and 7.5 per cent in 2005. Exports, meanwhile, are growing, and unemployment, although still in double figures, is well below the peak of 20 per cent reached in 2002.

All this turmoil necessarily had an impact on the real estate market. With the benefit of hindsight, the best time to have buy property in Argentina would have been in the dark days of June and July 2002, when prices were down 50 per cent from those at the start of the crisis. Although the market has since recovered substantially, property remains incredibly cheap: an apartment in downtown Buenos Aires, together with swimming pool and secure parking, costs a fraction of the equivalent in London. Take a trip out to the countryside, and the prices begin to look unbelievable. Although the long-term rental market is constrained by local salaries, which remain low, the market for short-term lets has been helped by the weaker peso, which has boosted tourism.

Buenos Aires, home to 3 million Porteños, is a cosmopolitan and bustling city with grand avenues and stylish restaurants that is more European than South American in flavour. A good choice is Recoleta, one of the most elegant and sought-after neighbourhoods, with a wide selection of restaurants, bars and nightclubs. By early 2006, prices, at around £1,000 per square metre, were already back at the pre-crisis highs of 1997, but still looking as if they had scope to rise further. Areas like Palermo Viejo and Las Cañitas are trendy but tend to appeal more to young tenants who could not afford to pay much rent.

The southern district of San Telmo, although picturesque, is frequented by students and others who have come to Buenos Aires to learn the tango, but does not generally appeal to expatriate business people. You could pick up a stylish 120-square-metre turn-of-the-last-century flat there for as little as £80,000, though. There are plenty of character buildings, in the process of being renovated, and with the city taking an active role in improving the area there is scope for capital appreciation. At the other end of the scale, one of the most expensive areas is Puerto Madero, a gigantic conglomerate, largely of new builds, on the banks of the Rio de la Plata river. A flat in a new development there could cost at least £1,800 per square metre.

There are plenty of other places to buy in a country that is the eighth largest in the world. Of particular interest are **Patagonia**, the vast steppe-like plain that straddles the border with Chile, and the **Mendoza region** in the west, home to over 2,000 *bodegas* (wineries) and with a history of wine-making that goes back 500 years. It is still possible to pick up a 30–40-acre property for as little as £40,000. Over the border in Uruguay, the resort of **Punta del Este**, the St-Tropez of Latin America, benefits from an extremely busy high season. It is possible to find a two-bedroom, 80-square-metre flat for around £50,000, and earn a 5–7 per cent return on your money by letting it in just January and February alone.

Property in Argentina is invariably priced in dollars, reducing the exchange rate risk. Buying can be a scary process for those used to the more sophisticated markets of western Europe or North America, not least because deals are almost invariably in cash under the table. Before buying, you must obtain a CDI number (the equivalent of a social security number in the UK or USA – a lawyer can arrange this for you, although it is possible to do it yourself). Estate agents are not generally especially efficient by British standards and not always honest; stories abound of properties being described on paper as larger than they really are, so always take your tape measure along to double-check. In a peculiarity of the market, buyers rather than sellers are charged commission by the agents, which works out at 3.63 per cent, including tax. After making a small deposit, buyers will typically pay a *boleto* of 30 per cent to secure the property, which effectively locks both sides into the deal. Completion is known as *escritura* and it is at this point that the title is actually transferred to your name.

Taxes are reasonable, with stamp duty of around 2.5 per cent (depending on the province) and notary's costs and fees of around 2–3 per cent. There is no capital gains tax levied on profits. Don't count on financing your purchase with a mortgage: in early 2006 they were available only to the locals. You probably would not want one anyway, because the terms are so poor.

Estate Agents

- **Andino Property, www.andinoproperty.com, t + 54 26 2743 7811.**
A selection of property for sale in the western region of Mendoza.

- **Apartments BA, www.apartmentsba.com, t + 54 11 5254 0100.** A wide range of property to let and buy in Buenos Aires and elsewhere in the country, together with plenty of useful information about Argentina.

- **Argentina Homes, www.argentinahomes.com, t + 54 11 4801 9291.** Very comprehensive site with property for sale and rent, maps and lots of useful information.

- **Mendoza Property, www.mendozaproperty.com, t + 54 26 2743 9088.** Agency run by a British expat, offering houses, *fincas* and *bodegas* in the Mendoza region.

Panama

Panama may be best known for its eponymous canal, but it also has much to offer investors. A small country that is home to just over 3 million people, it boasts a variety of natural attractions including snorkelling, deep-sea fishing, unspoilt national parks, and a strong sense of its Spanish heritage. Panama City, the capital, is a pleasant and thriving city. During the 1970s, Panama was a kind of Latin Casablanca, with arms-runners, drug lords and revolutionaries; the novelist Graham Greene was a frequent visitor. The place has become considerably tamer, if less colourful, since the Americans forcibly ousted General Manuel Noriega, the country's increasingly authoritarian leader, in 1989 and jailed him in Miami for drug-smuggling. Panama is now a stable democracy with considerable potential for tourist and residential development.

It also has economic potential. Located at the Caribbean-side entrance to the Panama Canal, the Colon Free Zone is the most important of its type in the western hemisphere, turning over more than US$6 billion worth of export and import transactions a year, while the country's international financial centre has made it the Switzerland of Latin America. The US presence has also left the country with excellent roads, a reliable telephone network, a modern banking system, nationwide mobile phone coverage and widespread high-speed Internet access. The economic and legal framework is good. Foreigners have the same property rights as the locals, while currency risk is minimised because Panama uses the US dollar. Purchasing costs should account for just 1.5–3 per cent of the sale price, while living costs are low.

Much of the property-buying interest has been concentrated on the string of pretty beaches of white sand and sapphire-blue waters along the **Pacific Coast** just outside Panama City. The best known include **Punta Chame**, **Gorgona**, **Coronado**, **Rio Mar**, **Santa Clara** and **Playa Blanca**. Prices vary widely: a new build 48-square-metre condo on Gorgona beach with a sea view could cost just

£20,000, and a seafront property close to the country's largest coral reefs around £140,000. There are also plenty of luxurious vacation homes for upwards of £700,000. A new-build apartment in Panama City could be a good investment, too. Panama still remains relatively undiscovered and prices look set to rise substantially as increasing numbers of American and other foreign investors move in.

Estate Agents

• **Century 21 Semusa Realty, www.semusarealty.com, t + 507 270 6050.** Panama City-based company with large range of property for sale, plus relocation services.

• **Happy Whale Real Estate Investments, www.happywhale.com.** Property for sale in Panama and Costa Rica.

• **Panama Realtor, www.panamarealtor.com, t + 507 265 8545.** A wide selection of properties for sale across Panama.

• **Panorama Panama, www.panoramapanama.com, t + 507 223 3648.** Agency specialising in property with high potential for tourism and private leisure activities.

• **Quality Investment, www.qualityinvestment.com.pa, t + 507 214 8833.** A wide choice of property for sale across Panama, together with lots of useful information about the country.

Belize

A sliver of land bordered by Mexico to the north and Guatemala to the west, the former British colony of Belize (known until 1973 as British Honduras) is one of the smallest countries in Latin America and is home to just 280,000 people. Although only 174 miles long, and 68 miles across at its broadest point, Belize offers a wide variety of landscape, from the Maya mountains in the north, through the savannah and sugar cane fields, to its incredible Caribbean coast. Just off the eastern shore lies the Barrier Reef, a wall of coral stretching almost 140 miles from Mexico to the Sapodilla Cayes. The climate is subtropical, with an average annual temperature of 26°C. Miami and Houston are two hours or so away by plane. Dotting the reef like punctuation marks are 175 *cayes* (pronounced keys), and, further out to sea, three coral atolls. The more developed areas are already popular with North American visitors, and growing numbers of Europeans are joining them. The main attractions are the scuba-diving, snorkelling and game-fishing. Many of Belize's coastal areas and islands are being developed into tourist resorts and luxury residential complexes; some are little more than islets of white coral sand and mangroves, home only to penguins and occasional fishermen diving for conch and lobster. Others, like

Ambergris Caye, are becoming increasingly lively, with an ample supply of bars, restaurants and small hotels.

Politically and economically stable, Belize offers a number of obvious attractions to investors: there is no income tax on rent or capital gains tax on sales, and there are no restrictions on land or property purchases by foreigners. There are also especially favourable tax rules for retirees (who need only be 45 and have a minimum income of US$2,000 a month). Thanks to its colonial past, Belize is English-speaking and has a legal system based on British common law.

Compared with other Caribbean countries, Belize is less developed and less expensive, but it is developing rapidly, with the government putting a particular emphasis on tourism. The number of flights to the United States and elsewhere in Latin America and the Caribbean is being increased, while the runway at Belize City Airport is being lengthened, to allow it to accommodate the larger 767 jets which cross the Atlantic; this will make direct flights to Europe more of a possibility.

A few British agencies have started selling property in Belize. One of the first projects is **Bella Maya** resort, set on six acres of landscaped beach and lagoon-front land on the **Placencia peninsula**, a short flight or three-hour drive by 4x4 from Belize City. Prices are around £1,500 per square metre. Some developers offer guaranteed yields, typically of around 8 per cent, although, given the length of the season, you may be able to achieve more by yourself through an agency. Local agents have a wide selection of second-hand property, at various prices depending on location and quality.

Estate Agents

- **Belize Real Estate, www.belizerealestate.com, t +** 011 501 227 2065. Agency offering a variety of properties and land for sale and some useful information about the country.

- **Bella Maya Resort, www.bellamayaresort.com**. Property for sale on the Placencia peninsula, direct from the developer.

- **Remax, www.realestate-belize.com**, t + 011 501 225 3555. A selection of houses, land and even whole islands for sale.

Index